W9-BUY-012

A Man
from
Another
Land

A Man
from
Another
Land

*How Finding My Roots
Changed My Life*

ISAIAH WASHINGTON

with Lavaille Lavette

CENTER
STREET

NEW YORK BOSTON NASHVILLE

Names and identifying details of some of the people portrayed in this book
have been changed.

Copyright © 2011 by Isaiah Washington
All rights reserved. Except as permitted under the U.S. Copyright Act of 1976,
no part of this publication may be reproduced, distributed, or transmitted in
any form or by any means, or stored in a database or retrieval system, without
the prior written permission of the publisher.

Center Street
Hachette Book Group
237 Park Avenue
New York, NY 10017

www.centerstreet.com

Center Street is a division of Hachette Book Group, Inc.
The Center Street name and logo are trademarks of Hachette Book Group, Inc.

Printed in the United States of America

First Edition: April 2011
10 9 8 7 6 5 4 3 2 1

The publisher is not responsible for websites (or their content) that are not
owned by the publisher.

Library of Congress Cataloging-in-Publication Data

Washington, Isaiah.
    A man from another land : how finding my roots changed my life / by Isaiah
Washington with Lavaille Lavette.—1st ed.
        p. cm.
    Includes bibliographical references.
    ISBN 978-1-59995-318-2
    1. Washington, Isaiah.   2. Actors—United States—Biography.   3. African
American actors—Biography.   I. Title.
    PN2287.W4523A3 2011
    792'.028'092—dc22
    [B]
                                                            2010039939

For my family, Jenisa M. Washington,
Isaiah Akin-Olu Washington,
Tyme Baraka Washington, Iman Sele Washington,
and the people of Sierra Leone,
with love and gratitude

ACKNOWLEDGMENTS

This book simply would not have been written without attorney Ricky Anderson's vision and Lavaille Lavette's support and assistance. Thank you Eloise Buckner for knowing I was a writer before I did. I would like to thank Professor Vera Katz, Harry Poe, Dianne Houston, Mr. and Mrs. Garland Poe, Moza Cooper, Gina Paige, Rick Kittles PhD, Professor Henry Louis Gates Jr., Dr. James McPherson, Dr. John Robertson, Carmen Smith, Jay Carson, Eric Nonacs, President William J. Clinton, Raymond Scott-Manga and the Manga family for adopting me, the people of Sierra Leone, Abdul Malik Abbott, Susan Whitson, First Lady Laura Bush, Sonya Gay Bourn, Bruce Gordon, Crispian Kirk, Hilal Basma, Ali Basma, Jackie Coker, Dr. Andre Panossian, Antonio K. Hubbard, Breton F. Washington, Adisa Septuri Jones, Dr. Sheku Kamara, Malcolm Bradford, Michael Caulfield, Mohamed Kamara, Ibrahim Sei Kamara, Henry Moriba Koroma, Duchess of York Sarah Ferguson, Jasmyne Cannick, Chandra Wilson, Johnathon Freeman, Max Abrams, Gonzalo Accame, Martin Proctor, Mark T. Laurent, Joe Opala, Minister Zainab Hawa Bangura, Congresswoman Barbara Lee, Congressman Donald M. Payne, Maria Elena Lamas and Tony Lamas, Noelle LuSane, Ian G. Campbell, Esther H. Vassar, Barbara Gothard PhD, Abdulai Bayraytay, Oluniyi Robbin-Coker,

Brian Gilpin, President Ernest Bai Koroma, Adel Nur, Lorne S. Wellington, Bertha L. Wellington, Alexis Idone, Lizette McBride, Gerrell Wilson, Kristle Jenkins, Eric Broyles, Paula Madison, Diahann Carroll, Barry and Dolly Segal, The Segal Family Foundation, MacDella Cooper, Sidney Poitier, Suzy Frank, Swami Turiyasangitananda (Alice Coltrane), Panduranga Henderson, Mirabai Henderson. A special thank-you to Kellie Tabron for your attention to details, the entire Hachette Book Group team for your guidance, my grandmother Savannah M. Holmes, my grandfather Willie H. Holmes, my grandaunt Gustavia. I would like to thank God for creating my father, Isiah Washington III, and having him meet my mother. And a very special thanks to my unbelievably patient and darling wife, Jenisa Marie Washington, my beautiful children, Isaiah Akin-Olu Washington, Tyme Baraka Washington, and Iman Sele Washington. Lastly, I would like to eternally thank my dear mother, Faye Marie McKee, and DNA.

CONTENTS

CONTENTS

A Man
from
Another
Land

CHAPTER 1

"What Part of Africa Are You From?"

For most of my life I have walked the streets of cities such as New York, DC, Chicago, Houston, LA, and others. I have traveled around the world, spending time in countries such as Germany, the Philippines, Japan, England, Australia, Namibia, South Africa, France, Singapore, South Korea, Thailand, and Sweden. Yet, while each of these places is very different, no matter where I traveled there was one thing that was always the same: everywhere I went, native Africans asked me, "What part of Africa are you from?" On buses, on planes, on the sets of my acting gigs, inevitably someone would stop and tell me I looked just like a close relative from West Africa.

I would reply as I always did, "I was born in Houston, Texas." And each time they would look at me as if I were lying. After each encounter, I was always left with a feeling that these Africans knew something that I didn't: I prayed that one day I would understand what it was they saw in me, what it was that made them believe I was from Africa.

"Gimme yo' money, you punk-ass faggot! Whatchu got?" One of the Frazier sisters shoved me to the ground. I was six years old and had just started walking myself to school. My mother would give me an extra quarter to buy a snack to go with my lunch, and every day, without fail, one of the Frazier sisters would beat me up and take it away from me.

The Frazier sisters were two light-skinned black girls from my neighborhood. Because my complexion was darker, many, including the Frazier sisters and their family, perceived me and my family as poor. They acted as if they were superior to me and took it upon themselves to subjugate me by calling me names like "little black monkey," "black sambo," "frog eyes," and "black boy" as they harassed me daily for my school money. They acted as if in order to walk the streets I had to "pay them a toll." They felt they owned the neighborhood because they were light skinned and perceived as better off than my darker-skinned self.

I was a laid-back, scrawny little kid with toothpick legs and kinky hair. I always avoided confrontations, even when they came right at me. I fought with my older sister, but when it came to anyone else, I was docile. I always ducked. Even though they were just a few years older, to me the Frazier sisters seemed like giants.

One day my grandmother, who we called Muh' Dear, happened to see what they were doing to me. As usual, the sisters had taken my money and taunted me all the way to the front gate of Muh' Dear's house. I walked up the front steps to the screen door, but when I tried to open it, it was locked. My grandmother stood right behind it and looked down at me, her eyes steeled with a hardness I had seen her reserve only for what she called the "triflin'-ass Negroes" in the neighborhood.

"You been runnin' home almost every day," she said. "It stops now."

"Muh' Dear, please..." I pleaded.

"No!" she said sternly.

I turned around and saw that the Frazier sisters were still standing at the gate. They were smirking at the fact that my grandmother was quietly scolding me. But they wouldn't have been smiling if they could have heard what she was saying. "If you don't fight those girls standing at my gate talkin' shit, you will never come in this house again."

I was afraid of the sisters for sure, but I was even more afraid of my grandmother. I tried to open the screen door again, but it wouldn't budge. Her foot was propped up against it. She was serious.

"Mickey," she said, using my family's nickname for me, "you betta get them nasty heifers out from in front of my gate."

That fifteen-step walk from the porch back to the gate felt like a mile. My eyes were already tearing up. I believed, one way or the other, my life was going to end. I slowly pushed open the gate.

"Whatchu want, punk-ass faggot?"

I took a deep breath, closed my eyes, and swung my *Hee Haw* metal lunch box as hard and as fast as I could. Fear turned to fire, or else I just got lucky, because my swings connected. I hit them both. I felt the vibration from the blows through my lunch box as they screamed and cried out. I opened my eyes to see them running off down the road.

I looked down at myself. My shirt was a little ripped, but otherwise there was no damage except to the thermos whose shiny glass insulation had cracked into a million pieces when it flew out of my lunch box and hit the ground. I didn't feel proud or boastful. I only did what I had to do...garner some respect.

I walked up to the gate, up the steps, and found Muh' Dear standing there with the screen door wide open. She didn't say a word. She just gave me a simple nod as I walked past her into the kitchen.

A MAN FROM ANOTHER LAND

My grandmother Savannah Mae Holmes was the true matriarch of the family and a culinary genius. She could "throw down" in the kitchen, as the kids say. She loved and doted on me, but she was also as tough as nails.

My grandmother despised the Frazier girls and their "light-skinned" family. They were a constant reminder of how she herself was treated badly by her two lighter-skinned sisters. Although her sister and my Aunt Gussie never treated me poorly when I spent summers with them in Conroe, Texas, I do remember being interrogated by Muh' Dear about being spoiled by my "highfalutin" grandaunt. Muh' Dear said her cooking was better than my Aunt Gussie's "rich whitefolk cooking."

None of this made sense to me. Light skin versus dark skin, "good hair" (soft, wavy, long) versus "bad hair" (short and kinky). The battles around these issues that played out in my family, church, school, and neighborhood confused me. To me people were people, what did it matter if they were light or dark, had straight hair or an afro?

Muh' Dear wore a wig all the time and insisted that my "nappy hair" be shaved from my head, fearing that it would bring me even more pain and problems than my dark skin would with people like the Frazier sisters. In fact, in all of my childhood photos, I am bald! The sentiment seemed to be that being dark skinned with kinky hair wasn't okay, but I wasn't quite sure why. I felt fine about who I was, it was other people that seemed to have a problem with me.

Serendipity or Destiny?

In 1972, when I was nine years old and living in my native Houston, Texas, I started having a recurring dream. I'd wake with the distinct feeling that I had been running from something, but I never knew what. The dream always had me running through a jungle or a forest. The terrain was always green, really green, and the ground was always a deep reddish brown color, like the dirt on my Aunt Gussie's farm in Conroe, Texas. The scent of sweat and dirt would permeate my nostrils.

There were always women and children in the dream, staring at me, pointing and looking as if they knew me but weren't sure that I belonged. I always ran the same path, never straying, always ending up in the same African village.

At first, I would have this dream only during Houston's extremely hot summers. But as I grew older I'd have it at other times; it followed me for years. I never told a soul about it for fear of being ridiculed or simply ignored. The dream started to occur so often that it became a kind of companion, a friend that I could rely on. I fondly named it "the Rerun."

It first occurred during the summer when bike riding was the favorite pastime in my neighborhood. I'd ride with my friends through heavily wooded areas, down "trails" that were really beaten down paths made by neighbors taking shortcuts through the woods.

I was never one to stay on the beaten path. I always wanted to take the uncharted course through the woods and beat my friends to whatever destination we had chosen. My quest to create my own path, to be first, usually meant suffering the penalty of huge welts or cuts on my face, arms, and legs. It was the price I paid for riding through the previously unexplored and unruly branches and rigid foliage.

Even at a young age, I was always trying to break barriers, aspiring to do things that people told me I couldn't, or others thought were strange or unattainable. I was willing to stay the course, take the unbeaten path no matter what got in my way, when others would give up and go home.

The sting from the vines lashing at my arms and legs seemed to urge me to pedal faster and faster. Not once did I ever consider retreating or worry about getting lost. Once, when charging through a particularly dense thicket, I stalled and lurched off my bike, landing hard on the dirt. My body itched and ached from the angry burrs that held fast to my clothes, skin, and hair. It was as if they were chastising me for disrupting their order. But, I remained undaunted, ignoring the pain of the razor-sharp weeds tearing at my hands as I yanked my bike's chain, pedals, and wheel spokes away from their snaking grasp and ripped them away from my legs.

I reached down and grabbed a piece of glass from a broken bottle I found lying on the ground near my leg and used it to chop away the weeds that still entangled my bicycle and me. Once free, I began to run using the bicycle as a makeshift plow, pushing and ripping my way forward as if my life depended on it. I had no idea where the hell I was or the path I took to get there. Gazing up I could see the sun begin to peek through the canopy of tall trees looking down on me. Suddenly I broke through to a cavernous opening in the forest that I thought just might lead me to our meeting place. I looked around, but none of my friends was in sight.

Was I late? Was I lost? No, I could see in the distance the greenery of Independence Heights (Studewood) that we were racing to. "Am I first?" I thought. "Yes!" Then I jumped on my Huffy and tore off the rest of the way as if I were on fire. I arrived at the park before the rest of my friends.

I lay down on the ground, sweating profusely, and tried to catch my breath, waiting for the others to arrive. As they rode up minutes later some of them looked at me, puzzled. "Ah, man! You did it again?" Then the usual litany of "He cheated!" "You're crazy!" "What happened to your face?" and "How did you get here so fast?" followed. I just looked at them, smiled confidently, and said, "What took you so long?"

They all jumped on top of me and took turns playfully

punching me. Nobody mentioned the scratches and welts on my face and body after that. I felt they just accepted me, even though I was different. Those scars represented something only I understood, endured for the privilege of being first.

They were a rite of passage, a precursor to the journey toward a different life, and a connection to a culture that would eventually confirm the inklings, the innate feelings I had inside about myself. Feelings that told me I could achieve greatness, that I was *from* greatness. Certainly, as a child, I could not yet *know* that as I would later, but even at nine years old I *felt* it.

In a way, I was proud of the scars on my face. They represented the fight in me, a pure, raw determination that kept me from ever giving up until I got what I wanted, until I came in first. I couldn't name it as a child, but in my neighborhood, at church, at home, I sensed a feeling of resignation. There was a veil of complacency over many of the people around me. They didn't expect much from their lives, and didn't expect much of me either. It seemed as if it was just enough for many of them to get by in life. They looked for work to put food on the table, but they had no thoughts of striving for a career; people would work to finish high school but not stretch themselves to attend college: some would get married to someone who was considered a good "provider," but they wouldn't seek to find a supportive, passionate love and life partner. Those attitudes are actually quite common in African American men and boys. Colonization taught us to smile more, bow more, and conceal our ambition in order to be accepted by those in power. My grandmother raised me and insisted that I be better than those around me at the time.

In the woods that day, a game of cops and robbers broke out. We threw small rocks at each other and I expertly dodged them. I was always the robber who refused to die when hit. This always led to an argument by the two sides. The slowest runners always suffered the worst consequences, eventually having some kind of unpleasant encounter with a big rock.

We took our rock throwing very seriously and often competed to see who could throw the farthest and most accurately. I was an extremely accurate thrower. I never aimed to hit my aggressor, rather I worked to whiz one by his head just to let him know the power of my throw. I mastered a thumb-and-index-finger technique that served me well when we played, and that could rival the power of any slingshot.

We concocted shields out of garbage can lids, car hubcaps, and cardboard boxes. Ultimately, someone would get hit in the head, hand, or face and the game would come to a screeching halt as we all gathered around the victim to assess the damage. A knot on the head or an open laceration would shut the game down immediately, and we'd turn our focus to erecting a solid story for the parents about what happened. If it was just a welt or minor scrape, we would just battle on. Thinking back on those days, I am still amazed at how invincible we thought we were as children.

Later that day, it began to rain while the sun continued to shine brightly. One of my friends shouted, "The devil is beating his wife!" This was what we said when the sun would shine but it would rain at the same time. This was an old wives' tale shared and believed by many people I knew growing up in the Independence Heights area of northeast Houston. It was a phenomenon that I would see many times in my life in different ways, both literally and figuratively. "Yep, she gettin' her ass whupped!" I replied as we all jumped on our bicycles. There were dark clouds looming on the horizon threatening to consume the sun at any moment.

Another race was on. We pedaled as fast as we could, trying to outride the rain and beat it home. This time I rode with the pack through the streets, glancing over my shoulder at the path

I made for myself earlier that day. I could feel the wind tickling the hard-earned scars on my hands and arms. I considered taking the treacherous path back, ensuring that I would beat them all home. But I had already proven my point, that I was different, willing to take chances, that I would do almost anything to come out on top.

I checked over my shoulder on the progress of the ominous rain clouds, and it seemed we were making little headway, not moving at all, as the storm continued to barrel toward us. I could smell the rain coming and feel its coolness as it caught up to us. I pedaled as hard as I could, faster and faster, dodging parked cars on the street and stray dogs running and barking alongside of us.

I felt a nip at my foot from one of the dogs, but I just nonchalantly tapped him on his nose with the tip of my sneaker, never losing my stride. Now just one hundred yards from our neighborhood street at Thirty-second and Airline, we were forced to stop at a busy intersection. As we waited for an opening in the high-speed traffic that would allow us to cross the road, I looked back to see huge raindrops marching down the middle of the street like a giant paintbrush coloring the once-dry concrete street a slick dark black. The rain hungrily came over us like an angled wall of scattered shimmering strings. It looked so ominous. Then, out of nowhere, growled a grinding rumble of thunder. As we looked up a flash of lightning streaked across the dark clouds...crack!

Frightened by the furor of the coming storm, I launched my bike into the crowded intersection, making it across to the other side just inches past the bumper of a honking, speeding car. Once again separated from the pack, I stopped and turned to see my friends become engulfed by the torrential downpour. It was as if the rain stopped moving and stalled on the other side of the highway. I watched my crew get drenched, like Moses watching Pharaoh's men being engulfed by the closing of the Red Sea.

In the spot where I sat on my bicycle, it was not raining at all. Not a drop. I sat there still in the sunshine. I blinked and then the rain started to fall on me too. Once the traffic slowed and my friends were able to join me, they just shook their heads, acknowledging I had won again. We all said our hurried and wet good-byes and rode off in different directions toward our homes on the block.

That day I simply had a burning desire to be first in a bike race. Today, as a man, I know that desire stems from the fact that I share a storied history, the same DNA, with great Africans and men of incredible courage. Men like Sengbe Pieh—Joseph Cinque as he was called during his historical trial—who had the bravery to lead the *Amistad* revolt. That history, that DNA, reflects a past of great accomplishment that eventually led me to my own place in history.

Why did I take that risk? Why did I not get hit by a car that day? Why did it seem to be raining on them and not on me? This situation has played out in so many different ways throughout my life and it still does.

That same summer I attended a party with my mother. As we entered the house, I immediately noticed a man with what I considered to be very strange hair, wearing nothing but a leather vest and bell-bottom jeans. He was cut, with huge muscles, and smelled of a burning mixture of sweet flowers that I found pleasant and intoxicating as we walked past him.

My mother said a brief hello to him and then moved on to greet other friends at the party, leaving me behind. The air was thick with the smell of barbecue sauce and hickory wood. I roamed around the house, bobbing my head to the loud music and grabbing food off the tables. But mostly I was transfixed by this strange-looking man. He noticed my stare and finally walked over to me.

"Hello, little brother," he said as he approached me, "What is your name?"

"Isaiah Washington," I answered.

He stepped back in mock surprise and with a broad smile replied, "Isaiah Washington! What a beautiful and powerful name, my brother! I hope that you grow and live up to it!"

He had what I thought then was a funny accent. I now know it as West Indian. And his strange hair, I now know to be African locks or dreadlocks as the Rastafarians called them. His intoxicating smell was oil of frankincense and myrrh.

I was drawn to something about him. Perhaps it was how he looked. His features and skin tone were similar to mine. The way he held himself was powerful, and at the same time he was very kind. He seemed a bit mysterious, and the way he spoke suggested he was quite intelligent. Years later, when I arrived in New York, I eventually found myself emulating him. The way he talked, the way he carried himself. He was different from anyone I knew at the time. This seemingly unimportant encounter would leave an indelible impression on me that would manifest itself fifteen years later when I would take on one of the most challenging and life changing projects of my life.

CHAPTER 2

Shades of Darkness

I had seen all the pictures about the exotic locales, gotten the run-down on the benefits, the money for college, and all of the great careers you could get after you got out of the military and joined the private sector. But I also got the speech that every recruiter gives, no matter what branch of the service you decide to join. It was the one about how you'll meet exotic women all over the world and get to fuck them just because you're wearing a uniform.

The pussy speech is more effective than any of those commercials they run during football games or ads they put in *Sports Illustrated*.

It was 1981. Ronald Reagan was our new president. The country was deep into a recession, and the cold war was at its height. We were watching out for the Russians, but at the same time we weren't at war with anybody. We were the richest, most powerful country in the world. Vietnam was far enough in the rearview mirror of our history that being in the military didn't seem like such a bad idea.

I sat there staring at the paperwork, realizing that I was about to sign away the next four years of my life. But once I thought about my life I figured this was my best option. Things at home were growing tenser every day. A fight between my mother and stepfather could break out anytime and erupt into violence. An offer to play college football that I expected never materialized. I did well in school. I was okay in math, a decent writer, and an excellent and avid student of history. My grades were fine, but not good enough for a full ride anywhere, and I couldn't afford college on my own. Taking out a bunch of student loans sounded too complicated. And unless I was somewhere playing Division 1 football, the best, I didn't really want to go to college. There was no one place in my life where it felt as if everything came together.

The economic downturn, particularly with the bottoming out of the oil market in Houston, Texas, made it nearly impossible to find any kind of decent-paying work in the city. I just didn't want to be there anymore. I knew I needed to do something. I knew it was time for me to leave, time for me to grow up, time for me to see the world. I put aside my dream of a college football career and joined the United States Air Force. I saw it as a chance for a clean break, a chance to start fresh, see the world, and learn what I was capable of.

"Do you need another pen, son?" The recruiter asked, wondering why I was hesitating.

"No, sir," I replied. "This one works just fine."

"You can keep it, if you want," he said.

I looked back down at the piece of paper. The blank line was just waiting there, waiting for my signature. I signed my name, Isaiah Washington. I looked at the blue and white ballpoint pen. "Aim High" was inscribed on the side of it.

I thought about myself on the cover of *Time* magazine as General Washington, the first black United States Air Force

Five-Star General. I imagined myself on TV, and my name being mentioned with pride. "Did you hear what amazing, courageous thing 'Mickey' did?"

This was my first step toward manhood. My graduating class of 1981 was the first graduating class of Willowridge High School. That bit of history came and went. The celebration cake had been eaten. The money from the gift certificates had been spent. Only the recruiter and I knew that I had joined the air force. I hadn't told anyone what I was going to do. I had yet to tell Mama. Now that I had graduated we had a lot more time to talk than we ever had before. She still considered me her baby, but she talked to me as if I were a man.

Three days before I was to report for basic training at Lackland Air Force Base in San Antonio, Texas, I finally got up the nerve to let the cat out of the bag. Mama was in the bathroom taking a bath, and I stood in the hallway and spoke to her through a crack in the door. My heart was beating so hard I could hear it pounding in my chest. "I'm leaving, Mama. I'm going to San Antonio."

"What the hell are you going all the way there for?" she asked.

"I got a job," I continued.

"A job? Boy, the post office is hiring right up the street. I checked for you. You know I'll let you stay here as long as you're working. You don't have to go all the way to no San Antonio."

"I have to go, Mama. I'm working for the government."

"Post office is a government job, son."

"I joined the air force, Mama."

There was a long silence. Then she screamed, "WHAT!"

I could hear the splash of water as she leaped out of the tub. She didn't even bother to dry herself off; she just grabbed her robe and pulled it around her. The door flung open, and she stood there, dripping wet.

"What did you do?" she asked.

"I joined the air force, Mama. I'm gonna be an aerospace engineer and a pilot."

I watched as an entire range of emotions washed over her face: anger, resentment, fear, sadness, and then, finally, acceptance.

"Why didn't you tell me?" she asked quietly.

"It's my life, Mama. I gotta decide what's best for me."

"What's best for you? Boy, you barely pee straight. Oh my God, you're just seventeen years old."

"I'll be eighteen in three months, Mama. I'm a man."

"Eighteen ain't no man, Mickey!"

I looked into her eyes. I knew she was going to be shocked, but I had no idea it was going to cause her this much pain. She started crying, sobbing like a baby. I felt helpless. I didn't know what to do. I loved my mama, but I knew it was time for me to get out and make my mark on the world, to make her proud of me, to live up to my name.

"You mad at Mama? Are you leaving 'cause of me? Are you tryin' to get away from me?" she pleaded.

"No, Mama, you can't afford to take care of me anymore. Just look after you now. It's gonna be all right, Mama. You'll see. I promise. I'm gonna be just fine. You're gonna see. I'm not gonna disappoint you like Daddy did. I'm not going to end up like my daddy. I'm gonna make you proud. You'll see."

I was ready for the world; at least I thought I was. Whether I was or not didn't matter, because it was too late to back out. "General Washington," I said under my breath. "General Washington."

The military provides one with a strong sense of extreme patriotism and the doctrine of taking and following orders. The only time you are an individual is on the weekends. I could not promote a particular party while I was serving. If I wanted to vote it had to be as an absentee in the state where I was from. I was eighteen years old; I could die for my country, but I could not legally buy alcohol. After just a short time in the air force, I knew that spending twenty years in the military was not going to be my purpose or legacy in life. After serving my four years, I left.

In 1985, I reentered civilian life. I like to say I had a "midlife crisis" at twenty-two years old. I knew my life was off track. I wanted to "find my purpose." I was certain the military wasn't my life's calling, but I had no idea what was. I was living in Gaithersburg, Maryland, working as a temp at IBM. A year later, in 1986, someone gave me a book called *History of the Theatre* by Oscar Brockett. I didn't know anything about acting or the world of theater. There was a picture and a name in the book...Ossie Davis. As I read about him, I learned about his Pan-African philosophy and his legacy at Howard University, where he founded a theater company, the Howard Players.

On that same day, a friend took me to see the movie *She's Gotta Have It*. I was inspired by the strong, complicated, dignified black characters that appeared on the screen. I was filled with so much pride that such an amazing and important work was written and directed by a black man. As I left the theater, I walked taller and felt an overwhelming sense of dignity. I also wanted to create art that would inspire people to see African Americans in the same way I saw those characters on the screen. I thought, "If this guy, Spike Lee, is doing this kind of work, then I want to do that too." I said to myself, "Ossie Davis is an actor with the Howard Players. Howard University is not too far from my house. This is what I want to do."

When I told people I wanted to be an actor, that I had a ten-year plan to work with Lee, the exciting new director, and that I would also one day meet the venerable Ossie Davis in person, they would just smirk, or raise their eyebrows, writing my comments off as mere persiflage. But I was undaunted by the naysayers, the people who told me I couldn't. I pursued my new dream with an unbridled focus, intent on gaining a platform to do what I really wanted, use my newfound artistry to eradicate stereotypes and educate the world about the complexities of the African American male and his humanity.

It was Davis's tenure at Howard that led me to apply to the university. In 1987, I became a student there. Just as no one believed I'd meet him, no one thought I'd go to college. Few people from my neighborhood went to college, and most of my family members barely made it through high school.

Later in my life, I would have the honor to meet Ossie Davis when working with him on the Spike Lee film *Get on the Bus*. And after Ossie Davis died, I was again honored that BET CEO Debra Lee chose me to give a tribute to him at my first and only BET Awards appearance.

My experience at Howard was not at all what I had hoped it would be. I soon discovered that just like back in my old neighborhood, people had in their minds degrees of blackness, ideas of what it meant to be "black." The campus culture—students, faculty, and administrators—included judgments of each other's "blackness." At Howard, I would soon discover just how black I was and how black I was not.

Things were not easy there on any level. I slept in my car for the first week because I had no money for student housing. I couldn't find a job that allowed me to attend classes by day and work at night. Socially, I felt cold and alienated. The term "African American" was not available to me yet. It seemed only my hue determined my relevance in the caste system that was campus culture, just like in the eyes of the Frazier sisters.

One night, thinking that I might find some camaraderie among other black "brothers," I attended a "smoker" for the Alpha Phi Alpha fraternity. However, it was immediately made very clear to me that entry into the group was not predicated on our shared history as black males. Rather, permission to pledge and join the line was contingent upon my ability to produce a valid American Express card. To the Alpha Phi Alphas, doing so would validate me and prove that I came from a wealthy family. I refused to respond to such an idiotic request and left.

I was later approached by another fraternity, Kappa Alpha Psi. To gain entry into that organization, I was required to subject myself to the "paper bag" test (a degrading test that blacks had been historically subjected to in order to determine if their skin color was light enough to gain entry into certain places or groups) and get an S-Curl (a popular hairstyle at the time which involved applying a chemical process to curl and soften the hair). When I refused to do either, they recommended that I join the Phi Beta Sigma fraternity, whose members, they said, "look like you."

The women of the Alpha Kappa Alpha sorority, made up mostly of lighter-skinned black women, treated me no better. They refused to even look my way while I was on campus, deeming me too dark to be from a wealthy family, and therefore not appropriate dating material.

Just as when I was a child, I couldn't figure out this obsession with the lightness or darkness of one's skin color, or why the texture of one's hair was so important. This idea of what supposedly constituted black beauty seemed idiotic to me.

I had no interest in pursuing membership in a fraternity, and instead turned my attention to other things. In addition to pursuing my acting career, I was increasingly intrigued by the continued questions I got from native West Africans on the streets of DC about my background. I focused on learning more about Africa and its people. While apathy was high among the general student body, I was growing more interested particularly in what was happening in South Africa.

Nelson Mandela had become, and still is, a source of great inspiration. I felt very connected to him and the plight of the South African people. And unlike the Alphas and the Kappas, the African people looked like me. Further, unlike the lighter-skinned students and others who looked at my dark skin with contempt and disdain, the African people I encountered almost always smiled at me and were happy to greet me.

I spent my time attending private meetings, planning and marching in antiapartheid protest rallies that were commonplace in DC at the time. I handed out flyers and "Free Nelson Mandela" buttons to help raise awareness of what was happening in South Africa. I even once played the part of a South African freedom fighter in the play *Tied-Apart* written by Clayton Le-Bouef. It ran for three weeks in a church playhouse, the Sanctuary Theatre.

Still things on campus grew increasingly difficult. I continued to find the so-called pedigreed students shallow, mean-spirited, and elitist. I ran out of money, and could not qualify for tuition assistance. I was told that to attend class, I would have to satisfy my tuition bill in full. Yet, at the same time, two of my classmates who had lighter complexions and "good hair" were allowed to remain in class, even though it was common knowledge among the students and faculty that neither had paid his full tuition. The deans, two light-skinned women, looked the other way. Apparently, the prevailing assumption at the school, shared with me by a darker-skinned professor, Joe Selmon, was that Mr. Carmichael and Mr. Miller would excel in Hollywood, in New York theater, and on TV as leading men.

Desperate to earn money, I was forced to take a job doing dinner theater with a company owned by Dr. Jeffrey Newman, a light-skinned Howard professor. The pay was minuscule, but the exposure and experience turned out to be a blessing.

At the close of each evening, I was entitled to a meal. One

night over dinner, one of my cast mates, a white woman, chided me for using the term "axed" when I spoke, instead of the appropriate "asked." I must have said something like, "I axed him for a ride," as opposed to "I asked him for a ride." This was how everyone said the word back home. I never realized I should say it a different way. Today, I thank her for bringing the error to my attention in such a loving and respectful way. From then on, I made sure to pronounce the word properly.

We would talk about various things as we ate. She was more interested than the majority of my African American peers at Howard were in the atrocities taking place under apartheid rule in South Africa. Their focus was on getting "the envelope" in the mail. I watched as many of them excitedly held it up to the light, feeling for a hard spot inside. If it was hard, it meant they had received a new American Express card and, in the eyes of the rest of the student body, were now legitimate. The times seemed to be all about those who were accepted and those who were denied.

But this was not my story. Still just in my early twenties, I had already experienced much. I had married at age twenty-one, separated, divorced three years later; worked as a Kelly's temp at IBM; dug ditches and worked on construction sites for the Tracy Labor Company; and served four years in the United States Air Force and been honorably discharged. I had acquired, and lost, all of the very credit cards that my peers lusted after.

On campus, I felt surrounded by psychosis and self-hatred based on one's skin color, family bank account, and status in the community. It was absurd to me to focus on these things when so many South Africans were being killed, raped, maimed, and displaced in their own country by whites.

One day I came across a quote from Mahatma Gandhi, "Be the change you want to see." It resonated with me. I realized that I couldn't focus on my fellow students' lack of understanding of the importance of Africa in terms of their own identity as African Americans. The quote became a call to action for me in my own life. *I had to become the change that I wanted to see.* Through my work, through my life, I had to become my own example.

As I learned and discovered more about Africa and the atrocities befalling my South African brothers and sisters, I continued to work to use my acting career to make "my dark skin" worthy of love and respect. I was sickened by what I saw happening there to dark-skinned people, people who looked like me. I wanted to use my work to become a living example of trying to effectively reconnect with the motherland. I knew clearly that I would have to remain disciplined and never deviate from my goal. Eventually, I would try, in my own way, to do what many great men before me—W. E. B. DuBois, Martin Luther King Jr., Marcus Garvey, and Malcolm X—had tried. Like them, I wanted to reverse the effects of the Middle Passage and slavery and elevate black men back to their former place in history, as kings, treated with all the respect that position garners.

At every step of my career, I have had to break down walls of ignorance and stereotypes. For years I was offered nothing but "evil thug roles." I took them so I could earn a living. My portrayals of "strong men" who also happened to be "dark skinned" is what eventually propelled my career forward. Those portrayals got the attention of Shonda Rhimes, the producer on *Grey's Anatomy.* They are what got me roles in films like *Dancing in September.* And it is what I believe will help me continue my quest toward making the concept of "dark-skinned" men obsolete through my art. My desire is for the world to see me and those who "look like" me as human beings. It is a quest I am still on today.

Howard University was just the beginning of my journey. While even today the school lists me as one of its "alumni," the truth is, I never graduated, nor have I ever received an honorary degree. After one semester, I dropped out. I didn't have the financial means to continue my education there, although, despite the social challenges on campus, I wanted to. I never want students to think that by "dropping out" of college as I did that they will easily become rich and famous anyway. It still bothers me today that I didn't finish. I have never been the kind of person who walks away from difficulty.

Still, I took much of what I learned at Howard into my continued transformation into adulthood. I left understanding that effecting great change, taking on challenges, stepping into unknown territory, and rising above difficult circumstances are what Africans have done since the beginning of time. As an African American man, I believe it is what I was born to do. I would eventually discover it is in my DNA.

After seeing *She's Gotta Have It* in 1986, I gave myself ten years to achieve my goal of appearing in a Spike Lee film. It was a goal I met—by 1996, I was not only a working actor, but I was shooting my fourth film with Lee, playing a gay African American Republican in *Get on the Bus*, following *Crooklyn*, *Clockers*, and *Girl 6*. But it took a lot of hard work to get there, and I had help along the way.

In 1987, when I was just twenty-four years old, Howard University drama teacher Professor Vera Katz took great interest in me as a student. She was a small-framed Jewish woman with reddish hair and a voice that packed a punch and she insisted that I meet a gentleman named Harry Poe.

My first impression of him was that he was a man of great discipline, a kind of taskmaster. He resembled the great theater director Mr. Lloyd Richards, who staged the original production of Lorraine Hansberry's *A Raisin in the Sun* in 1959 and directed numerous productions of August Wilson's plays, such as *Fences* and *Ma Rainey's Black Bottom.*

Harry loved shopping at Banana Republic. He always dressed as if he were going on safari—leather beret, starched jeans, white sneakers, and khaki utility shirts and vests. Apparently Richards made this look popular and was one of Harry's idols. Harry reminded me of a revolutionary still stuck in the 1960s, a martial arts instructor slash jazz musician. His receding afro, full beard, and potbelly made him look much older than his forty-two years. Even my mother commented on how old he looked after she came to visit.

In fact, Harry and my mother became good friends. She truly appreciated his support and careful watch over me, and to this day I remain grateful to him for that. With our eighteen-year age difference, Harry quickly became a father figure and a mentor to me. Through his Ebony Impromptu Theater, I was introduced to and performed staged productions with writer B. Mark Seabrooks, novelist Courtney Long (who gave me my first copy of *The Autobiography of Malcolm X*), and actresses Wendy Rachael Robinson and Robin McClamb, all talents and forces to be reckoned with.

Harry also further exposed me to various African peoples, such as the Akan of Ghana and the Yoruba of Nigeria, and African religions such as the Ifa divinations, and Vodu (Lucumi or Santeria). He insisted that I immerse myself in African studies and African art, and learn more about the Civil Rights Movement, the Black Panther Party, meditation, vegetarianism, Iyengar Yoga, and proper diction. He demanded that I study the writings of Paul Laurence Dunbar, James Baldwin, Richard Wright, Ralph Ellison, Langston Hughes, and the Harlem Renaissance.

In the summer of 1987, Harry allowed me to rent a room in his two-story duplex in the northeast section of Washington,

DC. He had a very large apartment that was filled with the squawking sounds of his parrot Iago and the many zebra finches, society finches, and parakeets he had. I remember feeling as if I were living in an aviary slash art museum.

I saw Harry as a serious, intelligent, private, kind man, who was quite eccentric in his ways and thinking. Harry loved rich, "light-skinned" women and often expressed his hope that I would marry a "light-skinned" woman for her money so that I would have financial support during the "lean periods" typical of an actor's career.

Like many of the students I encountered at Howard, Harry believed that a light-skinned, long-haired woman would open doors into the white man's world, signaling that I was a safe and assimilated dark-skinned man. I would laugh in his face when he went on his diatribes about the subject.

His lifestyle was all so new to me, yet, somehow, his home felt very familiar. Creativity and life were teeming from every corner of his place. I could hardly move without being stopped in my tracks, intrigued and enlightened by a framed lithograph, painting, book, or photograph. One day, I finally got up the nerve to ask Harry, "Why is it necessary to have nearly every inch of your wall space covered with various artifacts?"

He simply answered, "I need to see the beauty of our history, our literature, our art and be nourished by what I own of it."

His words landed on my ears as lightly as a feather, but their impact would transform me forever. I stood quietly, thinking to myself for a moment, allowing the words to resonate within me and then silently I repeated to myself, "nourished by what I own of it."

Harry taught me that if you want something, get a photo of it, hang it on your wall, and meditate on it every day. I fell in love with two paintings. The first was *Portrait of a Negress* (1800) by Marie-Guillemine Benoist. The moment I laid eyes on this beautiful painting I decided that my wife would look just like her and we would have a son. The second was *The Moorish Chief* (1878) by Eduard Charlemont. I immediately connected with this painting and began to see my spirit self in this image. I later had prints of both framed and displayed prominently in my apartment.

Harry and I spent many hours engaged in political and creative debate. Some conversations lasted from the afternoon well past midnight. The debates were interrupted only by his constant searching for some page in a book or article in the *Economist, Utne Reader*, or *Time* to help him make his point of view clear. I knew very little about what he was trying to teach me, but I sensed that his feeling of urgency matched mine in my desire to figure it all out...fast.

I always knew when my private lessons were over. If Harry found our conversations or me intruding on his TV time, he would silently retreat to his cluttered refrigerator to grab his trademark frozen mug filled with ice, a pomegranate, some tuna, and Breton crackers. He'd sit down, point the dusty remote at the TV, and start watching his favorite show, *The Honeymooners*. When this happened, I knew class was officially over. I would retreat to my room and drift off to sleep to the sound of Jackie Gleason's trademark threat, "One of these days, Alice! POW! Right in the kisser!"

One bitterly cold day in November, I finally found myself alone in the art-filled apartment. Harry was out of town for the holidays. I could not afford to travel back to my native Houston, so I stayed in DC and turned the heater to high. While it was freezing outside, I felt warm, surrounded by Harry's African art, black memorabilia, and *Jet* and *Ebony* magazines. It was the eve of Thanksgiving 1987. I turned on the TV and suddenly heard my last name. It was the heartbreaking news about the death of one of my heroes, Mayor Harold Washington. I sat in the kitchen, the smallest room of the apartment, watching Harry's tiny TV perched atop some open shelves that housed bags of sugar, rice, cookies, flour, beans, and various boxes of tea.

Hearing that the first African American mayor of Chicago had died left me feeling numb. I was so proud when Harold Washington took office. I remembered that no one expected him to win in 1983. Across the nation people argued about the impossibility of the city of Chicago ever having a black mayor. When he won, I felt as if a member of my family had been elected.

We had more in common than just our last names. When stationed at Clark Air Base in the Philippines from 1981 to 1983, I read an article somewhere that during World War II Harold Washington served in the United States Air Force. He helped build some of the very runways at Clark Air Base that I proudly traversed daily as a 431x1 Aircraft Maintenance Specialist.

Washington rose to the rank of First Sergeant while he served, definitely not an easy accomplishment for a black man in the 1940s. Prior to his becoming mayor, for me, Chicago was synonymous with Al Capone, the great migration, and urban blight. Seeing him at the helm changed my perception of Chicago and made me want to visit. Now he was dead. This beautiful African American man...gone forever.

I sat there alone, in the kitchen, feeling cheated, as if something was taken from me personally. I started crying, not really understanding why I cared so much. Still, I knew one day I would get to Chicago.

My relationship and conversations with Harry had ignited a thirst and passion for knowledge of self, my African self. To this day, for this, I am eternally grateful to him. However, he gave me an even bigger gift. When I announced I was going off to New York to pursue acting, even knowing I wasn't ready to compete with other more trained and seasoned actors there, unlike so many others—friends, family members, professors, strangers—who, in the past, hadn't hesitated to tell me what I was and wasn't capable of, Harry didn't talk me out of it.

Looking back, I realize that what happened on a bitter cold day in 1988 was actually quite miraculous. I auditioned for one of Harry's former students, Dianne Houston, and I got the job. It was a long-term gig with her CityKids Repertory Theater in New York City.

Living in New York was a major turning point in my life. For as far back as I can remember I wanted to know more about Africans. It had started when I was a young boy, with "the Rerun" which left me wanting to connect to and understand the dark-skinned people in my recurring dream. There was the strong, mysterious, dark-skinned man I met at the house party whose presence and persona never left my mind. And there was my awakening at Howard, where I learned more about Africans, the transatlantic slave trade, the horrors of apartheid, and the esteemed Nelson Mandela. I mistakenly thought that by studying at Howard I would find the answers I was looking for. But little did I know how serendipitous my time at Howard University would turn out to be, and how intricately woven the paths of those I had yet to meet in New York would also be in supporting my efforts to find my way. It was in New York that the foundation was laid for my Pan-African spirit.

CHAPTER 3

Aren't You Wolof?

In the summer of 1989, I lived in a loft in Brooklyn, New York. I would catch a bus to the Brooklyn Bridge subway stop and change for the A train for my journey into Manhattan. My old friend "the Rerun" was occurring nearly once a month and haunted me more intensely than ever before. One hot summer morning I awoke filled with anxiety, having had the recurring dream again for the umpteenth time. What did it mean? Feeling hopelessly inadequate and directionless in body and psyche, I decided to enroll in an African dance class to lift my spirits. I scrounged up some subway tokens, and headed out with the cash from one of my unemployment checks.

My heart raced at the thought of this new adventure. As I walked from Washington Street to Myrtle Avenue, I noticed people looking at me strangely. I put my head down and quickened my pace, ignoring the looks. Why were they staring at me? Was it the way I was dressed? I always wore a colorful kente cloth, either as a scarf during the cold winter months in New

York or as a sash or belt during the warmer weather. I took precious time to meticulously cut slits into the legs of all my jeans with my razor blade, and the stone-washed pair I wore that day was carefully ripped from my knees up to my thighs.

I had African locks with a cowrie shell dangling from one of them and the sides and back of my head were closely shaved. I wore a necklace with a cowrie shell centered on a square patch of leather. Most of my fingers had various types of sterling silver rings on them and my wrists were adorned with several bracelets fashioned out of leather, copper, and cowrie shells, which I bought while attending the annual African Festival at the Bedford-Stuyvesant Boys and Girls High School. I must have looked like a walking African jewelry store!

The bus arrived nearly full and I climbed aboard. I always enjoyed placing my token in the receptacle and watching it cling clang through the machine and disappear out of sight. It was always fun watching the bus driver slightly nod in appreciation to me and pretend not to notice our transaction and this marvelous piece of technology.

As I walked toward the middle of the bus, I immediately encountered a heavyset but extremely beautiful woman standing across from me. I had noticed her staring at me when I boarded. I tried to ignore her gaze, but she persisted in looking at me. More people boarded the bus and I was forced to move closer to her. She smiled and said something I didn't understand. I tried to avert my eyes away from hers, but she wasn't having it. Again, she said something in a language I did not recognize. Sensing her growing frustration with me I said, "Hey."

"Why won't you speak your language?" she said accusingly.

"Excuse me?"

She repeated, "Why won't you speak your language?"

"What language?" I asked.

"Aren't you Wolof?"

"Wolof? What's that?"

She laughed and said "You are American? You look like my people in Senegal! Are you sure you are not from Senegal? Where are you from?"

"I grew up in Houston, Texas."

"Texas?" she said, and then rolled her eyes as if she didn't believe me. Suddenly, the bus came to its final stop and she got up to disembark. As she brushed past me on the now over-crowded bus she said, "You are not from Texas, you are from West Africa!" And with that, she got off the bus and disappeared into the sea of humanity that scrambled underground to catch the subway train.

I was stunned, and left with a profound sense of confusion and curiosity about what had just transpired. Why was this woman so convinced that I was Wolof? What was it about me that evoked such a response from her?

The memory of her musical voice and bright smile pierced my previous cloud of anxiety, lifted it up, and blew it away from me. Voilà! My feelings of inadequacy dissipated like sugar on my tongue and sweetened my sense of self. There was something here I decided I must follow, a seed planted that I sensed I must cultivate. I was determined to not only find where Senegal was, but rapaciously learn everything I could about its food, culture, history, and its people. That year, I attended local seminars led by the famous Dr. Ben, the historian Dr. Yosef A. A. Ben-Jochannan, a Cornell University professor considered an expert on the ancient civilizations of Egypt and Africa.

I dreamed of saving up enough money to take a trip to Senegal and visit its slave castle on Gorée Island. One weekend, while out for a walk in Brooklyn, looking for a good lunch, I found myself at Keur N'Deye, a restaurant in Fort Greene. I discovered the owner, Salif Cisse, was from Senegal. He instantly made me feel like an old friend and introduced me to his wife, Marie Cisse. Salif gave me a menu and explained how tasty his *mafe* was. *Mafe* is couscous, brown rice, and my favorite *yassa*, a fish marinated in lemon sauce with onions. He recommended I wash it all down with a cold beer.

I was hooked. I ate there nearly every day and watched as his restaurant attracted many of my neighbors. Joie Lee, Spike Lee, Gary Dourdan, Erykah Badu, Randy Weston, and Stevie Wonder were all regulars. Salif told me so many stories about Senegal, that at times I felt as if I had lived there myself. He went from host to griot for me, deepening my knowledge and appreciation of Senegal and confirming for me that there was something relating to West Africa that I was supposed to do.

The following year, on June 22, 1990, I found myself understudying a role in the play *The Third Rhythm,* being performed at the legendary Apollo Theater in Harlem. During a somewhat unproductive rehearsal, our director decided we would cut the day short. Nelson Mandela was going to speak at a rally, not far from the theater, at the intersection of Martin Luther King Jr. and Adam Clayton Powell Jr. boulevards, also known as African Square. Gary Dourdan, a fellow actor, and I found an upper room at the theater. We watched out the window in silent awe at the sight of Nelson Mandela being carried down 125th Street atop a vehicle surrounded by bulletproof glass.

The sight of the huge crowds, standing behind barricades and cheering, "Mandela! Mandela!" at once intimidated and exhilarated me. There were so many people on the street that, literally, no one could move. It looked and felt surreal.

I realized at that moment that the flyers I distributed, the buttons I handed out, and the protest rallies I'd participated in while living in DC were now no longer necessary. Nelson Mandela was right there in the flesh, a mere fifty yards away from where I stood. He was free.

"Oh my God, is this really happening?" I wondered to myself. I felt an inalienable connection to Mandela at that moment. My strong sense of pride literally made me tremble. I knew that somehow my prayers, boycotts, and participation in rally meetings had helped to make this happen. I felt as if in my own small way I helped free Nelson Mandela. It felt good, really good. In that moment, the world stood still and everyone was on the same page. It was a page that read, "... with liberty and justice for all."

And on that glorious day Gary, a "light-skinned" brother, who sported a "nappy afro" and I shared a bond that transcended our hues.

As I got to know him, it became resoundingly clear to me that Gary was not interested in using *his* skin color to advance himself or his art. Gary was free. He was not like some of the "light-skinned" people I had previously met in my life—from the neighborhood, Howard University, and other places—who seemed to think their lighter skin color made them smarter or more insightful about how white people think, who used their skin color as a badge of honor, as a way to hold on to some *perceived power.* They were not *free.*

As I gazed down at the sea of people lining 125th Street, I realized that if Nelson Mandela could spend his entire life resisting bigotry through patience and the love of humanity, then why couldn't I do the same thing? I guessed that going forward whenever the misguided notion that lighter was somehow "better" revealed itself or made an appearance I would have to challenge and resist the notion, just as Mandela did, with elegance and dignity.

Nelson Mandela was free. Gary Dourdan was free. And as I stood there that day, watching all kinds of black people of every shade and hue cheering Mandela and his freedom—even whites in the crowd in Harlem were screaming his name—I was free too. It felt good. It felt natural. On that day we all were one people with one cause, and that cause was to resist bigotry, ignorance, and hate, and be free.

I now know that to overcome inequity and change the course of history is in my DNA, and the DNA of my people. I now know that just as bigotry from whites is dated, dangerous, and just plain silly, so is the bourgeois ideology of organizations such as "Jack and Jill"—formed in the 1930s by black prosperous families to provide their children access to teas, debutante balls, and other social practices of wealthy whites, from which they were excluded because of prejudice. The group's critics accused it of practicing its own brand of bigotry, favoring well-to-do and lighter-skinned blacks for membership.

The diversity train has taken off. People need to get on board or risk being run over by it.

My story is clear. Ignore Africa at your peril. Africa is in ALL of us and she is reaching out for help now in more ways than ever! Africa gave us the first civilizations and Africa will give each of us our freedom, just as she gave me mine. When we help Africa, we help ourselves.

W*hap, whap, whap*! I felt the sting of each measured blow on my back and my neck being administered by a very large and focused hand. I was strapped onto a machine hanging upside down in the darkness and unable to breathe. I was beginning to wonder whether I was going to die of asphyxiation or a broken neck.

Everything seemed to slow down and become very quiet. People were gathered around speaking in hushed tones and frantic whispers. The air was filled with urgency as someone hit me again and again.

I couldn't help but wonder, "Damn, is this what it felt like when I was born and not breathing? Did the doctor hang me upside down and violently spank me into existence? Shit, this sucks!"

This was not the first time I had experienced this feeling. I had nearly drowned twice in my life. But each time, someone or something always brought me back to life. This time, a peanut shell was threatening to kill me. A huge man was fighting back, hell bent on not letting me go. That man, my savior, was Mr. John Amos.

We were all backstage during an intermission at the Capital Repertory Theatre in Albany, New York. I was playing the part of Cory Maxson in August Wilson's *Fences* and John Amos was portraying the powerful patriarch Troy Maxson. Hundreds of people were patiently waiting in the audience for the second half of the play to begin. It would have been in extremely poor taste to die backstage before the paying audience could see how one of Wilson's greatest works ended.

The script called for my character to shell and eat peanuts onstage, listening intently as his father spoke. The monologue, designed to warn his son against the false hope and promises of the sports world, was delivered beautifully each night by Amos. Troy Maxson wanted his son, Cory, to focus on finding a real, steady-paying job. Cory had scholarship offers to play football and was confused as to why his father resented his chance for advancement.

I remember hearing the part in the dialogue where the father says, "You need to stop worrying if somebody likes you. You need to make sure that they pay you." At that moment I knew something was wrong. For a minute I thought John was speaking directly to me and not my character. I started to perspire and the room seemed different, as if every single person in the audience was looking not at me but right through me. I felt confused and desperately wanted to run off the stage and hide. I couldn't breathe. I tried to swallow, but nothing happened. Something was stuck in my throat.

My eyes began to water and I could see that John sensed

something was wrong. I wasn't supposed to actually cry at that moment, but my eyes were tearing up. He forged on as did I. All I could do was hold my breath to keep from gagging and choking onstage. There was no way that I was going to go down in this theater's history as the guy who embarrassed the hell out of Kunta Kinte (the central character John played in Alex Haley's *Roots*). To this day, I don't know how I managed to contain myself for the rest of act one of the play. When the lights finally went down, after what seemed like an eternity, I could hear the applause rise up as I ran off stage straight into the restroom.

As I was gasping and grabbing at my throat, someone gave me a glass of water. Another applied the Heimlich maneuver. Nothing worked. At this point, I could barely speak and panic was setting in. Some people watched on with shock on their faces, looking powerless as to what to do. Others smirked, acting as if they thought I was overreacting.

Luckily for me, John had a back problem and needed an elaborate machine that looked like a huge stretcher with ankle straps and hooks on the bottom of it. The stretcher was attached to a huge metal stand that allowed one to be strapped on and then literally flipped upside down. Apparently this contraption helped him stretch out his spine and back muscles.

The next thing I knew, John had strapped me to this thing and turned me upside down and then upright again with such force that I blacked out. The centrifugal force alone should have made that loathsome peanut shell fly up and out of my throat immediately. But nope, I was still choking.

A quiet hysteria filled the very same air that I needed to breathe. I could hear the weighted and growing concern in John's voice, "Someone needs to make an announcement, because we need to get this boy to the hospital."

"What? I hate hospitals!" I remember thinking, "Oh hell no, people die in hospitals!"

It was either my sheer will, or perhaps my fear of hospitals, that had me demanding, through my own version of sign language, to go back onstage and finish the play. I began to flail my arms all about trying to signal to them to let me up. Everyone backstage paused for a moment and then sprang into action. The show must go on! And that is exactly what we did.

The same calmness I felt as a child, plowing my way through the woods into unknown territory, washed over me. The last half of the show was probably the most focused and best stage performance of my career. I left my body—it was no longer responding to me as I wished. I called on my ancestors to get me through, to show me the way out of this. I wasn't ready to die. I prayed for assurance of more time on the earth to fulfill my purpose, and to become an influential artist. And they answered.

The final curtain came down and the executive director of the theater demanded that I see a doctor immediately. I was driven to the emergency room and X-rays confirmed that I had a sliver of peanut shell embedded in my esophagus. The doctor removed it, but the trauma of the choking had left me with a small laceration and a loose piece of skin that felt like a feather tickling the inside my throat whenever I spoke or swallowed. It bothered me for weeks.

I was put on twenty-four-hour watch. The theater arranged for the wardrobe mistress, Melissa Toth, to monitor me. She took very good care of me that evening. As we were talking she said, "You should become a writer."

I had heard that before. I asked, "Why do you think that? I'm an actor not a writer."

She smiled. "No. You are an artist. You can do whatever you want." She later gave me a copy of Walt Whitman's *Leaves of Grass*. It was a gesture that greatly resonated with me. A year later I found myself living at 231 Clermont Avenue between DeKalb and Willoughby streets, in Brooklyn. This was the landmark neighborhood where Walt Whitman lived and was inspired to write *Leaves of Grass*. I don't think it is an accident that I now write this book.

After we worked together and he so kindly challenged death on my behalf, John Amos, whose memory confirms mine on the choking incident, became a mentor and friend. Our relationship had special significance and actually began long before I met him in person for the first time.

It was 1976, I was thirteen years old and sitting at home in Houston watching the TV show *Good Times*. During a commercial break, there was a teaser for the five o'clock news about the death of a local man, fatally shot by his common law wife. Turns out, the man was my father. That's exactly how I learned that my biological father had died—at home, sitting on the couch after school, watching an episode of *Good Times*.

When I was three years old, after his beating my mother throughout their five-year marriage, my mother and I left him. My mother later told me that when she packed her bags to leave, she told him there would be a woman out there who would not tolerate what she endured from him, and that woman would probably take his life.

To me it is no surprise that when I learned of my biological father's death, I was watching my fantasy father on TV. I idolized James Evans Sr., John Amos's character on *Good Times,* and for years I wished he were my own father. They were complete opposites. While my father was aggressive and abusive, fighting everyone around him, James Evans Sr. used his strength to fight against the sting of poverty and racism in the Chicago projects that threatened to tear apart his family.

To me James Evans symbolized strength and character. I admired him, and with no strong black man close to me to look up to, with no one like him in my life, I looked up to him. As my life progressed, I would eventually learn that a man's character is his destiny. And I knew that one day, I would meet John Amos.

I feel extremely fortunate to have developed such a strong bond with John when I did. He exemplified strength of character in everything he did on film, television, and stage. It was his mentorship that laid the foundation for my transition from New York to Los Angeles. He helped me further understand my place in the world.

He would always say, "Your intensity can be a pain in the ass, son, but I love it! All you need is one vehicle and you are on your way. That is if your emotions don't become your worst enemy. You feel so deeply, son, but you have got to learn to contain it and make it laser sharp. Sharp enough to be felt through the screen. Can you do it? Huh?"

"Yes, I can do it," I replied.

"Can you be obsequious?" he asked me one day.

I looked up the word "obsequious"; definition: servile. The word "servile"; definition: humbly submissive.

I didn't understand. "Why on earth was John Amos asking me to be servile? He's Kunta Kinte, one of the strongest symbols of a black man ever on film! He's the guy who held up his newborn child toward the starry night sky and proclaimed, "Behold the only thing greater than yourself!" To me he exemplified strength, but he was telling me that I must figure out how to "conceal" mine.

Meeting John Amos was no accident. I was supposed to meet him; there was something I was to learn from him. He said I needed to appear affable and nonthreatening or there would be hell to pay. Hollywood never saw my strength as an asset; it already had Denzel Washington for that. Apparently, there was no room for another serious actor to become a "leading man" in the 1990s and I wasn't the happy and funny Will Smith type. John was right. I would figure out just how right years later when I found myself in the midst of a Hollywood controversy that spread out of control like a forest fire.

It is unflinchingly clear to me that there are no coincidences in life. We meet people for a reason and a season. We each have a message, a gift, and a purpose to share with the world. It is something that is undeniable and unique to every single one of us. For years I have used the words "ironic" or "serendipity" so much that it has become like a running joke I've told far too many times. I firmly believe that we are all given signs and dreams and put in situations that define who we were and who we are to become. All of it points us toward our destiny. All we need to do is listen carefully to the messages and follow our dreams. It is in our dreams that we find our true identities and where our destiny awaits.

Harry Poe had moved to New York City from DC as well. He became the creative director for the CityKids Repertory when Dianne Houston left to pursue her writing career in Los Angeles.

The cost of a New York apartment was, and still is, very expensive. Agreeing that it would be cheaper if we split the cost, Harry and I found a place together on Lincoln and Bedford streets in the Crown Heights section of Brooklyn. There was just one problem. I couldn't have overnight guests. I never knew the reason behind this; it was just one of Harry's rules. He was an extremely private man and I suppose did not want his space invaded by someone he didn't know or trust.

I once heard a story that he had been married to a woman who was part of the Washington, DC, bourgeoisie. They were reportedly known to throw lavish soirees at their huge home, for DC's politicos and community elites. The tale was that Harry refused to service his wife sexually after they married and rumors of his sexuality prompted her to file for divorce to save face. Harry's sexual orientation was never an issue or a discussion between us. I always considered Harry kind of asexual; I never saw him with a man or a woman. Many of Harry's protégés were gay, lesbian, or bisexual, but he had plenty of heterosexual friends and students too. He seemed to love money, people, and art far more than sex. I never thought much about whether or not someone was gay. I didn't really care one way or the other. We were all just struggling artists, theater people.

Harry fancied himself a Renaissance man like Langston Hughes and had delusions of grandeur, always talking about one day getting "his mansion." But as I got to know him, I began to see him as a very lonely and somewhat broken man trying to live vicariously through me. He talked about his mistakes as a young actor and how his hubris stalled his career. He never blamed his failures on racism; he just chalked them up to poor timing.

He had some health issues and suffered greatly from an ulcer. Harry was a complicated man. He would constantly remark that I wasn't "his type" and that he couldn't understand why he was so interested in me and my career. At times he chided me for being "too dark" and joked that I should stay out of the sun. This was a huge contradiction to his self-proclaimed African High Priest Akan demeanor. But Harry was full of contradictions. He would say, "Isaiah, I am incredibly human. I am probably the most human person you will ever know because I know that I am flawed. I know that I am perfect imperfection!"

I learned so much from Harry, but over time I began to resent his rules. I started spending many nights away from the apartment, staying at a girlfriend's place. I would stop by only to drop off my half of the rent.

The situation created extreme tension between us. Eventually, we stopped talking and I severed our ties. Our last argument was a crisp and philosophical one. Harry accused me of jeopardizing my career and losing focus on reaching my highest potential as an actor.

"You can be as big and successful as Oprah Winfrey, Eddie Murphy, or Denzel Washington!" Harry said.

"What the hell are you talking about?" I shot back. "I'm working as an actor all the time! I think I'm allowed to have some fun! I don't want to be successful like Oprah, Eddie, or Denzel; I want to be successful like me!"

What came out of Harry's mouth next sent me out the door. "Okay, then," he said. "It seems clear that I've been wasting my time with you if you don't want that level of success for yourself!"

I was floored and confused at his resolve. I walked past him, out the door, and never looked back. Like any son-and-father kind of relationship, I set out to prove him wrong as opposed to proving to myself that I was right. I felt that he was treating me like a child and not as a man. I had never had a father figure challenge me so completely. I didn't know what to do.

On April 29, 1992, Los Angeles erupted into chaos. I was riveted by the images on TV. The rioting was sparked by the acquittal of four Los Angeles police officers accused in the beating, caught on videotape, of African American motorist Rodney King.

A girlfriend gave me a brochure about Ayuko Babu and his newly formed nonprofit organization in LA called the Pan African Film Festival (PAFF). I sat there thumbing through the brochure, glancing back and forth between it and the TV reports, and read:

PAFF is a non-profit organization dedicated to promoting cultural and racial tolerance through film, art and creative expression. Each year the festival presents over 100 films from the US, Africa, the Caribbean, Latin America, Europe, the South Pacific and Canada. The goal is to present a wide range of creative works by black artists that help to promote positive images and work to destroy negative stereotypes. The festival also presents one of the country's largest fine art shows featuring prominent and emerging black artists and fine crafts people, poets, and story tellers.[1]

It was not the first time someone had mentioned the PAFF to me. It seemed I was hearing about this organization more and more, almost as much as I was hearing people tell me that I looked like a native Wolof out of Senegal.

I was especially interested in it because Ja'Net Du Bois, the actress and singer who portrayed Wilona on the hit TV show *Good Times*, was a cofounder and chairperson of the PAFF. I had great respect for her as an actress. She was also, of course, on the same TV show as my fantasy father John Amos. Together, all of these "coincidences" were a sign. My intuition told me that going to the PAFF would somehow lead me to someone or something that would get me closer to Africa.

Even while watching the reports of what was transpiring in LA, I thought to myself, "It is time for me to get to Los Angeles." I wanted to get to the PAFF. I watched the looting, burning, and hellish violence at the corner of Martin Luther King and South Normandie avenues. I watched, dubiously transfixed at this ignominy for the next three days. I couldn't believe my eyes. I could not digest the sheer inhumanity of what I witnessed. These people, the rioters, looked like me. Although I was just as angry at the injustice of the acquittal, my anger clearly did not burn in my heart as deeply as it did in theirs.

I will never forget the image of Reginald Denny being dragged out of his huge 18-wheeler truck and being mercilessly beaten and bludgeoned with a cinder block. I sat there watching in shock and in utter disbelief. The phone rang; it was a friend calling to tell me to call Dianne Houston immediately, she was trying to reach me. When I called her back, the message she gave me was shattering.

Harry Poe had died.

It was never really clear to me what he died of. He was found dead in his apartment, sitting in a yoga lotus position. They needed me to come and clean out the apartment and help his parents claim his remains.

The day I put my key in the lock of the door and stepped inside Harry's place, tears immediately leaped from my eyes. My knees buckled as I shut the door behind me. I stood there, leaning against the door, frozen, unable to move.

Then something in me said, "Start meditating." I sat down, closed my eyes, and quieted my mind. Twenty minutes later, I got up and walked into my old room, where faux paintings covered in bubble wrap were stacked to the ceiling. I cleared a path and stooped down to look under my old bed. I spotted a dead mouse that looked as if it had suffocated from all of the dust. I could barely breathe myself.

I began searching until I came across a file cabinet covered with old newspapers. It was unfamiliar to me. I opened it and discovered all of Harry's important personal documents. I never knew he had a middle name. It was Xavier. A voice in my head told me to give these things to his parents. I did.

After removing all the clutter from my old bed, I lay down in complete exhaustion. I felt shaken to my core and was trying very hard to understand what had just happened. In this apartment full of things, how was it I knew where to find *those* documents?

I turned my head, glanced to the right, and noticed two bullet holes in the window. Many copycat riots had spread around the nation during the riots in Los Angeles. While I was watching what was happening in LA on TV, apparently Crown Heights in Brooklyn, and uptown in east Harlem, were in the midst of riots of their own. The positioning of the holes told a frightening story. If I had been sleeping in the bed when those shots were fired, I would have been shot in the head, twice. I stood up slowly and followed the trajectory of the bullets to my old closet. As I suspected, the projectiles were still embedded in the Sheetrock.

This was all very difficult to process. The man who had become the closest thing I ever had to a father was gone, and I never got a chance to say good-bye. I had left him in this very apartment, in anger, and returned in sadness and regret.

I was still learning from Harry even after he was gone. His passing was pivotal in my understanding and acceptance of death, which would eventually help me prepare for my mother's death.

It was only two years later, in 1994, that I learned that she was terminally ill and had about seven years to live. Her life was now on the clock. I was running out of parents and there was absolutely nothing I could do about it.

"Yes I'll hold," I said. I had boldly placed a call to Mayor Richard Daley's office to formally file a civil complaint against a city yellow taxicab driver. I was working in Chicago. A dream had come true. I had finally made it to Mayor Harold Washington's city, just as I had promised myself I would back on that cold Thanksgiving eve in 1987, when I sat in Harry's tiny DC kitchen and learned of the mayor's death.

I was cast as Henry Antrobus in a production of Thornton Wilder's *Skin of Our Teeth*. The experience of Harry's death was still raw within me and was the driving force behind my performance that scared and intrigued the theatergoers at the Goodman Theatre in Chicago.

It was a very special production, not only for its color-blind casting, but it was also the fiftieth anniversary celebration of the Pulitzer Prize—winning play that originally debuted in 1942. My performance as the rejected and angry son was so visceral and ominous that it produced a great deal of controversy and left both the blue bloods and the African Americans boiling. The white season-ticket holders who "didn't get it," who misunderstood what we were trying to do, demanded we attend a special press conference to address the issues. The charge from some theatergoers was that we were destroying the true meaning that Wilder intended for the audience to receive. They bitterly accused me and the very talented director, David Petrarca, of changing the dialogue for Henry Antrobus.

We had not.

The African American theatergoers were outraged that Petrarca would cast me as Cain, the first killer, and for having the third and final acts set in postriot Los Angeles. To see so much sensitivity and ignorance exposed was great. It was exactly the kind of impact I had hoped to have when I became an actor. I think Mayor Harold Washington would have been proud of the play. The production was breaking down strict barriers, challenging septic attitudes, and changing perspectives in the city that he loved. There was just one problem. Someone didn't get the memo.

One particular night, after receiving rave reviews and a rousing fifteen-minute standing ovation, I floated off the stage. I hugged and congratulated everyone. Marcia Gay Harden had delivered a blistering performance that night as well.

I slowly got dressed, savoring every moment of the evening, and was the last to leave the Goodman Theatre. I asked the stage manager to call me a cab. Sure enough, it was there waiting for me by the stage door. I skipped down the stairs with the applause still ringing in my ears, and reached for the door handle.

It was locked.

I leaned down toward the passenger side window and looked in at the driver and asked him to open the door. The cabdriver looked me straight in the eyes, turned away, and stepped on the gas, nearly driving over my right foot and almost tearing my arm off.

I stood there in complete shock, motionless, as I watched that fool screech his tires and speed off down the empty street. My pants and peacoat kept the brisk, frigid Chicago air from cutting through my body, but my soul was left ice cold that night. I was too hurt to be angry. I had fallen in love with this city, its museums, its restaurants, its garlic festival, its people, and I thought it loved me.

"Hello? Yes. I'm still holding."

"Yes?"

"I would like to speak to the mayor, please. . . . What? No, he doesn't know me. My name is Isaiah Washington and I am in the play *Skin of Our Teeth* at the Goodman Theatre."

"Excuse me? *Skin of Our Teeth*?"

"Yes, at the Goodman Theatre."

"Yes."

"Well, I would like to file a civil complaint against a yellow cabdriver."

"What?"

"A taxicab driver refused to let me in his taxi and ran his car over my foot."

"Excuse me. Will you hold on, please?"

"Yes. I'll hold." Then, "Hello? Hello? Hello?"

This incident played itself out in places all over the country every day. A black man in America who couldn't get a cab was not an uncommon occurrence. Still, on this night in particular, when I felt so proud of what I had accomplished in the play, it only served to strengthen my resolve to change the way people viewed me and my dark skin.

When the play eventually ended I returned to New York.

I was lucky enough to be cast in the HBO film *Strapped*, Forest Whitaker's directorial debut. Interestingly enough, I canceled what would have been my first trip to West Africa to audition for him. I give him credit for helping start my film career. It was through my work in this film that Spike Lee first took notice of me. Years later, Forest would play another pivotal role in my life and provide me with the chance to publicly thank and honor him through another kind of work, work that had little to do with acting but had everything to do with celebrating and empowering black people in Africa.

Another dream manifested in my life a year later. It was one of the hottest summers on record in New York when I got a part in Spike Lee's critically acclaimed film *Crooklyn*.

As I stood on the set during a scene, a flying camera crashed right into my head! The scene required me to walk up a flight of stairs, outside a brownstone, while shaking hands with some neighborhood kids who idolized my character, Vic Powell. I chose to wear shades during the scene and wasn't clear on the direction of the camera.

It was my very first scene on my first day and I was a nervous wreck. I heard "Action!" and I took one...two...three...four steps, then WHAM!

Everything stopped.

I thought to myself, "What the hell was that?"

"Cut! Cut! Cut!" Spike bellowed.

I tried to maintain my composure as Spike ran up to me screaming.

"What the hell are you doing? You missed your mark! Look, this is your mark! I gotta camera on a Louma Crane and it's going to fly over your head and stop in front of you! You understand?"

"Yeah, I got it." I said. "Hit my mark."

"Do you know what a mark is?" Spike asked.

I lied and said, "Yes, of course I know what a mark is."

"What is it?" he barked at me.

I paused and, then guessing, pointed down at the bright yellow piece of tape on the upper step where he and I were standing.

"Well then hit it and don't fuck up my shot again. If you do, you will be out of focus." And with that he ambled away.

I never missed my mark again.

My opportunity to work with Spike Lee blew the minds of many of the people who, when I pronounced back in 1986 that I would, told me, "You're dreaming!"

Much has been written and said about Mr. Spike Lee and not all of it is good. Spike isn't perfect, but none of us are. I'm confident that his body of work, rather than what the critics write, will stand the test of time and ultimately define his legacy. His passion inspired me to become an actor, to be bold, be beautiful, and be intelligent, to stand up for what I believed in and creatively challenge systems that marginalize all people. And for that, I remain eternally grateful to him.

Thanks to Spike and the second film I made with him, *Clockers*, Hollywood and the world took notice of me. I set my sights on Los Angeles and my friend and mentor, John Amos, was there to support me.

One night, while I was staying at his home in Sherman Oaks, John invited me to take a late-night drive with him. As we drove around Los Angeles's Crenshaw district, in his dark green Volkswagen Beetle, he pointed out places to eat cheaply like the M & M Soul Food restaurant near Village Green and Phillips Barbecue in Leimert Park; he showed me the Eso Won Bookstore at 900 North La Brea and then the future home of the Magic Johnson Theater.

As we drove, he shared some valuable insights about his experiences in Hollywood, some good, some bad, and some funny. That night I told him that, as a child, I always knew that I would meet him. He seemed a little uncomfortable at first. "Where are your people from?" he asked. I told him mostly Louisiana and Virginia on my father's side and that my great-grandmother Miss Della's maiden name was Amos. She was born August 1, 1888, and married my great-grandfather, Mr. John Brown, born June 11, 1888. Her brother, a Mr. Otto Amos, was born October 15, 1874.

John pulled the car over and said, "Damn, son, we may be family." We both sat in silence marveling at this serendipitous moment and watching some firefighters battle flames on the roof of a burning house. We didn't say a word. We just sat silently watching the silhouette of one of the firefighters engulfed by the smoke. His shadow was cast high up onto the smoke as if it were a canvas. It made him look as if he were a twenty-foot-tall giant. He seemed determined to save the sanctity and tranquillity of that home but was rendered powerless by the sheer ferocity of the flames dancing and searing their way through the wood-shingled roof. We could feel the heat from where we sat in the car.

The smell of the burning wood and the sight of this firefighter's battle brought tears to my eyes. "There will be no wins tonight," I thought to myself, "only losses for the family that lived there and for the firefighters who struggled so hard."

We drove on.

The next day I found myself alone in John's cavernous house. It was a sunny, beautiful California day. I stood at the kitchen sink making myself a turkey sandwich and marveling at how great life was. Suddenly, a loud rumbling seemed to come from the back of the house. It sounded as if the floor were going to erupt and explode beneath me. I instinctively grabbed my case knife tighter to protect myself.

Silence.

Then again, the rumbling came toward me and continued on under my feet. I ran out of the kitchen, terrified. It was so loud, so foreign, and so threatening. I reached for the telephone, preparing to dial 911, then suddenly felt ridiculous and cringed at my stupidity standing there holding the case knife and the phone tightly in my hands. What the hell was I going to say? "Hello, Operator? There is a giant noise rumbling under my house, can you send someone to help me please?"

I soon calmed down, realizing this was one of the tremors or shock waves I had heard about, stemming from the 6.6 earthquake that hit Northridge, Sherman Oaks, and other surrounding areas at 4:30 a.m. on January 17, 1994, Martin Luther King's holiday.

When I later told John about my reaction, he didn't laugh at my fear at all. He told me that during the earthquake he walked outside and saw that all of the water in his pool had been thrown completely out. He said that he slept in that same pool that night, too afraid to go back inside the house. I walked outside and looked at the very large pool and tried to imagine its contents forced out of it. I couldn't.

I called B. Mark Seabrooks, whom I knew from my Ebony Impromptu Theater days, and told him that I was going to try to make a go of it in LA. Mark had been a fixture in Harry's duplex long before I showed up. Harry had a seemingly unquenchable sweet tooth and Mark supplied him with a never-ending stream of cakes that he baked himself.

I tried desperately to find an affordable car and my own apartment. I felt as if I had overstayed my welcome at John's place and tried to split my sleepovers between there and Mark's house. Eventually, I ran out of spending money and had to cash in a few stocks to purchase a plane ticket back to New York.

A few days before I planned to leave Los Angeles, I had a conversation with a woman at a party. She said, "You must come back next year for the Pan African Film Festival in February." I thought, "You gotta be kidding me.... There is this Pan African Film Festival thing again."

As soon as I returned to my humble apartment in Fort Greene, "the Rerun" was back and in full force. Though it was usually a sign that I was back on to discovering something new and important in my life, I would later learn that the dream was a sign that I was on track to fulfilling my destiny.

I didn't make it to the Pan African Film Festival in 1995, but I did meet Jenisa Marie Garland. And on February 14, 1996, we were married.

When Jenisa saw my framed copy of *Portrait of a Negress,* even she had to acknowledge her resemblance to it. She also shivered at the powerful likeness that I had to *The Moorish Chief.*

CHAPTER 4

Notes on Namibia: My First Trip to Africa

Finally, in 1996, I made my first appearance at the fourth annual Pan African Film Festival. I remember walking the red carpet directly behind the actor Laurence Fishburne. I admired his ceremonial African dress and was awed by how regal he appeared in it. These kinds of encounters only fanned the flames of my desire to know as much as I could about Africa. It deepened the still undiscovered connection I felt to African people, and my dream of visiting the continent.

In addition to the powerful films and art I saw at the festival, this is also where I met a woman who would, soon after, literally change my life. Her name was Moza Mjasiri Cooper. Moza is a stout, caramel-colored woman with braided hair that she always pulls up elegantly atop her head. Her Tanzanian accent fluttered through the air like a hummingbird's wings making a sound that called to me. Moza could convince me to do her bidding in thirty seconds flat. She is one of the most incredibly positive human beings I have ever met. Whenever I see her she is smiling and happy; she is like a breath of fresh air. I had only just met her when she invited me to come to her native Tanzania and meet her relatives. I think, like the lady on the bus in Brooklyn who decided I was from Senegal, she had decided that Tanzania was my homeland.

Because of Moza, I made every effort to attend and support the PAFF every year. I had resigned myself to the fact that this would be my only way to ever see Africa. At the time, I was an actor trying to build his career, and I had no money and no contacts to make such a trip on my own. I thought that by attending this festival I might meet someone who could open a door of opportunity for me. I saw the PAFF as a form of international networking.

I was right.

In December 1998, I received a call from a director named Elaine Proctor. She wanted me as a lead in her new film *Kin*. It would be shot entirely on location in Namibia. I was blown away! The timing, however, could not have been worse. It meant leaving my pregnant wife for three months.

After a fitful night of stop-and-start sleep, I woke at 3:30 a.m. then drifted in and out of consciousness until the alarm rang an hour later. Jenisa and I held one another tightly, lovingly. She whispered a prayer for my travel in my ear.

I climbed into the shower just before five. Eddie, my cat, was alarmingly sedate. He seemed to sense that I was leaving for a longer time than usual and he let me off easy, sparing me his usual howling cry for food the moment he opened his eyes.

The doorbell rang at 5:15 a.m. sharp. I was dressed and ready to go! Jenisa walked into the living room, tears running down her face. Seeing her cry killed me softly; she was usually so strong. I said, "Please don't do that, we said we would not be sad." I hugged her. We exchanged our final kisses and hugs. I hated good-byes.

I was now getting into the vehicle that would catapult me toward my dream, Africa, the motherland. Ironically, I found myself climbing inside a Lincoln Town Car. I laughed to myself at the symbolism—President Lincoln freed the slaves and now a Lincoln limo was bringing me, a free man, to the airport for my return to Africa. It was ironic.

American Airlines flight 898 was turbulent and the movie *What Dreams May Come* with Robin Williams and Cuba Gooding Jr. was playing on the monitors. The film was actually quite moving. I forced myself to hold back the tears that were virtually popping out of my eyes. Love conquers all; that was the movie's message.

Four hours and twenty minutes to Miami. I felt a little as I imagined my unborn son, Isaiah Akin-Olu Washington, felt all snuggled up in his mother's womb. My wife Jenisa and my mother Faye's prayers for my safety had me feeling securely wrapped in love and protection. I sensed the hand of God on me as we flew.

The pilot was extremely apologetic when, over the PA, he announced a delay. I laughed a little, thinking to myself, "Pity the man and his machines as I ride on the wings of God." When we landed I realized that I had been daydreaming and missed the announcement about my connecting gate. I tried to locate the flight going to Cape Town, South Africa, on the terminal monitor but couldn't. I found a desk attendant and asked for help and she directed me to gate E8.

As I walked toward the gate, I noticed a very long line. As I approached the end, slightly unsure that I should be waiting in it, I saw others already boarding. It was 4:22 p.m. and the flight was scheduled to leave at 5:00 p.m. There were two older passengers in front of me complaining about how unsafe the flight would be if "all these people were allowed on with all their pieces of carry-on luggage."

"South African Airlines used to only allow two pieces at a time," the woman snorted. "It couldn't possibly be safe with all this extra weight!"

I was very excited and looking forward to my time in Africa; finally I was going to step foot on the very soil I had been dreaming of, protesting for, studying about for so many years. I could barely contain myself. I was anxious with fear and anticipation of the unknown.

When I finally boarded the plane, there was an announcement over the PA system that the trip would take thirteen hours and fifty minutes. I thought to myself, "How interesting. It took fourteen weeks for the slave traders to get my ancestors to America via the Middle Passage and will take only fourteen hours for me to return to Africa."

A stroke of good fortune found me seated next to a very interesting man: Ivahn Van Niekerk, a native Afrikaner (a white South African), a fine ostrich leather dealer, and a zoologist who worked to protect the antelope. He seemed to recognize me from my movies and was quite well informed about the film industry.

During our conversation, he mentioned that his sister was steadfast in filmmaking in South Africa. He seemed like a nice enough chap. He was very proud to be an Afrikaner. He swore that he would never live anywhere else. "My country is one of the most beautiful countries in the world," he said proudly.

I reflexively thought, "His country?"

I was so anxious I found it hard to sleep. "God, let me sleep!" I wanted to arrive feeling rested and refreshed so that I could take in all Africa had to offer. I ended up reading instead. As I looked out the window, I could see the deep orange hue of the morning sun beginning to rise over the horizon. I kept checking my watch, wondering what Jenisa was going to do that day, her birthday. I sent her silent wishes, "Happy birthday, my dear Jenisa."

I looked at my watch again, six more hours to go. There was a show on the airplane's TV about Namibia's wildlife. My mind wandered to thoughts of my trip. Ivahn leaned over to say something, and the sound of his voice brought my thoughts back to the present.

"That beetle they are talking about is called a dung beetle," he said. He went on to explain that the insect ate cow excrement and was very important ecologically to the region. After breaking chunks of it open it rolls the dung over and over and then deposits its eggs. The hatchlings devour the larvae of flies and other parasites before they evolve. As I stared at the screen it occurred to me that this dung beetle was in fact a "scarab," an ancient symbol for the Egyptian pharaohs, once highly revered as a god and a source of power and good fortune.

I checked my watch, two hours to go! The flight attendant served plates of assorted fruit, with tea and coffee, and the sleeping passengers began to stir and awaken. The sun was now completely up and shining brightly through the windows, illuminating the cabin and flooding it with a glow. Ivahn suggested I take a photo of Table Mountain as we passed over Cape Town. He also allowed me to take his photograph before we disembarked. We shook hands. I reached for my carry-on bag, and when I looked up Ivahn was gone.

My first impression of Cape Town was that it looked very much like many other cities I had traveled to. If I hadn't known for sure I was in Africa, I am not sure I could have guessed it. There were tall buildings and the city was busy with activity, cars, and people rushing here and there.

I was delighted to find, despite the warnings of the old couple in Miami, that all my bags had made it to Africa. The producer of the movie was the former wife of the great playwright David Hare, Ms. Margaret Matheson. She was a very tall and sturdy Englishwoman with salt-and-pepper hair. Margaret was waiting there at the airport reception area along with my driver, Thami. Thami was a very nice South African man who was quick with a smile, and who gave me a fast education on where not to walk after dark. He seemed to be quite good at and secure in what he did. He was very knowledgeable of the current events and political upheavals that plagued South Africa. As we drove through the airport gates en route to the hotel, he pointed out a huge shantytown directly outside the entrance of the airport. There were hundreds of shanties built alongside the road, row after row of rickety little shacks. The level of abject poverty was shocking. The sight of it made me sad.

Thami talked of a new group of extremists called the People Against Gangsterism and Drugs (PAGAD), a group of Arab Muslims who resided in Cape Town. The group had taken it upon themselves to rid Cape Town of its drug problem using terrorist acts. Their primary focus was the complete destruction of the drug dealers' "fronts" and "camps." Unfortunately, many innocent people had died in the crossfire.

The PAGAD members were fully armed and at the time numbered five hundred strong.

According to Thami, they made it known that if the police ever tried to intervene in their activities they would declare war in Cape Town. The irony was that while we rode, and I listened to this story, I thought about, and could understand, why the Boers and Cecil Rhodes wanted to kill every Zulu in sight and take over this land for themselves. It was easily one of the most beautiful, green, lush places I had ever seen. I was there only for a short time, but driving through the streets of Cape Town gave me a nirvana-like feeling, it was almost mystical.

I arrived at the Vineyard Hotel in Cape Town, a wonderful little place with lush gardens, trickling water fountains, and a patio area overlooking Table Mountain. To call this setting beautiful and serene is an understatement! I called Jenisa to let her know I had arrived safely. Fatigued from the long trip, I decided to lie down to catch a bit of a nap. As I began to drift off to sleep, I was startled back to consciousness by a ringing phone. It was someone from the production office telling me that Elaine Proctor, the writer, producer, and director of *Kin,* the film I was there to work on, would be delayed for thirty minutes.

Kin is the story of a female conservationist who is an Afrikaner, and a corporate lawyer who is African American. While hunting elephant poachers, they fall in love with each other, despite the disapproval of the local people.

A few minutes later, just as I started to drift off for a second time, the phone rang again. It was Elaine calling. Elaine is a very beautiful, intelligent, and good-hearted woman. She said she was waiting for me in the lobby and suggested we have dinner. I agreed. I cleaned up some and went down to the lobby to meet Elaine and Miranda Otto, an Australian actress, also in the film, who seemed very nice and was quite pretty in an odd kind of way.

We dined at an East Indian restaurant called Bukhara. There I also met other film crew members Amy Vincent, the director of photography, a self-described American vegetarian, and her camera operator, a splendid, seven-foot-tall African American man named Brian Pitts. The love and respect they shared between them was a joy to watch; even if the image of the two of them walking side by side gave a whole new meaning to the epithet "Mutt and Jeff."

I was particularly excited to work with Amy. She did a great job shooting Kasi Lemmon's *Eve's Bayou.* Amy was an intense woman with a very warm smile. She wore a trademark straw cowboy hat and in temperatures of 120 degrees would outwork every single man on the set. Her fearlessness, stamina, creativity, professionalism, and focus behind the camera were remarkable to watch.

After dinner, we all were driven to a club called La Med near the beach, where it was drag queen night. The place was complete with cross dressing, freaky dancing, and mate swapping. I wasn't impressed. I thought that the gay clubs in New York did this much better. When we arrived there the door attendant gave us a number to place on our chest. If a stranger "fancied" you they could call out your number. "No way!" I thought to myself. I wondered, "What is wrong with these people? There is an AIDS epidemic here!"

As we enjoyed the music and our drinks, my hosts told me the story of Gugu Dlamini, an AIDS activist who was beaten to death by her neighbors after revealing her HIV-positive status on Zulu television in 1998. Gugu Dlamini tried desperately to educate her people about their sexual behavior. (Many South African men refused to practice safe sex.) She was murdered for her efforts. Township denial, cultural resistance, fears, and ignorance had allowed the AIDS virus to reach an incredible high point in the country, amassing huge emotional and psychological turmoil that wasn't being addressed within the community. Those discovered to have contracted HIV were banished from their homes, ostracized, beaten, or even killed. I made a mental note to research Dlamini's name.

Back at the hotel, I couldn't sleep. I was keyed up from the long trip and anticipation of taking still another leg of the journey to Namibia in just a few hours. I repacked my bags for the flight to Epupa Falls the next morning. After another night of little sleep, I was up before the sun, at 4:00 a.m.

It was quiet and heavenly still.

Nothing was moving but the wind, or should I say its sibling, the breeze. Sunrise was still a few minutes away. We loaded up the truck that would take us to the airport and I realized that I'd left my Canon ELPH point-and-shoot in the rear seat of our driver's truck the night before. "Lucky," the driver said when we discovered it still there and intact.

It was a short drive to Eros Airport. Craig Matthews and his assistant, Janet, arrived in their car, filled to capacity with provisions for the camp we would set up in Epupa Falls. Craig was a thin, muscular Englishman, who had worked photojournaling the Himba tribe for many years. He was fluent in the Himba language and served as liaison and consultant for our film. Since the tribe had no formal knowledge of television or radio equipment, Craig and Janet planned to stay in Epupa Falls to inform the tribe on the technical aspects of filmmaking.

We unloaded Craig's car only to discover that most of the food he and Janet brought for the camp, his television camera, a few pairs of Elaine's shoes, and a few other assorted articles would have to be left behind. An unexpected traveler, the wife of one of our pilots, had shown up. Since all of the seats had been assigned we had to make adjustments.

Amanda was our pilot for the first three-hour flight. She was very easygoing, confident, and reassuring to those in our group who were nervous about flying. As our single-prop Centurion II cranked up and taxied, wobbling down the runway, I had the sensation that I was outside of my body. My stomach tightened. I was nervous, I was excited, and I was in Africa! Elaine revealed to me how afraid she was of small planes. I don't think I was much of a comfort to her; most of my experience was with much bigger planes, the United States Air Force T-38 and the F-4 Phantom. My anxiety was more about not knowing exactly what to feel.

I took some great photographs of Cecil, the pilot of the other plane, carrying Amy and Janet, as he flew alongside the plane that carried Craig, Elaine, and me. I also got my first aerial view of the Himba dwellings. From the plane the villages or *omganda* (homesteads) looked like ant beds. The dung-and-tree-branch huts or *ondjuwo* (houses) were inside a circled fence made from the branches of the mopane tree, a necessary staple and building resource for the Himba people in Kaokoland.

Amanda pointed out a mountain range known as the Zebra Mountains. They got their name because of the black rock formations alongside of the mopane trees that truly resembled the zebra. She also showed us a mountain in southern Angola which stood eight thousand feet high. This mountain, she told us, should never be pointed at, for legend was that it may bring on extremely bad luck.

As we approached Epupa Falls, Amanda maneuvered our aircraft in a series of forty-five-degree-angle turns so that I could get some clean shots of magnificent waterfalls cascading off several cliffs. Unlike arriving in South Africa, and feeling Cape Town could have been any city, my reaction to setting foot in Namibia was quite different. Once we landed, I got off the plane and dropped down onto one knee, feeling an uncontrollable need to kiss the ground of Mother Africa. "I'm home again," I whispered. Tears of joy ran down my cheeks.

Enya, our caretaker, an Afrikaner, met our plane and drove us to the Epupa camp. Once there, we unloaded the boxes of food and luggage and were assigned to tents. I had tent #7, toilet #3. My tent was pitched adjacent to the Kunene River. I removed my boots and stepped inside my new mosquito-proof dwelling.

Later, as I sat at the edge of the river and meditated, I contemplated my blessings and my work ahead. While my eyes were closed, I felt a rough pull on my arms. The force was so strong it almost knocked me into the river.

What the hell was that? Startled, I stood up looking around for a prankster, but there was no one in sight. I stood there, looking across the river for several minutes, and began to have the most intense déjà vu moment I'd ever had. It was as if I had been in this very spot before. It was a fleeting sensation but very powerful. It startled me physically and emotionally, like I had just woken up from a bad dream.

Back at the camp, we got word that our contracted driver had damaged his truck coming to Epupa and now refused to drive us anywhere. Craig tried to negotiate with him, but he seemed to be having a nervous breakdown. They let him leave. Instead, we borrowed Enya's 4x4, and Elaine, Amy, Craig, Cornelius—our interpreter, an African man who loved to dress in red shirts— and I loaded in and headed out. Before Craig had driven two kilometers, the equivalent of just over a mile, Cornelius's Himba brother passed us on the road and stopped to chat with Craig for twenty minutes. In Africa, when you come upon someone you know, it is considered good manners to stop and chat for a while before moving on to your next destination. I learned very quickly that one cannot be in a hurry in Africa!

We proceeded for a short time but then stopped again, to talk with Cornelius's cousins and nephews in their village. We got out of the truck to say hello. I greeted the men first, then the grandmother, the children, and finally the younger women as is customary in African culture. There was a Himba woman named Uamahuno. She was a tall, thin, statuesque beauty with smooth dark brown, reddish skin and big bright penetrating eyes. I secretly referred to her as the Whitney Houston of Namibia. She stood off in the distance holding her baby. She allowed Amy and me to take a photograph of her little boy and her.

The noonday sun was incredibly hot. After chatting, taking photos, and drinking the customary offering of goat's milk, we climbed back into the truck and drove deeper into the Kaoko-land, picking up and dropping off other villagers along the way. Uamahuno had joined us on our journey. She began to sing a beautiful tribal song in Herero, her native language. It was lyrical, rhythmic, like "row, row, row, your boat"...I couldn't understand a word of it, but it soothed me as we drove through this hot, unfamiliar, and foreign land.

Our next stop was the Himba Chief Kapika's *omganda*. It was a stunning structure, very large and sturdy, almost like a prehistoric ranch. Chief Kapika wasn't there, but his semi-blind brother came out to greet us and asked us to retrieve some water for him. We obliged. Apparently Chief Kapika had traveled to Tanzania, the place I heard so much about from Moza Cooper. Craig and I were both a little disappointed not to have the chance to meet him.

We drove on, stopping to deliver medicine and blankets to people to whom Craig had promised them on his last visit, and handing out food, tobacco, T-shirts, and chocolates. We also continued to serve as something of a local taxi service, giving countless villagers a lift from one place to another.

People eyed me with great curiosity. I later learned that I may have been the first African American to visit this Himba village. One of the first things I noticed was the red ocher smeared all over the women's bodies. They were elegant, mysterious, rugged, majestic, and sensuous beings. I couldn't stop staring at the *erembe,* the headdresses, that sat high on the heads of married women, and their goatskin skirts, called *ozombuku,* and the front aprons they called *outuhira.* They wore beautiful bands on their ankles, copper jewelry on their wrists, huge leather-and-wire ornaments on their backs called *omaha,* and *ohumba,* huge white conch shells between their bare breasts.

For a minute or two, as we drove deeper into the country looking for Kehapa, one of the councils in command during Chief Kapika's absence, I felt as if I had been sent back in time. At the same time I felt strangely at home and safe, and incredibly humbled. These people had absolutely nothing but their children and, if they were lucky, a few cattle. Yet they seemed to be at peace. I felt they were looking at me as if I were too complicated. I was unable to speak their language and was overdressed for the conditions. There were goatskins drying in the sun, hanging from the mopane trees. The leaves of the trees were also used to make whistles, as Cornelius demonstrated for us. The Himba could not manage this common American trick without the leaves because they remove four of their bottom teeth, a cultural sign of beauty.

The day was long and hot, and the already long drive was made even longer because Craig knew almost every person we passed on the road. And each of them ran over to greet our 4x4 and have a chat. He had produced a documentary on the Himba people and was in the process of negotiating with them, on Elaine's behalf, to organize payment and travel for twenty-five villagers to be extras in the movie we were there to film.

As we approached what looked like the nearest small "town," Cornelius let out a scream at the sight of a man sitting in front of a pool hall and storefront. It turned out it was Chief Kapika himself! He was more beautiful and regal than I ever imagined he would be. He had coal black skin wrinkled by the intense heat of the sun, with epicanthic folds in his eyelids. He had a face you would expect to see in China, Korea, or Japan, not in Namibia, or anywhere in Africa for that matter. Were it not for his deep, dark, pecan-colored skin, he could have easily been mistaken as Asian. He looked as if he could have been Chinese. As he was known for his slyness, it is possible he had instructed his people to tell the "foreigners" he was "out of town." The Himba people were adamantly opposed to a dam that Westerners were seeking to build in the Kunene River. Perhaps he thought his absence would forestall such efforts.

Cornelius insisted that we all get out of the truck and greet the latter-day king, and I humbly did so. Chief Kapika remained seated. He stayed extremely still and watchful, a placid smile on his face. Likely cautious of strangers, after enduring years of negative effects from Western politics, as well as wage labor, drought, war, and the loss of thousands of cattle, he had many reasons to mistrust our group of outsiders.

Following our chat with the chief, we proceeded to drop off more goods. We met with Kehapa, who was in command in the absence of Chief Kapika, and Craig proceeded to engage in a two-hour negotiation. The chief was amazing to watch. Kehapa and another disgruntled councilman argued their concerns about the "foreigners" stealing the Himba culture and selling it abroad for personal gain, leaving them exploited once again. Finally, somehow, everyone came to an agreement. I totally understood the angry council's concerns and Kehapa's desire to take advantage of this money-making opportunity. They were extremely proud and graceful people.

Our final stop for the day was back in town to pick up Chief Kapika. We were to bring him back to his *omganda* and begin negotiations all over again! Finally, after an hour of further discussions, we loaded up the 4x4 and set off back to our camp. We were all hungry again; the quick lunch and water break we had enjoyed earlier in the day, by a riverbed, was now a faded and dry memory. As dry and constantly changing as the harsh terrain we drove through. The long journey left us feeling extremely fatigued. "My God! How have these people survived this land for all these centuries?" I thought to myself. "It's so hot!" Amazing grace is all I could think of.

Uamahuno managed to accompany us on our entire adventure. She seemed to be quite taken with me, even though she was happily married to three husbands. We headed toward the camp, dropping off villagers who had hitched a ride at some point on our journey. Uamahuno was the last Himba to get off. I watched in the side view mirror as she seemed to reluctantly step down from the Jeep. She turned and said something in her native tongue to Cornelius and then gestured for Craig to turn the 4x4 toward her *omganda*. Craig declined and shook his head no.

I reached for her outstretched hand and shook it firmly, yet gently, conscious to convey as much respect as possible. She then gestured for me to get out and "sleep" with her people that night. I was deeply moved and profoundly shaken by this Himba woman's generosity. I politely declined her very earnest invitation. She then proceeded to open my door and gestured for me to get out! I sat there frozen, blushing, honored and proud that this traditional woman saw something in my spirit that made her extend herself without shame or apologies. But, graciously, I declined again.

It seemed like forever passed before my door was finally closed. I saw Craig smile at her and say, "Not tonight." I was rendered speechless. As we drove off, I waved at Uamahuno, thinking about how much I loved my wife and the African women of the world. I know that from America to the motherland, black women are truly goddesses and a force of nature.

As we returned to the Epupa camp, I felt as though I were floating as I made my way to my tent. I sat quietly on my bed for a while, pondering the day's many gifts. The sheer vastness of the Kaokoland and the Himba people, nomads of Namibia, overwhelmed me. For a long time, I simply and desperately tried to digest it all. I was thrilled to finally be in Africa, and working on a film. The pay was $175,000, more money than I had ever made. I knew I could take care of my expectant wife and my family waiting for me back in LA, where I had moved. I had to resist the unmistakable pull on my spirit to stand up, walk across the Kunene River right into Angola, and never look back. It would be seven years before I understood that this was more than an idle thought. For now, I was shaken to the core, humbled, educated, and forever changed. "There is something here that I must do," I thought to myself.

I just wasn't quite sure what it was.

Silently, I thanked God for using Elaine Proctor to get me to Africa. Later, at dinner, I personally thanked her. She simply smiled and responded, "Pleasure." We were all seated around a table, Craig, Janet, Elaine, Miranda (the Australian actress), and Amy, all to my left, and Enya, who had prepared a wonderful dinner of roasted potatoes, green beans, and rice, to my right. Three crude, loud-speaking Germans, quite curious as to why I was there, were seated across from me. I gave them a cordial glance every now and then but continued to eat and converse with Amy and Enya. But they seemed to get louder and cruder. Then, failing to get our attention, they soon quieted down.

I finished off my second helping of the delicious food and noticed that Elaine was totally engrossed in an intense conversation with Cecil, our other pilot. She was explaining to him what *Kin*, the movie we were all there to make, was about. He seemed genuinely interested and curious. Elaine later explained that he was a purely ignorant representation of the old South African racist regime. That's all I needed to hear. Armed with that bit of information, I thought of what fun I could have with him. I planned to kill him with kindness and a bit of African American bravado too.

Also that night, I finally got a chance to chat with Craig. He spoke candidly and in great detail about dealing with the Himba people, Chief Kapika, and his news-breaking photojournalism during apartheid. He told me of the Himba women and their annual 125-kilometer, five-day walk toward the Angolan border to retrieve horns filled with red ocher.

They mix the ocher with butterfat and cover their entire bodies with it, including their long locks of hair that hang past their shoulders. In the Himba culture, a woman's hair is a

cherished symbol of beauty. Craig explained to me that cultur-
ally the Himba women were not allowed to have water touch
their bodies from birth until death. I was stunned by this fact and
found it hard to believe, because the Himba women's hygiene
was impeccable! In fact, they emanated only the earthly scent of
iron ore.

Craig also talked about his wife and four kids back in Cape
Town. Missing Jenisa so much, I asked him how he could spend
all that time away from his family. He looked at me and simply
replied, "This, Isaiah, is my passion!" His words lingered there
in the warm African night air. I looked out the window and
decided to take a walk outside. I lit up a cigar and leaned against
a dusty Land Rover. My mind wandered back to my experience
at the Kunene River the night I first arrived. I looked up at the
starry night sky and heard myself say aloud, "Behold, the only
thing that is greater than yourself."

For the next two months I remained captivated by what I saw
of the power of this mysterious and ancient land, Africa. I witnessed the magic of the moon and the sun rising together. I
ran along an uneven fence and watched as it rained on one side
of the fence and not on the other, just as it had on either side of
the street when I was a little boy riding bikes with my friends
back in Houston. I jumped back and forth over the fence standing first in the rain and then in the dry wind and sunshine. "The
devil is beating his wife," I thought to myself.

There was an Ovambo man on the set. The Ovambo live in
parts of southern Africa, especially in Angola and Namibia. He
intensely admonished me daily, demanding I speak my "native
language" and refusing to believe that I was American.

When my satellite phone didn't work, I watched elder
Himba women read the entrails of a goat and ensure me that my

pregnant wife, Jenisa, was fine. I traveled for hours across the Namib-Naukluft Desert to Walvis Bay and Swakopmund without seeing a single other vehicle, only ostriches and baboons. One day I climbed sand dune #7 in Sossusvlei, Namibia, and captured one of the dung beetles I first learned about from Ivahn Van Niekerk on the plane ride over. I later brought it home with me to Los Angeles, hoping it would bring me good fortune. It was there, sitting at the top of the dune, where I vowed to someday return to Africa and help my people.

CHAPTER 5

Moza Cooper and the DNA Test

It was October 2004. My career and my life had been steadily on the rise in the almost seven years since my first trip to Africa. I had appeared in several critically acclaimed films including *True Crime* directed by Clint Eastwood, Warren Beatty's *Bulworth,* and *Romeo Must Die.* I was now shooting episodes of my new TV show, *Grey's Anatomy,* and I felt at peace. Life was pretty damn good.

I received a call from the Pan African Film Festival's Moza Cooper. She left a message that I had been selected to receive the 2005 Canada Lee Award and that I should call her. I was confused and a bit taken aback. Ironically, I had just finished reading Mona Z. Smith's book, *Becoming Something: The Story of Canada Lee.* Lee was among the most respected African American actors of the 1940s, and a tireless civil rights activist. Yet he is mostly unknown today, reduced to a historical footnote. His death was one of a handful directly attributable to "the blacklist" of the late forties and fifties.

Lee was a Renaissance man: a violin prodigy, successful jockey, and champion boxer who became an actor and shot to stardom in Orson Welles's Broadway production *Native Son*. His meteoric rise to fame was followed by a tragic fall. When he was labeled a Communist by the FBI and House Un-American Activities Committee in 1949 and condemned in the press, his career was ruined. He died penniless at forty-five years old.

When I talked to Moza, she could hear me preparing to decline the honor so she said, "We are doing the award ceremony differently this year, Isaiah. This year we are asking the recipients to take a DNA test that would reveal their ancestral lineage to the African peoples. Will you do it?"

I said, "DNA test? Canada Lee? Moza...thank you for considering me, but I think I have to pass."

She was not easily deterred. "No, no, no, Isaiah!" she was practically shouting. "You have to do this. You are perfect for this." I hung up and thought to myself, "I'm perfect to do what? To get blacklisted?" The next day, I called Gina Paige of African Ancestry, founded in 2003 by Gina and Dr. Rick Kittles and specializing in helping people trace their African roots.

Gina explained to me how the testing process worked. I expressed my concerns about cloning and having my DNA out there somewhere to possibly fall into the wrong hands. But when she explained, "African Ancestry is a privately owned company with no attachments to any forensic or government institution," I sighed in relief. "It takes about three hundred parts to test for ancestral links in our database and about three billion parts to clone a human being, Isaiah," she said in her unique below-the-Mason-Dixon-Line drawl. "What makes you think that someone would want to clone you anyway?" she asked.

I paused for a moment and then laughed out loud at myself. And with that, I agreed to take the test. I hung up feeling like Christmas had come early.

Two weeks later the kit arrived. It contained two small envelopes for two long cotton swabs, a FedEx envelope, and a return label addressed to African Ancestry. The instructions were inside. It was a surprisingly simple process. I rinsed out my mouth with water as directed and then swabbed the inside of my cheek with each of the cotton swabs, careful to follow the warning to let each one dry before placing them in the envelopes and sealing them up to send back. I was anxious to get my results and learn which peoples and which land in Africa I had originated from.

On the evening of February 12, 2005, I stood tightly gripping the African staff that was the PAFF Canada Lee Award I had just received. Dr. Kittles approached me holding a reddish brown–colored folder. The room at the Magic Johnson Theater, in Baldwin Hills, California, seemed to go still. It felt like no one was breathing as Dr. Kittles started to speak. My ears were ringing loudly with anticipation and my heart pounded hard in my chest. "Sss..." is all I heard before I had the feeling a scream was about to explode from my body. I pride myself for my ability to think fast on my feet, so I quickly covered my mouth and buckled over.

Did he say Senegal? Of course, I had heard that on the streets of New York and DC for years; there had been the lady on the bus who was certain I was Wolof, from Senegal, West Africa. But no, wait, what was that? What did he say? *Sierra* what? I blinked my eyes a few times as if that would help me hear him better. I waited a second...then I heard Dr. Kittles say, "Sierra Leone."

WHAM! Another surge of energy tried to leap out of me. I instinctively cupped my hand over my mouth even tighter as if to prevent the hundreds of spirits that were all trying to speak through me at once. It was all I could do not to pass out. I began to feel dizzy, and my legs felt weak; still, I refused to succumb. I felt transformed and complete at that moment. I took a deep breath, my blood pressure slowly lowered, and I heard him say, "Isaiah, your results show that you share ancestry with the Mende and Temne peoples of Sierra Leone."

I couldn't stop smiling. I stood there next to actress Vanessa Williams and Congresswoman Diane Watson, who had both just received the results of their DNA tests from Dr. Kittles as well. He told me I shared 99.9 percent ancestry with the Mende and Temne peoples of Sierra Leone on my maternal side. And, on my paternal side I shared 99.3 percent with the Mbundu people of Angola.

Now I understood that intense feeling of connection I felt with Angola. It all made more sense. Perhaps it was my DNA rebooting my memory of my father's lineage of the Mbundu across the Kunene River in Angola. Or maybe this was the reason for my intense feeling of emotion when I first stepped foot on Namibia's soil back in 1999, as well as the incredible and unexplainable experience I had while meditating at the Kunene's banks. Had my DNA given me that connection? Did my DNA "remember" that place?

I was stunned. I stood there, in a tailored suit, with my beautiful wife, my manager, Eric Nelson, and a camera crew from ABC News watching me. I couldn't believe what I was hearing. No European? No Native American? I was nearly 100 percent African? Was this really happening?

It was. It was scientifically official. Not only did I now know where my ancestors were from, but so did a room full of other people.

I felt reborn that night. No longer did I need cowrie shells hanging from my locks, African jewelry, African dance classes, or African drumming circles. There would be no more need to hang portraits of Negresses or Moorish chiefs or wear kente cloth around my neck. All the external things that I thought I needed to connect me to Africa were now unnecessary. Africa had been inside of me all along. She was inside my DNA. She was beckoning me and guiding me my entire life through my dreams.

And for my dreams to come true, I decided I needed to go and see the country of my ancestors, Sengbe Pieh's people—my people—for myself.

I started to ask myself, "Could DNA be the bridge that closes the gap between Africans and African Americans?" I thought about the possibility of helping to create a radical break with the international capitalist system and the idea of "taking back" Sierra Leone from its colonialist constructs. I started to imagine myself with a group of competent American businesspeople helping Sierra Leone achieve its economic development goals one village at a time. I wondered if African Americans could come together long enough to help rebuild a nation only the size of South Carolina and show the world how and why we were able to build pre-European civilizations centuries ago.

I decided that I would be the guinea pig in my own experiment and see just how much of an impact I could make over the next ten years. I closed my eyes and began to meditate. In my mind's eye I saw images of "the Rerun." "This is it," I thought to myself. "This is what I was born to do. This is my purpose."

CHAPTER 6

Now What?

It is difficult to explain the sense of oneness I felt with the people of Sierra Leone, even though I had yet to visit the country. For eight months I conducted intense research, learning all I could about it, its people, and its history. The Portuguese gave Sierra Leone its name in 1462. It means "Lion Mountain." Those same Portuguese goods traders turned into slave traders during the 1550s, making Sierra Leone the "testing ground" to kick off the transatlantic slave trade.

The story that interested me most was that of Sengbe Pieh, later known as Joseph Cinque, who was the most well known defendant in the case of the slave ship *La Amistad*. Like me, he was a child of Sierra Leone.

The case involved fifty-three Africans who were abducted from Sierra Leone in February 1839 by Portuguese slave hunters to be sold as slaves in Havana, Cuba. About five months into the journey, the Africans took control of the ship, killing the captain and the cook in the process, and ordered the ship to return to

Africa. When the ship was captured by a U.S. brig off the coast of New York, the Africans were initially imprisoned on charges of murder which were later dismissed. Yet the Africans were still held as "property" even though they had been made slaves illegally. Former president John Quincy Adams represented the Africans.[2]

I had some awareness that Sengbe Pieh was the Mende leader who led the revolt on the slave ship *La Amistad,* but as I read more about him, it hit me. "Wait a minute," I thought. "This guy is one of my ancestors!"

I believe we owe Sengbe Pieh and the people of Sierra Leone a huge debt for the courage that many, including the great Professor Joe Opala, a Sierra Leonean expert and historian at James Madison University, considered to be the beginnings of the Civil Rights Movement. I would later have the honor to meet and work with Professor Opala.

I pulled the book *Africana: The Encyclopedia of the African and African American Experience,* edited by Kwame Anthony Appiah and Henry Louis Gates Jr., off my shelf and read about the history, politics, language, and culture of Sierra Leone.

I discovered that in 1839 Lewis Tappan, a wealthy New York merchant and prominent abolitionist, for whom the Tappan Zee Bridge is named, launched a campaign to defend the *Amistad* Africans and created the Amistad Committee. Three long trials later, the United States Supreme Court issued its final verdict in the *Amistad* case on March 9, 1841, that the Africans on board were kidnapped and transported illegally. The captives at last were free! John Quincy Adams had overturned President Van Buren's attempt to have the *Amistad* Africans sentenced to death for mutiny.

Sengbe Pieh became such a public figure in the United States that the newspapers compared him to the heroes of ancient Greece and Rome. Pieh's cause and return to Sierra Leone garnered the attention of thousands of people and raised millions of dollars for the Amistad Committee and its Mende missions. The first Mende mission arrived in Freetown with Sengbe Pieh in 1842, designed to persuade their new African friends to adopt the American dress and manners. This attempt failed once the *Amistad* Africans became anxious to return to their individual villages. The Amistad Committee evolved into the American Missionary Association and built the most celebrated schools of its time—the Harford School for Girls and the Albert Academy, which predated the government-run Bo School by several years.

The village of Bo the school is named for has an interesting story behind its name which I found on the Web site www.sierra-leone.org. The peoples of Bo have a reputation for warmth and determination, and the town is named after its generosity.

An elephant was killed close to what is now known as Bo Parking Ground. People from the surrounding villages came to receive their share. Because the meat was so large, the hunter spent days distributing it and the words "bo-lor" (which in Mende language means "this is yours," with reference to the meat) was said so much that the elders and visitors decided to name the place Bo. "Bo-lor" in Mende also translates to "this is Bo."[3]

The impact of this quest for excellence left its mark in the United States. Two important examples are Sierra Leoneans Barnabas Root and Thomas Tucker, who both attended the original Mende Mission School. Root became a powerful pastor for the Congregational Mission Church for Freedmen in Alabama and later returned to Sierra Leone. Thomas Tucker stayed on in America and along with Thomas Van Gibbs founded the State Normal College for Colored Students at Tallahassee, Florida, in

1877. Thomas Tucker was the first president of the college which grew into the present-day Florida A&M University.

The freedom of the *Amistad* Africans made a further impact on the United States. In 1846, the American Missionary Association was the best organized abolitionist society in the United States. After the Civil War, the association established more than five hundred schools and colleges in the South for the education of newly emancipated slaves. Eventually, these schools evolved into universities—Clark, Atlanta, Howard, Fisk, and Dillard—and Hampton Institute, just to name a few. Thousands of African Americans owe their higher education to Sengbe Pieh and the *Amistad* case.

I read everything I could get my hands on that was written by Joseph Opala, and I would have the pleasure of meeting him in person a few years later in 2006. Joe suggested that these institutions educated the young reformers who started the civil rights movement. Morehouse College was another beneficiary of the *Amistad* case. Martin Luther King Jr. was a Morehouse man. The connection between Sierra Leone and historically black colleges and universities is direct and the importance for African Americans, all Americans for that matter, is clear.

I also read about the history of diamond mining. It seems the first diamonds were discovered in the riverbeds of India. They were discovered in Africa in 1866, when a fifteen-year-old boy found a transparent stone on his father's farm on the south bank of the Orange River. In the next fifteen years, diamond mining dramatically increased, with Africa producing more diamonds than India had produced in the previous two thousand years. To this day, diamond mining is one of Africa's most important industries.

"Diamond" comes from the Greek word *adamas,* meaning

unconquerable. Diamonds are made up of pure carbon and are the hardest natural substance known to man.

Like many cultures around the world, as Americans we think of diamonds as a symbol of wealth, a sign of love and romance. But at the same time, they also have something of a sinister side and are at the core of one of the darkest periods in my Africa's history. Used as capital by rebels to buy weapons, diamonds have funded some of the country's bloodiest and deadliest wars including in Angola, the Republic of Congo, and my new homeland, Sierra Leone.

De Beers, a London-based company, is the largest producer of diamonds. You often see De Beers featured in magazine and TV advertisements, especially around Valentine's Day and Christmas. The company's first chairman, Cecil Rhodes, was an Englishman who founded De Beers Consolidated Mines Ltd. By 1888, he enjoyed a monopoly over Africa's diamond production. He formed the London Diamond Syndicate, a cartel of the largest group of diamond merchants of the time, and essentially controlled both sides of the diamond market by manipulating the supply and demand.

When Sir Ernest Oppenheimer took over the company in 1929, he followed Rhodes's example and formed the Central Selling Organization (CSO), which served to expand De Beers's control by incorporating more diamond sellers and producers into the cartel. When the Great Depression hit, De Beers had a bigger supply of diamonds than there was demand for them and the company was forced to shut down many of its mines. The problem was it was still obligated by contract to buy diamonds from members of the CSO.

In 1939, Oppenheimer's son Harry took over the company after his father's death. He initiated a U.S. marketing campaign to expand the market for diamonds to include the middle class as well as the rich. A copywriter who worked for him came up with the now famous advertising slogan "A Diamond Is Forever."

De Beers's successful marketing campaign became very popular around the world. In fact, it became too popular. The increase in demand put it under pressure to keep pace with the number of new mines being discovered and exploited by the cartel, and as a result De Beers had to stockpile a large amount of its own diamonds. After the Department of Justice charged it with violating U.S. antitrust laws, De Beers had to reduce its U.S. presence, restructure, and rethink its marketing strategy.

The relationship between my homeland and De Beers started in 1935 when the company legally assumed complete control over the mining prospects in Sierra Leone for the next ninety-nine years. But when Lebanese traders figured out the immense potential profits to be made by smuggling diamonds out of the country, Sierra Leone soon became a hotbed of illicit diamond mining and trading. Foreign companies were forced to provide security for their own mines and personnel. By the 1950s, Sierra Leone's government had essentially given up trying to police its diamond industry with the exception of two places: the Kono diamond district and the Freetown diamond export center. As a result, illegitimate diamonds, taken from the secured cities of Kono and Freetown, were diverted to Liberia—and an illegal diamond pipeline between Sierra Leone and Liberia was born. The government tried to stem the tide of illegal activity by introducing the Alluvial Mining Scheme in 1956, empowering local miners to receive mining and trading licenses. However, rather than bringing order to the legal diamond trade as hoped, it only served to increase the number of illegal miners and strengthen the Liberian pipeline.

When Sierra Leone gained independence from Great Britain in 1961, diamond smuggling became a political and economic pariah for the country. Populist Siaka Stevens became prime minister and, to gain power officially, encouraged illicit mining. He nationalized the diamond mines and De Beers's Sierra Leone

Selection Trust (SLST) by creating the National Diamond Mining Co. (NDMC), giving himself and his key adviser, Jamil Mohammed, a Lebanese businessman, control of the diamond mines. Under Stevens's rule, legal diamond trading decreased from over two million carats in 1970 to less than fifty thousand carats about twenty years later. When Stevens left office after seventeen years, De Beers "officially" withdrew from Sierra Leone and sold its remaining shares to the Precious Metals Mining Co., controlled by Mohammed.

The high level of corruption and illicit diamond mining made the country attractive to rebels, and in 1991 civil war erupted. The Revolutionary United Front (RUF), a group of one hundred fighters from Sierra Leone and Liberia, headed by a savage and brutal leader, Foday Sankoh, an ex–army sergeant, began its reign of terror. The RUF claimed to represent the urban dispossessed and promised poor Sierra Leoneans that unlike the current corrupt government, it would offer a greater share of the wealth from diamonds. But Sankoh and the RUF routinely subjected people to mutilation and amputation. The RUF used systematic rape of women and girls as a tool to terrorize the population into submission, breaking apart families and communities. Many more women were abducted and forced to travel with the rebels as sex slaves, often gang-raped, tortured, and threatened with death if they tried to escape. Women and girls who escaped or were released now often suffer a variety of consequences including HIV/AIDS and other sexually transmitted diseases, as well as serious gynecological problems. Many also suffer from posttraumatic stress disorder and extreme anxiety, and find themselves ostracized by their families and communities. A high percentage of the survivors are now single mothers of what are referred to as "rebel babies." The RUF used profits from diamond smuggling to fund its rebellion, knowing control of the diamond trade meant control of the country.

Under pressure from the United Nations and the U.S., Sankoh and President Ahmad Tejan Kabbah signed a peace treaty in 1996 and three years later they signed the Lome Accord in July 1999. To avoid a death sentence for Sankoh, the RUF agreed to surrender its rebel forces in exchange for a share in Sierra Leone's government. In the deal, brokered by Reverend Jesse Jackson acting as a special envoy, Sankoh became chairman of the Strategic Mineral Resources Commission and essentially controlled most of Sierra Leone's diamond exports. But peace was short-lived, lasting only about seven months. The RUF, having never surrendered its forces as agreed, revived its attacks and the fight for diamond mine control raged on. In response, the UN issued a ban on the purchase of nongovernmental diamonds from Sierra Leone.[4]

Time to Go Home

I continued to read one horror story after another about my ancestral land's history, before and after it declared its independence from British rule in 1961. Now that I knew I was 99.9 percent Mende and Temne, it was time for me to go and see for myself what so many West Africans had seen in me for so many years. It was time for me to go home again. I had no idea how this trip to Sierra Leone would come together, but I prayed and planned to have everything and everyone I needed to make the journey.

One afternoon, I sat in my trailer reading and waiting to be called back to the set of my very popular TV show. Then it hit me...access. I had access to capital that could help many people in need. I picked up my cell phone and called Ms. Carmen Smith, an ABC executive. Carmen was a fan of my work on four Spike Lee films, and my work starring opposite actors such as Clint Eastwood and Warren Beatty, as well as Jennifer

Lopez and George Clooney in the critically acclaimed film *Out of Sight*. She respected that body of work before I had ever considered doing television. In fact, it was that same résumé that brought Shonda Rhimes, my boss and executive producer, to insist that I be on her show.

"I recently took a DNA test with an organization called African Ancestry Inc., a genetic-testing company," I explained to Carmen. "I discovered that I share an ancestral link to the Mende and Temne peoples of Sierra Leone. I want to travel there and document what I hear and see. I feel as if I am in a unique position to help the people of Sierra Leone and make a change there." I told her I wanted to put a delegation and camera crew together.

Carmen was immediately intrigued and supportive. She was already aware of my philanthropic work with various charities and organizations. At the time I had a PSA running on WABC TV where I acted as a spokesperson for the Los Angeles Regional Food Bank. The LA Food Bank provides the basic food requirements for anyone who needs help. I was beyond surprised when I realized how few people were even aware that this organization existed. I produced and filmed the PSA *The Construction Accident* using $75,000 out of my own pocket. I knew that I could use my celebrity as an outreach to those who may be in trouble but were too embarrassed to ask for help. I recalled times that I, as a student, and later as a struggling actor, knew firsthand what it meant to be homeless and hungry. I recalled sleeping in my car my first week at Howard University, unable to afford food.

Carmen told me she thought I would qualify for a grant that ABC Entertainment Group funded. I applied for a $30,000 grant as a first-time director of a documentary. She made sure that my application and new dream were ushered through as quickly and efficiently as possible. As an African American woman, Carmen shared my passion for trying to reconnect with Africa, and she was there for me every step of the way. ABC Entertainment Group awarded me the $30,000 within six weeks. It is important to note that what I was planning to do had been done many times since 1787 and written about extensively in James T. Campbell's book *Middle Passages: African American Journeys to Africa, 1787–2005*. I was not the first African American man to feel this pull, this need to connect with my homeland. Having been kidnapped and brought as slaves to the United States, African Americans are the only "immigrants" who do not have a continent they can claim as their own. Our history was destroyed because of slavery. This knowledge of my ancestry, of my DNA, changed that for me. Like my Italian, Irish, Scottish, and other European sisters and brothers, I too wanted to know and understand where I came from. I began to wonder if I could help reverse the Middle Passage.

In May 2005, ABC News invited me to attend my first White House Correspondents' Dinner in Washington, DC. As I looked around the room and at all the famous faces in attendance, and listened to First Lady Laura Bush roast President George W. Bush, I began to think of Edward R. Murrow's famous 1958 speech to the Radio and Television News Directors Association. It reminded me that I now had access. That night, he said:

> To those who say people wouldn't look; they wouldn't be interested; they're too complacent, indifferent and insulated, I can only reply: there is, in one reporter's opinion, considerable evidence against that contention. But even if they are right, what have they got to lose? Because if they are right, and this instrument is good for nothing but to entertain, amuse and insulate, then the tube is flickering now and we will soon see that the whole struggle is lost.

This instrument can teach, it can illuminate; yes, and it can even inspire. But it can do so only to the extent that humans are determined to use it to those ends.

Otherwise it is merely wires and lights in a box.[5]

After that first White House Correspondents' Dinner, I called Tavis Smiley to enlist his help in throwing out a very large net to see what I could catch that would help me with my Sierra Leone project.

On June 27, 2005, I appeared on *The Tavis Smiley Show* on PBS. We engaged in typical show business talk for a bit. We talked about how I came to acting, discovering the legacy of Ossie Davis, and my first glimpse of Spike Lee's work. We discussed my career and my struggle to find strong, intelligent roles, and some of the films I had made, and talked about the major success of my hit TV show.

Then the conversation turned to my search for my African roots. Tavis said that he had spoken to a few African Americans who had recently done some digging to find their roots. He asked me what I had found. "What does it do for you?" he inquired. "My mind goes back to *Roots* obviously. What does it do for you to have, at a certain point in your life, discovered what those roots are for Isaiah Washington?"

I explained to him that through the mitochondrial DNA on my maternal side I was "directly related to the Mende and Temne peoples out of Sierra Leone. The most famous Mende to date is Joseph Cinque, who took over the *Amistad,* so I'm connected to that wonderful legacy, and on my paternal side, my father's side and all his father's fathers are Mbundu, or Kimbundu, out of Angola, and I can't wait to get to both of the countries to see what I can invest in."

Then he wanted to know what it had done for me. "Wow," I thought to myself, "how could I even put that into words?" But

I tried: "Freedom, man. A quiet power for me. I've been searching for a long time, Tavis. I've gone from locks to goatees to this
to proving that I'm African and I'm African American, and I no
longer have to hold on to these very outward kind of scenarios
anymore or all the literature and rhetoric. I've found a bookend
to all the literature that I've ever read about Africa, 'cause now
I don't have to go 'Soweto,' or wear kente cloth, or hang out at
all of the African film festivals and African festivals all over the
world, because I'm very clear now that inside me there's Angola
and Sierra Leone. And that if I can, with my black dollars, I'd
like to be able to go back and help in some kind of way."[6]

Within a week of the interview with Tavis, I received a message from my manager, Eric Nelson, that a Mr. Brian Morris,
consultant to the Matthew 6 Foundation and Public Affairs
Counsel in the United States to the Republic of Sierra Leone,
saw my interview on the show and wanted a meeting with me as
soon as possible. I agreed.

I called Maeyen Bassey, a producer friend of mine, and
asked her to grab her camera and document everything. While
I couldn't always articulate my need to connect with Africa, I
was beginning to understand that reconnecting with my Sierra
Leonean roots was my life's purpose. I wanted to serve as a living example for others who had the same desire and passion to
connect with their African ancestry. I knew this meeting would
somehow serve as my "first step" at reconnecting with my ancestral home.

CHAPTER 7

Power People

M aeyen had the camera rolling as I walked up to Brian Morris's room at the Beverly Wilshire Hotel and knocked on the door. She tucked herself into a far corner so Brian or his wife would not be uncomfortable. I was not about to lose any of this conversation. I had the sense that this was the start of something big, that from this moment, my life would be monumentally different, that I would be a man changed forever.

"Thank you for meeting with me," I said. "Why did you reach out to me?" I asked quickly.

Brian blinked, glancing at his wife, who seemed desperate to stay out of camera shot. I assured them I planned to use the footage only to document an interesting and historical journey.

It soon became clear why Brian had contacted me. He thought that as a well-known African American interested in Sierra Leone, I could help make his job as a public affairs consultant to the Republic of Sierra Leone a little easier.

"I think I could help facilitate your trip," he said. I was thrilled. We ended the meeting agreeing to keep in touch.

After a few subsequent conversations I sensed that Brian's agenda regarding my relationship to Sierra Leone was not in line with my own. He intended for me to merely be a "celebrity face" for the Matthew 6 Foundation. Reportedly, the organization had been building new homes throughout Sierra Leone for several years. During the eleven-year war, the organization took a big loss and was looking to attract new investors.

It would have been easy for me to simply say no thanks and step back from Brian, but something inside me told me to wait and let this thing play out. I had a sense that Brian Morris was pivotal to my destiny. I just wasn't sure how.

Eventually Brian arranged a meeting with Brian Haney, Matthew 6's president. The day before the meeting, Brian warned me that Haney suffered from narcolepsy and that I should not be alarmed if he suddenly fell asleep. The three of us sat down for dinner at the Mondrian Hotel on Sunset Boulevard and for the next three hours I explained my plan to reconnect with Sierra Leone, and why DNA testing could finally help bridge the gap between Africans and African Americans.

Haney never dozed off or lost focus during the entire meeting. After dinner, he excused himself; Brian and I watched as this little nebbish of a man practically skipped off to the men's room.

Brian looked at me quizzically and said, "I have never seen him stay awake this long in a meeting."

"Maybe the meetings he falls asleep in are just plain old boring," I said, wiping my mouth with my napkin. Maybe it was Brian's slow and pensive midwestern voice that overcame Haney with somnolence.

Later that week, Brian called, sounding more animated than usual. "There is a fellow Sierra Leonean I think you should meet," he said. "Mr. Raymond Scott-Manga." He was a retired Boeing aerospace engineer who lived in Seattle, Washington, and who still had strong family ties in Sierra Leone. He was expecting my call.

I hung up with Brian and dialed Mr. Manga. When he answered, I was immediately struck by the high energy in his voice. He spoke so rhythmically that the words wrapped around me like an upbeat melody, as if he had a perpetual jocular grin on his face.

Our conversation flowed easily from one subject to another as he slowly revealed some of our shared history and the layers of his own life's journey. We began the conversation as complete strangers, but as we shared our thoughts, our words and stories overlapped as we spoke. Raymond admitted he was unfamiliar with most of my work but had seen a few episodes of my TV show. "Isaiah, I didn't know your name," he said, "but I told my wife that you looked like a Mende man."

I wasn't sure if he was just flattering me or truly being genuine. It didn't matter. I knew instinctively that Raymond Scott-Manga would be instrumental in facilitating my destiny and entry into Sierra Leone.

On April 26, 2006, *People* magazine named me one of its "World's 50 Most Beautiful People." A few days later the magazine flew me to DC to attend the White House Correspondents' Dinner. This time, I had my own agenda in mind: spreading the word about my plans to visit Sierra Leone and finding people in power who knew how to navigate the Hill.

Steve Ross turned out to be just what the doctor ordered. Steve works for the Artists and Athletes Alliance and is very well connected. He arranged for me to tour the White House and introduced me to several key people in President George

W. Bush's administration. During the White House Corre-spondents' reception I shook hands with Helen Thomas, the legendary correspondent, and had the chance to meet John McLaughlin, Wolf Blitzer, and Jake Tapper. I shared a laugh with rapper Chris "Ludacris" Bridges and fellow actor Terrence Howard. Greta Van Susteren, who turned out to be a fan, and I were introduced by her husband, John P. Coale, and I shared my love of literature with Joe Pantoliano, who gave me some tips on vintage book collecting.

People magazine's managing editor, Larry Hackett, arranged for me to sit next to Jeffrey D. Sachs, the economist of the Earth Institute at Columbia University and author of *The End of Poverty*. He was enthusiastic about my plans for a trip to Sierra Leone and asked if I was familiar with his UN Millennium Project and promised to send me a copy of his book. "Call my office and leave your mailing address," he said, handing me his card.

As I thanked him, Steve Jones, from ABC News Radio, appeared at the table. "Hello, Isaiah," he said. "I see you made it back, but I have a much better table for you than this one!" I laughed, stood up, and gave him a big hug. "I want to introduce you to the next mayor of Washington, DC, Mr. Adrian Fenty." I excused myself and followed him; he looked ahead and then to his left and motioned with his head for me to do the same. It is considered "unprofessional" to point at anyone at this kind of high-powered event. "I think you know that guy over there sur-rounded by fans." I could see a crowd clamoring around George Clooney.

I walked over to his table, perfectly placed in the center of the ballroom near the stage, and waited for him to notice me. "Isaiah! Hey, it's good to see ya! What are ya up too these days?" said George.

"Oh," I replied, "I'm playing a doctor on this little TV show and I'm preparing to go do some work in Sierra Leone."

George said, "Sierra Leone, hey, be careful in that country."

"Yeah, I know all about its reputation," I assured him, "I'm going with my eyes and ears open."

The event was about to begin. I jetted back to my table. Comedy Central's Stephen Colbert was the featured entertainer for the dinner that evening and he brought the house down with some of his usual biting quips.

I also met a lady named Ms. Ashley Tate-Gilmore that night. She worked for Senator Obama and was a huge supporter of my efforts in Sierra Leone and a huge fan of my TV show. Ms. Tate-Gilmore would soon become a pivotal player in my date with destiny.

After dinner, I headed over to the Bloomberg News after party at the Embassy of the Republic of Macedonia to do some networking. Since it was my second consecutive Correspondents' Dinner, I felt like a seasoned political insider and was welcomed as such. As I stepped outside to enjoy a cigar, a young man introduced himself as Jay Carson. He worked in the office of former president William J. Clinton. He handed me a card and said to give him a call the next time I was in New York. My mind began to race. As I firmly shook his hand, I said, "Thanks, Jay. This is very forward, but do you think President Clinton could give me some advice on his experience with Sierra Leone?"

"What do you need to know?" he asked.

I explained that I wanted Clinton's thoughts on the safety of a visit to Sierra Leone. Jay set up a meeting with Clinton's foreign policy adviser, Eric Nonacs, for mid-May, when I was already planning to visit in New York to promote my TV show.

The next day, I pulled out the business card Jeffrey Sachs had handed to me. He had the longest job title of anyone that I had ever seen in my entire life! Director of the Earth Institute, Quetelet Professor of Sustainable Development, and Professor of Health Policy. I dialed the office number and left a message.

Then I tried his personal mobile phone. To my surprise, he picked up.

"Isaiah! How are you?" His voice always sounded positive, like a joyful smile.

I asked if we could meet for lunch during my trip to New York to continue our conversation about Sierra Leone and his Millennium Development Goals. He told me to call his office and set something up. "Thank you, Professor Sachs," I told him, "this means a lot to me."

On May 15, 2006, I took the red-eye from LA so I'd have twenty-four hours before my promotional obligations for ABC began. After checking in to the Trump International Hotel & Tower in New York, I quickly checked my notes on Sierra Leone and jumped in the shower. I arrived at Jean Georges a few minutes early and waited at the bar for Jeffrey to arrive. I picked up a copy of the *New York Times* that had been left on the seat next to me. Immediately I noticed a two-page ad by Bausch & Lomb, the contact lens company.

Bausch & Lomb Contact Lens Solution, ReNu with Moistureloc, Removed from Market—Found to Cause Severe Eye Infections.

That day Bausch & Lomb announced its decision to permanently remove all ReNu with Moistureloc products from shelves worldwide. I checked the stock exchange quotes for BOL, the company's ticker symbol. The stock's price had plummeted on the negative news. I quickly dialed my business manager, Mark Kaplan, and instructed him to immediately buy five hundred shares. I knew that when the stock came back up I was golden.

"You're the boss," he said.

I didn't know why at the time, but I hung up thinking I might need to fall back on that money.

Jeffrey arrived right on time. During our lunch he shared some very detailed insights on what to expect when dealing with a poor nation in Africa. He suggested I stop using my own money to fund my mission and look for interested investors.

Now I understood. The Bausch & Lomb shares could serve that purpose.

"Trying to rebuild a poor nation's village is very expensive," he explained. "Maybe you should try and use your celebrity to get yourself on the board of a major oil company."

I was confused. "Why an oil company?"

A huge smile spread across his face, "Those guys have lots of money," he said, his eyes squinting behind his glasses.

When asked how to do that, he said, "Isaiah! You are a celebrity, my friend, just pick up the phone and call, like you did me. I told Angelina and Bono the same thing. Use your celebrity for good." He left me with a copy of his Millennium Development Goals, checked his watch, and dashed off to another meeting.

"I can't wait to read this man's book," I thought to myself.

Two days later, I took a taxi from the Trump hotel up Broadway to Harlem. As I walked down 125th Street, I immediately spotted the Apollo Theater.

It was a different Harlem from the one I remembered. Gone were many of the mom-and-pop establishments, replaced with Starbucks, Old Navy, and other big chain stores. Harlem had changed, I suppose, just as I had. People stopped and shook my hand and asked for autographs. One man asked a passerby if she would use her camera phone to take a picture of the two us. I wondered how he would get the photograph from this total stranger. I was even more surprised when she agreed to do it!

I told him he didn't need a picture, "I'll just give you a hug. Is that cool?" He stepped back, blinked, paused for several seconds, and then he opened his arms wide. I hugged him as if he were an old friend. "You the man! You hear me? YOU-ARE-THE-MAN!" he shouted as he made his way down the block. I gave hugs and signed phone bill envelopes and the backs of some T-shirts too. "Wow," I thought to myself, "I'm in Harlem signing autographs!" I had come a long way.

I recalled how I had felt the day, fifteen years ago, when I stood with Gary Dourdan at the window of the Apollo and saw Nelson Mandela's motorcade go by the crowds of cheering people. The air had been filled with pride and anticipation. I felt much the same way on this day. I was now standing in front of the William J. Clinton Foundation building, ready to meet the former president himself.

Jay greeted me in the lobby and together we rode the elevator up to the office. After offering me a soda, he explained that Clinton was not able to meet with me personally but wanted to speak with me on the phone after I sat with Eric Nonacs, his foreign policy expert.

Jay showed me Clinton's large and impressive office with its amazing view of New York City. It was filled with mementos and photographs of Clinton standing with a who's who of political icons. After a tour of the rest of the foundation, Jay walked me to Eric Nonacs's office. Eric asked what I hoped to achieve in Sierra Leone.

I explained my plan of doing a "meet and greet" around the country, traveling wherever I could to meet people and local leaders and let them know who I was, and why Sierra Leone was important, and that Raymond Scott-Manga would escort me to the State House to meet with President Ahmad Tejan Kabbah.

Eric cautioned that I should keep alert and be sure not to promise anything that I could not deliver. He also made a point to say I should make sure I didn't do or say anything that would cause me any "media liability."

"What is media liability?" I asked.

"Media liability," he explained, "is saying or doing anything that would damage your ability to maintain goodwill with the Sierra Leone government and/or the people there, by embarrassing them or yourself."

I shook his hand and thanked him for his time and Jay asked if I was ready to speak to President Clinton. "Absolutely!" I said.

Jay gave me a number to call and left me in an empty office.

"Hello, it's Robert Bogast, the President is expecting your call, can you hold for a minute?" he said. After about a minute he returned, "Isaiah, the President is ready to speak with you."

Then I heard it, that famous trademark voice that sounded like a mixture of Elvis Presley and a smooth Southern charmer. "Isaiah," he said, "just tell me one thang. Is Dr. Burke's hand gonna work again? I need to know if Dr. Burke is coming back, baby!" He chuckled. "I-I-I Isaiah, I gotta tell ya your show is the only show that Hillary and I watch together in bed before we go to sleep."

"Oh wow," I said, "that's very nice to hear, Mr. President, and, yes, Dr. Burke is coming back, but I can't tell you anything more about his hand. You're going to have to wait and see."

"Well, I hope so," he said, "because, man, that is really a well-written show!"

"Thank you, Mr. President, thank you very much."

"I hear you are making a lot of my staff very happy being there. My guys are taking good care of you, I hope?"

I told him that Jay and Eric had been amazing and thanked him for his support.

"Jay tells me that you are preparing to go to Sierra Leone," he said.

"Yes, sir," I replied.

"That's good, Isaiah. Sierra Leone is a beautiful country,

I wish I could have done more for Rwanda and Sierra Leone while I was president. I really wish I could have done more." He told me he was doing something with the American Heart Association and that he wanted to tell me more about it when I got back from Sierra Leone. I agreed.

"Good," he said. "Well, you keep doing what you are doing, Isaiah. God will bless you for it and if you need anything, do not hesitate to call my office. Keep up the good work."

"I appreciate your support, sir," I said.

Then he said good-bye.

Robert Bogast returned to the line. "The President really enjoyed speaking with you, Isaiah," he said. "If you need anything don't hesitate to call us. Take care." And the line went dead.

I sat in the empty office for several minutes, just taking it all in. "I just talked to President Bill Clinton," I thought to myself. I took photos with a few more staffers, answered a few questions about my TV show, and left. Later that evening, back at my hotel, I read an e-mail from Jay thanking me for my visit and for spending time with the staff, and mentioning that President Clinton really enjoyed our chat.

I hit reply and sent Jay a thank-you. Then I walked into the bathroom, and stood there staring at my reflection, looking into the eyes of the man in the mirror. "This is it," I said. "So, what do I do now?"

I thought back to the many times I had ridden my bicycle into unknown territory, making a new path. I thought of the Rastafarian man at the house party back in Houston who had told me I had to live up to my name. I recalled hearing about my father's death on the news, joining the military to become the next General Washington, to attend Howard University, meeting Vera Katz, Harry Poe, Spike Lee, and John Amos. I thought about my wife, Jenisa, and my three children, and about my mother's last words to me on her deathbed. She said, "Spread the love, son. Spread the love." That was it. My mother would give the shirt off of her back to anyone who needed it.

I turned on the faucet and watched the water run down the drain for several minutes. I reached down, cupped my hands, and splashed a handful on my face. Switching it off, I reached for a towel and just stood there, looking at myself in the mirror. "A team," I said to my reflection. "I need a team. God," I prayed, "I need to put together a team."

I felt a jolt of energy and walked out of the bathroom and reached for my black binder, the "bible" where I kept all of my notes and papers on Sierra Leone. I pulled out a yellow steno pad and a pen and began to scan through everything I had learned so far about the country.

"What do we know?" I asked myself. I then proceeded to make a list of the types of people I would need. A chief of security, someone who had access to the Justice Department and the U.S. embassy to gather sensitive intelligence on Sierra Leone. I wrote down Antonio K. Hubbard, my longtime friend, who was a year behind me in high school and the quarterback of our football team. Antonio served in the U.S. Marine Corps and did a tour of duty in Kuwait during the Gulf War. His nickname is "007" and he is highly trained in hand-to-hand combat, counterintelligence, surveillance, and gun and knife weapons. Who better to head up our security detail?

I also needed someone to look at the infrastructure in Sierra Leone and make an assessment of the buildings. I remembered meeting an architect at a Los Angeles fund-raiser, Breton F. Washington of the SmithGroup. Breton was one of the architects who designed the newly built state-of-the-art Saint John's

Health Center in Santa Monica, California. He was a very smart and genuine man. I wrote down his name.

I needed a doctor to look out for all of us, and someone who could help the people on the ground. I thought of Dr. Andre Panossian, a cleft lip and palate specialist who worked as a technical consultant on my TV show, lending his assistance and guidance on how to make the surgeries authentic. He regularly traveled around the world donating his skills as a reconstructive plastic surgeon specializing in children's cleft palates. I nicknamed him "Top Gun" while we were in Sierra Leone. He was a very likable man and an incredibly talented surgeon.

NAACP president Bruce Gordon and I had already discussed my plans to visit Sierra Leone, and he recommended that I bring NAACP human rights attorney Crispian Kirk. Crispian had extensive knowledge on global human rights issues. He was a very smart attorney and very well connected on Capitol Hill. I added him to the list. A journalist, Jackie Coker, had interviewed me for the magazine *Africa Journal*. She worked for Corporate Council on Africa, and, more importantly, she was Sierra Leonean. I added her to my list.

I needed a camera crew to document the entire trip. Sonya Gay Bourn was a line producer on my PSA for the Los Angeles Regional Food Bank. She was a very smart, dynamic, tall, fair-skinned Southerner with a great sense of humor, and she made me laugh. Sonya would prove to be instrumental in planning my first trip to Sierra Leone. She had exceptional organizational skills and I trusted her judgment on many important issues regarding the budget and film production. I wrote her name down.

I called Jeff Vespa, of the world-renowned celebrity photography company WireImage in Los Angeles. He gave me the name of a former Associated Press photographer, Michael Caulfield. Michael was highly recommended as a great photojournalist, also very smart, and had a great "gung ho" kind of energy. I wrote his name down too.

This would be my team: Antonio K. Hubbard, security; Breton F. Washington, infrastructure; Dr. Andre Panossian, health care; Crispian Kirk, legal; Jackie Coker, journalist; Sonya Gay Bourn, film production; and Michael Caulfield, photographer. Now I just needed one more important thing. I needed some visas, and I needed them fast. I had called Congresswoman Diane Watson's office months before for support but I hadn't heard back. She had received her DNA results on the same evening I had, so I thought she might be able to help me cut through "red tape" if I encountered it. Then I thought of my hometown, Houston, Texas. I'd received a lot of support from fans back home. It was a long shot, but I reached for my phone and called Congressman Kevin Brady, a representative from Texas. His assistant, Ms. Jessica Peetoom, picked up.

"This is Isaiah Washington," I said, "may I speak with Congressman Kevin Brady please?"

"Oh, ahh, may I ask what this call is regarding?" she said hesitantly. I sensed by the slight stumble in her voice, she might be a fan of my TV show. I thought, "Wow! This TV show is really working for me."

"Yes," I continued, "I am planning a trip to Sierra Leone and I was wondering if the congressman could help me acquire some visas for my crew as soon as possible."

She explained that Congressman Brady wasn't available but that she would have him return the call. I gave her my number, thanked her, and hung up.

Forty-five minutes later, before I had time to wonder if anyone would call back, my mobile phone rang. "Hello, Isaiah, this is Kevin Brady returning your call. I hear you are doing some work in Sierra Leone."

"Yes, sir, I am trying to go at the end of this month."

"Oh, that's just around the corner."

I said, "Yes, sir, it is."

"Well, I think I can make a few calls to some friends in the embassy and see if I can be of any help. I just want to say that I think what you are doing is commendable. I have done quite a bit of humanitarian work in Central America myself. I am also impressed with your work with United Way down here in Texas. We took in a lot of people in need here in Texas after Hurricane Katrina hit. I saw your United Way commercial running all day every day on TV. It really made us feel good to see that one of our own in Hollywood cared."

"It was an honor to be of service, sir."

He said, "If I come up with anything soon, can I call you on this number?"

"Yes, sir, this is the best number to reach me on."

And with that we hung up. I sat down on the edge of my bed. There was still one more question I needed to answer for myself. Why had I always felt that deep connection, before I knew the results of the DNA test. Did my DNA have memory?

CHAPTER 8

DNA Has Memory

The wheels for my trip to Sierra Leone were in motion. I would make more calls to Congressman Brady and everyone else on my list, in between shooting scenes on my TV show. Luckily, within days, everyone I wanted was able to commit to me and Sierra Leone. I was able to get my visas expedited with lightning speed.

Still, I found myself dogged by the question: Could my DNA be the reason for my dream, "the Rerun"? Could it be responsible for the sensations I felt while meditating beside the Kunene River? Could DNA control and guide an individual's destiny? I needed answers.

When researching my role as Dr. Preston Burke I had read everything I could get my hands on about the medical community. I had come across the name of one of the world's top neurosurgeons, Dr. Keith Black. I decided to make a cold call to his office and see if he would meet with me.

I Googled his name and learned he was the chairman of the

Department of Neurosurgery for the Maxine Dunitz Neurosurgical Institute at Cedars-Sinai Hospital in Los Angeles. I locked his office number in my mobile phone, pressed dial, and left a message. After playing phone tag with his assistant for a day or two, we finally connected on the same day I was to do an incredibly intense surgical scene on my TV show.

Dressed in my yellow surgical cap and dark blue scrubs, I slipped inside a small darkened closet on the set and pulled out my Treo cell phone. I lowered my speaking voice so as not to be overheard and called Dr. Black's office. His assistant answered.

"Hello, is Dr. Keith Black available? This is Isaiah Washington."

"The Isaiah Washington from—"

"Yes," I said, interrupting. I was getting used to this surprised response to my calls.

She put me on hold for a moment and then returned asking, "Can I ask you what this call is regarding?"

"I need to ask Dr. Black if DNA has memory."

"I'm sorry, you need to do what?" she asked.

I went on to explain. "I have a theory that DNA has memory and I would like to speak to Dr. Keith Black about it since he is a brain surgeon."

She told me he was still in surgery but asked for my number. "You know," she said, "I really love what you are doing on the show, but Dr. Black doesn't watch many medical shows, so he may not know who you are."

"Yes," I said, assuring her that was all right, "from what I have read, Dr. Black is a bona fide genius and I'm glad that he is very busy saving 'real' lives. I'm glad that he doesn't have a lot of time to watch TV, you know what I mean?"

"Yes, of course." She continued, "I know Dr. Black would want to meet you, Mr. Washington, but please understand that he is a very, very busy man and may only have ten or fifteen minutes to give you."

"Whatever amount of time he can give me would be an honor."

She promised to get back to me with a time Dr. Black and I could meet. I thanked her and hung up.

"Rehearsal's up!" I heard a voice shout. I turned off my phone and proceeded to mentally prepare for a surgery of my own.

A week later I found myself getting off the elevator and standing in front of a beautiful and welcoming door with the metal letters reading The Maxine Dunitz Neurosurgical Institute. Dr. Black's assistant greeted me, offered me a seat, and asked if I'd like something to drink. When his assistant said, "Dr. Black will see you now," I stepped into Dr. Keith Black's office.

His back was turned to me as I entered. "Have a seat," he said, not turning around. I sat down, waiting to see his face. He was preoccupied with some paperwork that I could hear rustling but could not see. To my left, I saw a photograph of what I assumed was his daughter standing next to an airplane. I thought, "Is this guy a pilot too?" Finally, he turned around and I was stunned at what I saw. Dr. Black looked a lot like me!

"Hey, man," he said. "I will be with you in a second. I just have to do something really quick. Go ahead, what is it you wanted to ask me?" I was too busy trying not to stare when I heard myself say, "Okay. Um ... Dr. Black—"

He interrupted. "Call me Keith."

I said, "Okay, I was just wondering if you shared the same opinion that DNA has memory." Now at his computer multitasking, without hesitation or looking up at me, he said, "Yes, it does."

I said, "It does?" I felt an immediate sense of relief, of validation. It was as if I let out a long breath that I hadn't realized I'd been holding. It was similar to the way I'd felt when I first saw a Spike Lee film and decided to become an actor. I just knew. I had found the thing I had been looking for.

He stood up, walked back to his desk, and sat down to face me. I couldn't help but notice that his blue scrubs, white medical coat, and eyeglasses looked very much like my wardrobe for Dr. Preston Burke. His eyebrows were thicker than mine and his voice soft, studied, and calming. I didn't dare bring this up in our conversation for fear of being perceived as a weirdo.

I had to work hard to maintain my faltering composure. I explained my ancestral link with the Mende and Temne peoples through a DNA test and that I was planning a trip to Sierra Leone to see the country and the people for myself.

"That's great, man," he said. "My daughter is doing an internship in Gabon right now. I have been working in Gabon for nearly twenty years. I love it there."

"Really?" I asked. "Why Gabon?"

"I don't know, I just feel at home there," he said matter-of-factly. "I have diplomatic status there and the president of Gabon and I are very close. I will be working in Gabon for many years to come."

"Would you be interested in taking a DNA test to see if there is any ancestral link to explain why you are so connected to Gabon?" Without hesitation Dr. Black agreed. I was dumb-founded by how casual he was about it. I was blown away by his explanation of the brain and how it allows us to see, hear, and smell with confidence and speed. I was thinking to myself, "This is the sexiest shit I have ever heard!"

When he finished, to make sure that he understood I recognized his genius and respected it, I licked my dry lips and said, "Keith, I know that you are smarter than me, but spiritually speaking, I think I can keep up with you."

Dr. Black's head slightly fell back and he laughed so coolly that it made me laugh too. His door opened and his assistant stuck her head in. I assumed this was an in-house tactic used to allow him to make his escape if I proved unworthy of his precious time. But to my surprise, Dr. Black gave his assistant an "It's okay" nod and she quickly retreated, closing the door behind her. I admired his subtlety.

I had surpassed the ten- or fifteen-minute meeting time Dr. Black's assistant said to expect. "That was funny, Isaiah," he said, smiling. "Yes, I know scientifically everything one needs to know about the brain, but no one knows what makes the brain work or what makes the heart beat. I wanted to know more about the connection between the mind, body, and spirit. I started reading up on various massage techniques. I took up meditation, studied Eastern cultures and their alternative herbal medicines. I read voraciously about naturopathic and homeo-pathic treatments and acupuncture."

Dr. Black took off his glasses and began to clean them as if for effect or to remove any barriers between us. As he talked I never took my eyes off of his. He put his glasses back on and told me a story. "Isaiah, I was once meditating and found myself looking down at my own body. I heard or sensed a voice say, 'If you want more knowledge, you will have to leave your body and go through the roof.' I was so startled. I thought to myself, 'No thanks! I think I'll stick around, you know, down here a little while longer.' That's when I decided that I would try to do less cutting and incorporate more holistic remedies."

The door would open again and again, and each time Dr. Black silently sent his assistant away. I couldn't help but notice how poised and precise he was. He never seemed to waste any movements. His stillness drew me in deeper. "I'm interested to know my genetic connection to our people," he continued, "I have been thinking about it for a long time. I'm really curious to see what they find. How much are the tests?"

I assured him it was on me. "You sure?" he asked.

"It would be my pleasure," I told him. I asked if he was familiar with the book *The Journey of Man* by Spencer Wells, a book Mr. Sidney Poitier had given me.

He smiled widely. "You know Sidney?"

"Yes," I said. "I even debated with him in his own house, trying to persuade him to take the DNA test."

"Did he take it?" he asked.

"No," I said. "He told me that I will achieve everything that I'm trying to do, but in the end I will find that we are all brothers and for me to never forget that."

"Wow," Dr. Black said. "I love Sidney. You know I taught Sidney how to sail. You sail?"

"No," I said, "but my son has learned."

"You scuba dive?" he asked.

"No, but I would love to learn at some point."

Dr. Black looked straight into my eyes and said, "Isaiah, you must dive with me one day. You just have to. It's beautiful. There is so much life down there."

The door opened again and the assistant was not as easily sent away this time. Apparently, Dr. Black and I had been talking for nearly an hour and a half! She walked in and stood at the door waiting for me to get up and follow her out. Dr. Black and I stood up and shook hands. "Hey, man, we need to do this again sometime," he said.

"I hope so," I replied.

"Keith," I asked as I started to leave, "can I go out into the world and say that DNA has memory?"

"Yes," he answered immediately.

I turned to go, paused one more time. "Just one more thing. When I do this thing, when I say that DNA has memory, will you back me up if I need you to?"

He smiled and said, "Absolutely."

I promised him I would ask African Ancestry to expedite his results. Then I walked out of his office feeling as if I were floating on a cloud.

For a long time, I just sat quietly in my car in the parking garage of Cedars-Sinai, unable to yet drive away. As I considered what had just transpired, it hit me: after receiving my DNA results, I no longer felt like an outsider in the world.

Where I had once felt as if no matter where I went, no matter what group I was with, I never quite belonged, now knowing where I came from did more than strengthen my sense of nationalism; it strengthened me as a man, as a person. A strong me, in turn, strengthened my sense of fatherhood. A strong me strengthened my ability to be a better husband, teacher, leader, and friend. A strong me strengthened my sense of globalism. *I know my place*...my place in the world.

CHAPTER 9

Reversing the Middle Passage

I t was May 20, 2006, just before noon. The sun was high in
the sky and shining brightly, an awesome rehearsal for the
upcoming summer. My eldest son, Akin, and my son, Tyme,
had been awake since 6:30 a.m. and I sensed they knew Daddy
was leaving today. They played peacefully as Jenisa and I lazed
away in bed. My daughter, Iman, was awake as well. She had
this habit of looking at me, doing what looks like a double take,
and then she nestles close under my arm, stretching her arms
and legs out like a cat shaking off its slumber. Iman threw up her
hands, a sign for me to pick her up. Jenisa got up and proceeded
to make us a wonderful breakfast. I said a few silent blessings and
took in the simple wonder of this morning with my family.

My ride to Los Angeles International Airport was smooth
and traffic free; and the Virgin Atlantic check-in was simple
and fast. I met up with the team: Antonio K. Hubbard, Sonya
Gay Bourn, Breton F. Washington, Dr. Andre Panossian, and
Michael Caulfield. Two others had been added to the group as

well. Adisa Jones, my soundman, came highly recommended. He was a very animated, fun-loving African American man. A very spiritual person, he was well connected to the Agape International spiritual community and had close ties with various Kemetic organizations. Adisa loved him some African culture. I knew the moment I met him he would be the perfect person for the project. Gary Livneh would be the cameraman. He was a good-looking version of Henry Kissinger. Our interview had lasted about two hours. I originally had someone else in mind for the project but he was not available. I needed to make a decision quickly, so Gary was the guy.

Everyone was present and accounted for. Jackie Coker and Raymond Scott-Manga were already on the ground in Sierra Leone and attorney Crispian Kirk, whose connecting flight was delayed, was on his way. The Virgin Atlantic lounge was quiet and comfortable. Everyone on the team, including me, was excited and ready to go. After so much planning, it was hard to believe that this was finally happening.

About a half hour before we were scheduled to board Sonya gave me the news that Crispian had finally arrived into Los Angeles and was picking up his bags. "Yes!" I thought to myself. "He was going to make the flight!" The team was in place when he arrived at the gate. With anxious anticipation we awaited our turn to board. I bought a beer and watched Crispian drink his down rather rapidly.

I remembered an article about Sierra Leone that I wanted to share with Crispian. As we were boarding I reached into my bag to pull it out, and as I turned to hand it to him, I noticed he didn't look so good. Just before we stepped through the cabin door, he became disoriented and suddenly began to collapse. I grabbed him and held him up, pinning him against the wall for support. "Don't move!" I told him. I frantically ran down the Jetway and grabbed Dr. Panossian and Antonio before they boarded.

They calmly followed me back to where I had left Crispian. He was still leaning there against the wall of the Jetway. As we walked him back out into the airport Crispian immediately collapsed to the floor and started to convulse and wet himself. Dr. Panossian took his pulse. His blood pressure was falling rapidly. We called the paramedics.

I heard, "Last call for boarding," the announcement that the plane was leaving. It took everything I had not to cancel the trip. How could I leave not just one, but three good men behind? Antonio assured me that he would take care of everything and meet us in London. I saw the determination and resolve in his eyes. It was the same look I had seen many times before playing football together back in Texas.

"Is he going to be okay?" I asked, still not sure what to do.

Antonio said, "Nothing is going to happen to him on my watch. Now get on that plane."

I did. Ironically, just as I boarded, my phone rang. I could see in the display that it was Dr. Gene Allen of the trauma ward at Centinela Hospital. I met Dr. Allen while doing research for my TV show, shadowing him as he made his rounds treating actual patients. He taught me so much, including how to suture and how to administer intravenous antibiotics. He was calling to wish me a safe trip to Sierra Leone. The plane was taxiing down the runway, but I answered anyway. The flight attendant immediately asked me to turn the phone off. I did. But just before the airplane began its ascent I hurriedly turned it back on and texted Dr. Allen a message: "On runway taxiing on Virgin Atlantic to SL. NAACP attorney collapsed in airport at gate 23A. Had to leave him behind with my doc and DEA agent. Name is Cris Kirk if he comes thru ur trauma ward." I pressed the send button and nothing happened. The plane was now climbing fast. I just sat there staring at the phone hard. "Please God, please send. Please send. Send now!" I prayed silently to myself.

The frozen text flickered and disappeared. Then a "No Signal" prompter popped up.

Somehow, the text went through.

Needless to say, the flight to London was intense. I had gone from feelings of excitement and anticipation to a controlled panic. Once we were at cruising altitude of thirty-five thousand feet, I quickly unbuckled my seat belt and went to tell the rest of the team what had happened. I returned to my seat and made several attempts to call Dr. Panossian on the airplane phone. I tried ten times in eight hours. The airplane phone never worked.

We couldn't land at Heathrow Airport in London soon enough. The plane touched down in a pouring rainstorm. The moment we got off I rushed to a phone to check on Crispian, Antonio, and Dr. Panossian. No answer.

I settled into my hotel room and put in a call to Jenisa. I tried six times to reach her, but there was no answer there either. Where was she? I was on pins and needles. I had barely slept on the plane and was a nervous wreck. This was not at all how I pictured this trip would begin.

I placed another call to Dr. Panossian and, finally, he answered. Apparently Sonya, my producer, had given Crispian two Ambien, a prescription sleep medication, to help him rest on the plane. Unfortunately, he had taken them on an empty stomach. By the time he arrived in Los Angeles, going on twenty-four hours of no sleep, drinking a beer caused him to collapse. Dr. Panossian reassured me that Crispian was fine to fly. I believed him. What a relief. I went to sleep.

The next morning brought a cloudy day but no sign of the heavy rains we landed in the day before. I was not happy, I needed that rain! If our flight out of Gatwick wasn't delayed, Crispian, Antonio, and Dr. Panossian's flight wouldn't arrive in time to join us.

Sonya suggested I might have to plan to go on to Sierra

Leone without them. We checked out of our rooms in bright sunshine. I looked at the sky through the hotel lobby atrium and said, "Sonya, it will rain and our flight will be delayed and those guys are going to Freetown with us." She blinked. "I don't think so, hon." And I watched her as she turned and walked away.

"It will rain," I said to myself, it had to. Twenty minutes before we were scheduled to board an announcement came over the airport's PA system. Our flight had been delayed due to heavy rain. I looked at Sonya. She just shrugged. Everyone else sat there, staring at me in complete disbelief.

Just then, I turned to see three of the most beautiful faces I could imagine: Crispian Kirk, Antonio K. Hubbard, and Dr. Andre Panossian were all walking toward me, smiling. I looked up toward the sky and smiled. Like so many times in my life when things seemed hopeless—as when as a kid I had to do battle with the Frazier sisters, or when I found myself sleeping in my car at Howard unable to pay tuition, or when I struggled to become a working actor—in the end it turned out all right. "Okay, people," I said, "it's time to go to Sierra Leone."

It was May 22, 2006, when wheels touched down and the team and I arrived at Lungi International Airport in Freetown, Sierra Leone. I was so happy I could not stop smiling. At times everything seemed to be in slow motion, as if I were watching a movie, except it wasn't a movie, it was happening, and to me! I felt like a little boy about to unwrap a gift I had been hoping and wishing for all year long.

I grabbed my bags and thanked the Astraeus Airlines pilot. "Astraeus" in Greek mythology is the Titan god of the dusk. It was nighttime, but as we descended the plane's stairs, the tarmac was lit up like noontime by the flashing bulbs of my photographer. The name of the airlines, the light in the darkness, it all felt like a good omen.

We were fast-tracked through customs and ushered to a VIP room, where we waited for Jackie Coker and Raymond Scott-Manga to pick us up. I looked around at the small, humble airport, very basic by American standards. It looked very much like a storefront church in Brooklyn, with Plexiglas windows and 1950s-style walls and furniture. It was very hot and crowded with people, but I didn't care. I had finally arrived. "I really am in Sierra Leone," I thought to myself.

Just as we were gathering our luggage, I heard the energetic, rhythmic voice of Raymond Scott-Manga screaming, "Izayyyyyyyahhhhhh!" I turned to see his trademark grin as he walked toward me.

I grabbed him, lifting him up off his feet exclaiming, "I'm here, babyyyyyy!" I put him down and then grabbed Jackie and gave her a big hug too. I introduced them to the team. It was a moment of euphoria, hugs and handshakes, and laughter. I will never forget it.

The VIP representative was a very professional Sierra Leonean woman who took care of returning our passports to us. She expertly escorted us to the van that would take us from the Lungi International Airport to the ferry. The ferry, a large hovercraft, looked like a huge boat built on top of an enormous black inner tube. I climbed out of the van and made my way to an overhang where many people were sitting on white plastic chairs, waiting for the ferry to depart. I found a chair and sat down, and tried to take it all in.

"I'm in Sierra Leone," I thought to myself again, "one of the poorest and most stigmatized countries in the world." I still couldn't believe after so much preparation and hard work I had finally arrived.

Raymond walked over and asked, "Do you want something to drink? A beer?"

"If it's local, yes," I replied. "I will try whatever you suggest."

With that, he walked to the kiosk and placed his order. I gazed out at the pitch-black surroundings and was immediately lured toward the sound of waves crashing on the beach. I walked toward the sound and my eyes began to adjust to the darkness. The ambient light from the waiting area created a twilight effect along the beach. I noticed something moving down at my feet. I strained to see it but couldn't quite make it out, I had ventured too far from the light. Suddenly, as my eyes adjusted a little more, I could see it was a sand crab.

Then another appeared, and then another. They were everywhere, surrounding me. I turned and shouted toward the waiting area, "Hey, guys, come look. There are hundreds of crabs over here!" The locals looked at me quizzically as if to say, "Crazy American, of course they are there, they come out every night." I didn't think anyone from my team heard me until, FLASH! My photographer snapped a picture of me standing there in the dark. The crabs retreated down into the sand so quickly it was as if they had been a figment of my imagination. "Michael," I said excitedly, "did you see that? Did you see all of those crabs?"

"Huh?" he asked. "Crabs, what crabs?" I stood there looking at him, trying to figure out if he was messing with me. He tried to keep a straight face but couldn't. "Yeah, man, I saw them." He chuckled. We had a good laugh. Michael began chasing some of the crabs crawling in the darkness a few feet away.

I found myself looking out into the night, listening to the crashing of the waves, and wondering what tomorrow's rising sun would bring.

Sonya's shrill Southern voice shattered my meditation, "Heigh-ho!" she shouted. "Come on everyone, the bags have been loaded and it's time to go!"

We boarded the ferry, walking into the dimly lit cabin filled to capacity with passengers. Up ahead, I could see Sonya standing with the ferry captain. I joined them, shaking his hand and asking, "Man, how long does it take to learn how to navigate this thing?"

He replied, "Oh, I have been in the navy for seventeen years and piloted almost every kind of water vessel. Not long." He was a tall man, about six foot four, with a striking face and presence. He resembled Henry Cele, the South African actor who portrayed Shaka in the film *Shaka Zulu*.

We finished our chat and I found a seat. Making sure that my camera was rolling, I immediately began to interview a young Sierra Leonean man sitting next to me. "If you could change five things in this country," I asked him, "what would they be?"

"End corruption, create more jobs, build more schools, end malaria, and create clean water systems," he answered. Without any urging the young man willingly began to discuss the many concerns he had about the cleanliness of his beloved country. He told me a story that still haunts me today. He had gathered a bundle of long grass from his mother's village. He set it on fire and walked into his home to do battle with the burdensome and treacherous mosquitoes that plague the local villages. He explained that he used the fire and smoke from the grass to swat and kill the cloud of buzzing mosquitoes in the darkness. When he'd finally finished swinging at the air invaded by his attackers, he stood there, out of breath, and turned on the lights. What he saw terrified him. The floor was completely covered, blackened with hundreds of dead mosquitoes.

He spoke to my camera and me with such determination that if the world could hear his stories his life would immediately change. I sensed that there was so much more he wanted to say, but the ferry was docking and our journey had come to an end. As we arrived and prepared to disembark, I didn't know what to say to him. I just gave him a hug.

The utter sadness and shock I felt hearing his story was obliterated by the face of a woman who approached me asking for a photo and an autograph. I was stunned. She looked just like my Aunt Gloria back in Houston! The resemblance was so uncanny; she even walked the same way. Her voice and even her goldtoothed smile were my aunt's. I couldn't stop staring at her, the sight of her made me feel a little wobbly. She said something to Raymond in Mende, and I could tell by her body language that my gaze was making her uncomfortable.

"Raymond," I said, "please tell her that she looks just like my Aunt Gloria back in the United States!" He translated and a broad smile crossed her face. She grabbed me and hugged so tightly I thought she might bruise a rib or two. She was very strong for her five-and-a-half-foot frame.

The team's bags were loaded into a waiting van and I climbed into a 4x4 with Raymond. I noticed candles burning in kiosks or in front of shanty entrances as we drove through the streets. "Why are there so many candles burning tonight?" I naively asked Raymond.

"Isaiah, these people have to use candles every night. There is no electricity in Freetown."

"You're kidding me," I said, astounded. "No electricity at all?"

"The only people who have electricity are those who can afford to have generators," he explained. "The candles you see are those of people who have no jobs and no money for that."

As we drove deeper into the city of Freetown, along the dark streets congested with pedestrians, I could feel my mood darken with every mile. I took a deep breath, trying to forestall the anxiety that was beginning to suffocate my previous excitement. Raymond turned the red Dodge Ram down an alley, coming to a stop at a huge white steel gate. He honked his horn. A security guard appeared in response and opened it. As the vehicle slowly rolled inside, I could see ominous rows of coiled steel barbed wire illuminated by the car's headlamps, making the wire look as if it were floating in midair. My eyes tracked this image along the top of the high cement walls now separating me from the rest of Sierra Leone. What looked like a high-security compound turned out to be the Hotel Barmoi. This is where I would spend my very first night in my newfound homeland, and it would be my home for the next ten days.

CHAPTER 10

Heart of Darkness,
Ray of Light

I awoke at the hotel in Freetown, on May 23, 2006, to heavy knocking at my door. It was Sonya. "We have a little problem," she said. The 750 pounds of boxes filled with gifts that I had sent over for my meet and greets with the local people and officials were "lost." Customs couldn't seem to locate the shipment. She explained that Raymond was convinced that it had arrived, but we might need to "pay taxes" on it.

"Those boxes are filled with gifts for the villagers!" I said, exasperated. "All the sneakers donated by NIKE, the boxes of Children's Tylenol and soccer balls are missing? I can't deal with this right now!" I was scheduled to go with Raymond to speak to a group of students at Fourah Bay College.

After my speech about 150 of them mobbed me. Their excited energy did little to calm me down. I signed as many autographs as I could before Raymond insisted that we go.

As we drove through the town I saw piles of rubbish along the roads as far as the eye could see. Signs along the road warned about HIV and stood next to signs that read Welcome to Sweet Salone, the country's nickname. It was hard to take in how filthy Freetown was. I wondered how people could live this way. Culture shock was setting in fast.

Raymond drove us to meet with his uncle, Minister Sidikie Brima, who was responsible for local government and community development. Sierra Leone customs told Sonya that our 750 pounds' worth of gifts had been "found," but we would need the signature of a government official in order to waive the tax for release. Raymond said we could get that signature after I met Minister Brima.

We walked into the dated and sparsely furnished office building and climbed the stairs. The heat and humidity tugged at my shirt now soaking wet with perspiration. After a short wait, the minister finished up a meeting with—from what I could see through the office door—a disgruntled local businessman.

To my surprise, Minister Brima appeared quite comfortable in front of the camera and the American entourage invading his office. He smiled and coolly invited us all in. After introductions, I asked Crispian, as the team's human rights attorney, to lead the meeting. Crispian asked very good and pointed questions, and Minister Brima responded with equally good answers. What impressed me most about the minister was his clarity, and the eloquent way he spoke about the eleven-year civil war and endemic corruption that had severely hurt his country's reputation. He appeared to be a reasonable man. When I arrived in Sierra Leone I learned there were plans under way to hold a ceremony to make me an honorary chief. As an "honorary chief" I would be adopted into the family but exempt from the full responsibilities of the chiefdom. I decided to address our customs issue head-on, since he would later become my "uncle" by tribal induction.

"Minister Brima," I said, "I really appreciate your candid dialogue about poor governance and corruption here in Sierra Leone. Having said that, I need to know why my medicine for children, shoes, and toys are being held in customs for a fee? These are gifts to express my goodwill. I don't intend on selling or making a profit on any of these items. I'm told by Sonya here that we would need a government official to sign a letter of release, which we have here with us. So for the sake of timing, I was wondering if you could call the people in customs and find out what is going on."

Then Raymond did something remarkably smart. He pulled out his mobile and speed dialed the number for the Sierra Leone customs office. While my cameras were rolling, he got up and handed the phone to Minister Brima. Minister Brima had no choice but to take the call.

"Hello? Uh-huh...This is Minister Sidikie Brima. No... no...yes...yes, well we need to get that...What? Uh-huh. Uh-huh. Yes, he is sitting right here in front of me. Yes, I am on camera now. Okay. Okay. Yes, we need to get that released as soon as possible. Yes, I will do that. Bye."

Minister Brima hung up the phone and said to us, "I was told that they have located your goods and that they need me to sign a waiver, then you have to take the letter of release and waiver to them. After that, your goods will be released to you. It may take you a few days to get all of the necessary paperwork."

Sonya jumped up and presented all of the paperwork needed for release of our goods. "Minister Brima," she said politely, and curtsied. "I have all the required documents right here. All we need is your signatures."

Minister Brima got up from his office chair and walked toward his desk, where Sonya was standing, waiting with a pen in her hand and the documents at the ready. He smiled at Sonya, sat down at his desk, and slowly looked over each document.

"Everything looks in order," he said. And with that he selected one of his own pens from his desk and signed and initialed all the paperwork. I looked at my team and thought, "Damn, now that was the most gangster move I have ever seen in my life. I think we just strong-armed a government official in Sierra Leone!"

We happily drove to customs and proudly presented our signed documents. We were assured that we could pick up our goods the next day. I returned to Hotel Barmoi, exhausted. I opened the curtains and stepped out of my room onto the patio. There was a pool, white plastic chairs and tables thoughtfully placed around the area, a bar, and the most magnificent view of Fourah Bay.

I went downstairs, ordered a beer, and noticed a familiar voice on the TV over the bartender's head. The reception was poor, but I finally realized that the person speaking was me! The bartender was watching a repeat episode from my TV show. I paid for my beer, tipped the barkeep, and walked toward the patio's edge to look down at a drop of about forty feet to jagged rocks below me. I sat down on the low stone wall lined with plants. Suddenly, I heard a voice as gravelly and ancient as time say, "Please, sir, do not sit there. It's dangerous." I turned to see who was chastising me. A well-dressed, stout man walked toward me. His body seemed to sway from left to right as if it were trying to constantly right itself from some hidden inertia brought on by his bowed legs. I was curious to know who this was telling me to step away from the edge with such authority. I wondered if he was afraid I was going to jump.

We shook hands. He introduced himself as the owner and manager of Hotel Barmoi, a retired physician, Dr. Sheku T. Kamara. He asked if my room was okay and I assured him it was. He looked away from me, gazing out at the sun setting on the bay. "It's beautiful, isn't it?" he asked. I agreed that it was.

Without looking at me, he said, "Welcome home, Mr.

Washington. If you need anything, please don't hesitate to ask for it." With that he ambled away, leaving me with my thoughts. I tried to put what I had experienced so far into some kind of perspective. I failed. The juxtaposition of the beautiful spirits of the Sierra Leonean people and the abominable blight I saw was simply overwhelming.

It was hard to digest what I had seen on my first full day in Sweet Salone. I recalled the filthy chickens I saw feeding off of scrawny pig feces. Those same pigs roamed through stench-filled trash piled high right next to a shanty where children played with a battered and patched-up soccer ball. Many children were sick with runny noses and large scabs and sores all over their bodies. Flies fed off their open wounds.

I saw insanity darting its sunken eyes at me with its mouth distorted and slack. I witnessed a woman having sex for money in an alley in broad daylight, and blind, malnourished old women being led by children with missing limbs while they begged for money or food. There were countless men, women, and children in wheelchairs, crippled by polio.

I saw wealthy businessmen refuse to give clean water to children, forcing them to fend for themselves at a broken dirty water pipe spewing muddy water. There were schoolgirls in bright green and blue uniforms, wearing filthy, dirty sandals and clutching their books as they walked to school past burning, smoking trash heaps. And there were other children, with beautiful, beaming smiles, selling fruits and vegetables along those chaotic, busy roads.

Yet even in these worst of circumstances, in these horrific conditions, I also saw hope. The Sierra Leonean people were so down that up was the only direction they could go. Their resilient spirits were chained to a broken, war-torn landscape, but I saw my face in their faces, and I knew that I was witnessing all of this so I could return time and time again and help change it.

*　　*　　*

THUNK! Something hit the side of our red 4x4 hard.

"What the hell was that?" I asked Raymond.

"Rock," he said blandly.

"Rock? Someone threw a rock at us?" I asked, incredulous.

"Kids," he answered.

I later learned that locals threw rocks at our vehicles when they saw the camera pointed at them. They were convinced that the camera was "stealing their souls."

Raymond steered the Jeep into the parking lot. I noticed a sign for DHL, the express shipping service. Sonya went inside with our paperwork signed by Minister Brima. I stayed in the Dodge Ram looking over some notes and discussing the shots for the day with my cameraman. About twenty minutes had passed before Sonya reemerged to inform us that the manager in charge to release our 750 pounds' worth of gifts and medicine was unavailable.

"What?" I shouted. "There has to be someone who can sign off on this. This is crazy!" I noticed the reflection in the side rearview mirror of the *Oprah* signature on the blue T-shirt I was wearing, and I got an idea. I jumped out of the truck and turned to my cameraman, "Guy, you rolling?"

"Yep," he said. "Adisa, sound good?" Adisa nodded his headphone-adorned head up and down. "Let's go!" I said. I strutted into the DHL office with my film crew close behind.

"Hello, is the manager here?" I asked a group of women sitting behind a desk. Stunned by the camera crew, they sat there, staring like zombies, barely answering. "You speak English?" I asked. They shook their heads no. "Okay, is there another person in charge who speaks English, because I'm here doing a show for Oprah Winfrey." I pointed at the signature on my T-shirt.

The women's eyes grew wide as they recognized Oprah's

signature from her talk show. Luckily for me, I had just appeared on the show a week earlier and was given one of her signature shirts. One of the women stood up, walked to the back of the office, and disappeared. A few minutes later she returned with a gentleman who looked very confused. "Hello, sir, you speak English?" I asked.

"Yes," he answered tentatively.

"I'm trying to pick up my goods over at customs," I explained. "But I'm told that your office has to sign off on our paperwork first. Oprah wouldn't be happy if we fall behind with our schedule. I'm told that your other manager is out, but as you can see"—I gestured toward the camera—"you will be on the *Oprah Show* instead of the other guy. How cool is that?"

There are few people in the world who can resist the opportunity to appear on *The Oprah Winfrey Show*. We got signatures on our paperwork and then set off to retrieve our 750 pounds' worth of gifts and medicine. The black market was going to have to wait. "I'm going to get my shit *today*," I thought to myself.

As we drove to the building and got out to deliver our letters of release, I heard a man shout something at us in Mende. I didn't understand what he said, but I immediately sensed the anger behind it. I asked Raymond, "What did he just say?"

"He's crazy," Raymond said. "Just ignore him."

"Don't do that, tell me what he said. He looks angry," I protested.

Raymond tried to ignore me, but I persisted. "*Tell me what he said*," I said again, now irritated. Raymond appeared embarrassed; reluctantly he explained. He said, "'You people always come with all of your cameras, take a lot of pictures, and nothing changes after you leave.'"

I looked back at the man. When our eyes met I felt as if he were staring right through my soul. I let him get a good look at my face. Then, to his surprise, I walked right up to him and said,

"I know you don't understand me, but I am not 'you people.' My name is Isaiah Washington and I'm here for you."

I called out to my camera crew and told them to follow me. I wanted to walk through the streets and connect with the people. My photographer took off in front of me and started snapping away. I caught up to him and saw what he was photographing. It was some homeless children who looked very sick; mucus was caked inside of their noses and on top of their lips. Insects were feeding off of the open sores on their arms and legs. Michael was so excited about the shots that he nearly knocked me over as I stood behind.

"I got it," he said proudly.

I looked at him. "No you don't."

"Come on, this is great stuff!" he protested.

"You're not here for the ugly, I brought you here to find the beautiful, and I want you to find the beautiful, do you understand?"

"Isaiah, this is—"

I interrupted, "Michael! These people are not *National Geographic, Time,* AP, UPI, or *Newsweek* subjects. These are my people, do you understand? They don't know me, but they are my people! I don't want the world to see any more of this shit. Find the beautiful!"

Michael's posture seemed to change, his adrenaline subsided. He stood there for a moment, looking into my eyes, and said, "Okay, I get it, I get it. Find the beautiful."

I walked away seeing but trying to ignore the photographic gold mine of pain. When I arrived back at the SUV, Sonya informed me that everything was done; we could pick up our goods early the next morning.

We piled back into the vehicles and drove out onto the streets of Freetown. I saw the man who cursed us upon our arrival standing by the side of the parking lot. He smiled ever so slightly and waved good-bye. I hate good-byes, so I threw him a wink. We weren't twenty feet outside of the parking lot before we were forced to come to a complete stop, stuck in a traffic jam. A commotion between some locals had spilled out into the hot streets and we couldn't get past. I looked back to see Guy filming as Raymond banged on his horn and screamed for the people to move out of our way.

I was about to ask Raymond what was going on when I heard Adisa exclaim, "Oh my God!"

"What? What's wrong?" My heart was pounding; the adrenaline started pumping through my veins.

When I turned to look at him, Adisa was straining his neck from the backseat of the Dodge Ram, trying to look at something.

"What is it? What's wrong?" I asked.

"It's the little girl I gave money to!" he screamed.

"How much did you give her?" I screamed back, immediately understanding the seriousness of the situation.

"I gave her a few dollars," he said. "I didn't have any leones."

I exploded, "American dollars? You gave her American dollars? Are you trying to get her killed!"

I yelled, "Raymond, stop the car!" But he kept driving. "Raymond!" I screamed, "Stop the car!"

"Isaiah, you stay in the car, I will handle this."

Raymond got out and walked toward the swarming crowd. But with so many people he found himself jammed in front of our SUV unable to move. The little girl's screams were killing me. Ignoring Raymond's instruction, I jumped out of the SUV and started pushing and shoving my way toward the center of the mob. As I broke through the crowd, I was horrified to see a terrified little girl desperately trying to fight off a fully grown man as he yanked viciously at her flimsy yellow dress. He was trying to rip it off her right there in the street, in broad daylight!

I was too pissed off to worry about being shocked. "Hey! Stop that! Leave her alone!" I yelled. The anger rang in my ears so loudly that I barely heard Raymond screaming for me to get back in the car. It was too late. I was totally locked on the aggressor. I pushed several people away from me and put my hand over the black pouch at my hip that secured nothing but a halogen flashlight. "Stop it!" I said in as menacing a voice as I could muster.

The man turned toward me and stared at me through yellowed, jaundiced eyes full of desperation and rage. I looked straight back at him, my gaze daring him to put his hands on that girl just once more. He stared back, blinked, glanced quickly at my right hand firmly placed on the pouch on my right hip, looked back at the girl, and then slowly back at me.

I was thinking, "Yeah, muthafucka, it's a gun all right and I will blow your head clean off before I let you hurt this little girl any more than you already have!"

He took a step toward me, testing my bluff.

I steadied myself and popped the Velcro strap covering my flashlight. The tearing sound startled him and the crowd around us. I stood there, staring at him, stark still. He morphed, in my mind, into my stepfather. "GET! OFF! MY! MAMA!" were the words choking in my mouth, but not my mouth as the man Isaiah Washington, rather as the teenager Mickey. My mind raced back.

I ran headlong and flew through the air just as the ball was landing in the wide receiver's hand. We connected while still in midair and landed together on the ground with an authoritative thud. The whistle blew. I stood up and looked down at him lying there on the ground, out of breath. My hit had knocked the wind out of him.

I turned and jogged back toward the sideline. Coach Narcisse ran over to meet me, screaming, "Goddamnit, number 57! It's only practice. Light contact. Remember? Light contact!"

I smirked. I wasn't trying to do my teammate any harm, but I didn't care. If you threw or ran the ball anywhere near my zone, I was going to try to get you. Football was such a rush for me. There was just something about putting on pads and a helmet and being allowed to slam myself at someone running full speed, hitting him so hard I knocked him out of his cleats.

My mother had married my stepfather when I was eight years old. I liked him then because my mother told me he was a "provider." As I got older, I became more and more disillusioned with my mother and stepfather's sham of a marriage. I knew they were both cheating on each other, I had heard the fights. I couldn't take how he treated her. My grandfather, Pa-Pa, was getting older, and it wasn't as easy as it used to be for him to get around. My sister, Savannah, was long gone, she moved out when I was eleven and went to live with Muh' Dear and Pa-Pa because she didn't get along with my stepfather.

There were days I wanted to scream and smash my head through a wall.

But with football I didn't have to. Instead, I could take those feelings of angst and frustration and unleash them on some unsuspecting quarterback. Football was like legislated anarchy. It was pure violence, controlled chaos. I thought it was beautiful.

I was fast as hell, so I loved running. With my height and speed, I could have been a tight end. I had really good instincts, a specific mind for plays, so playing quarterback was also an option. But there was one problem with all of those positions—they were offensive, you got hit; you rarely got to hit back.

As a defensive end, I learned to be creative on every snap of the ball. There was nothing sweeter in the world than sacking a quarterback, blocking a pass, or causing a fumble. To watch my opponents' shoulders crumble when I took the ball away was intoxicating. But the best part was the hits. On the surface I was tall and skinny—but line me up and I could flatten someone twice my size. Force is equal to mass times velocity. I didn't have a lot of mass, but my speed equaled out the equation.

My idols were Baylor's Mike Singletary and the Oakland Raiders' Jack Tatum. Singletary, a middle linebacker, was a thinking man's thug. The middle linebacker was the defensive coordinator on the field. He called the audibles to make sure coverage was ready, and at the same time he had to be hard, and had to possess a "kill the quarterback" mentality. Singletary was small but aggressive, and when it came time to drop the sledgehammer on somebody, he added plenty of finesse to it.

Jack Tatum was pure fear. Animalistic. Carnivorous. There were players who faced him who said they didn't even like watching old game tapes where they played against him, it was too upsetting. I saw him put one of his bone-crushing hits on Earl Campbell, the running back of the Houston Oilers. He hit him so hard, and with so much force, that the sound of it rang up to the topmost rafters of the Astrodome! WACKALACK!

I played defensive end for the Willowridge Eagles and modeled my style of play after a mix of both men. I wanted to have Tatum's brutality with Singletary's single-minded ambition to make plays through sheer will. I was 175 pounds, but I could hit like a man twice my size. When I made a hit, I wasn't happy unless I left a gash in my opponent's helmet, in fact I cracked two Riddell helmets in my day.

Opponents were so afraid of my ferocity that they stopped lining up one-on-one with me for fear they would leave the game injured. Players began to double-team me. They didn't need to be concerned. I wasn't trying to hurt anybody. I was just trying to hit somebody. Every opponent was the person who shot my father. At every snap, I would think about my stepfather beating my mother and my blood would boil over with anger and resentment.

It wasn't that I was violent, in fact, far from it. Off the field I wasn't aggressive at all. I opened doors, carried groceries, cut yards, and said, "Yes, ma'am. No, ma'am." But I needed an outlet. And I couldn't find it at school, or in church, or by hanging out with the few friends that I had back then.

The football field became the best place to release my frustration. I could let it all hang out and people cheered me for it. It was my sanctuary. It was my stage. And we're talking about big-city high school football in Texas, where football is like a religion. To play varsity football, and to be good at it, meant you were a star. We walked through the halls wearing our varsity jackets in our school's blue and silver colors. We had our own exclusive lunch table and the girls all knew my name. On Friday night, under the tall, square, massive white lights, thousands of people packed the stands to see the game. It was the first time I ever truly felt as if I was a part of something special. The nods, the smiles, the slaps on the back, and the admiration for a good tackle or a sack felt like heaven to me. It was a blanket I could wrap myself in— the love was enough to counter the increasing silence and growing tension and violence I faced at home.

We had some good players on the team—running back Thurman Thomas, who was two years behind me, not only ended up going pro, but became the star running back for the Buffalo Bills and was inducted into the Pro Football Hall of Fame in Canton, Ohio.

Scouts from major Texas colleges, and from all over the nation, started showing up to our practices and games. I met a few, some asked me questions about my good grades, high test scores, my speed, and my ability to shut down a corner. I was certain offer letters to play at their schools would come, I was sure of it...but they never did.

There were times that my coaches took me and other players off the field during practice and in games, seemingly inopportune times that would completely throw off my rhythm. It would be a long time later when I found out why players who didn't have close to my ability were all of a sudden getting so much playing time. I didn't know why I was being frozen out. All I knew was that my dream of playing professional football was dying in front of my eyes. I was named All-District Honorable Mention. "Honorable Mention"? Well, that just wasn't good enough for me—my goal was to go pro.

Unlike many players who dreamed of taking their game to the big time, money wasn't what I was after. What I wanted was recognition, that feeling that comes from people admiring you for doing something better than anyone else.

After my father died, I couldn't shake the image of him lying in a casket. I was determined to be somebody—anybody—and to make the name Isaiah Washington mean something. I didn't want to end up like him, a quick blurb on the news about another violent Negro death. I wanted my life to be about something more than a few sentences' worth of mention in the local newspaper.

One Sunday afternoon, like so many other young men my age, I was watching football. I stared intently at the screen, singularly focused on every play. It was the one thing my stepfather and I could still do together without wanting to fight each other. We were watching Warren Moon, the Houston Oilers quarterback, do some serious damage to the other team. We reveled in the fact that Moon was a black man. At the time it was the closest thing to having a black president. After Moon completed a long pass, the other team called a time-out, and the broadcast paused for a commercial break.

Instead of the "Be All You Can Be" army commercial or the "The Few. The Proud. The Marines." commercial, there was a spot for the U.S. Air Force. "Aim High" was the slogan. After seeing it, I couldn't get it out of my mind. I don't know what it was about it that so captivated me. Maybe it was the beautiful F-15 Eagle that did unbelievable and graceful maneuvers. Maybe it was seeing the tall man wearing the elegant, crisp dark blue uniform that, to me, looked so much better than the drab greens that army personnel wore. Maybe it was the book I read about the Tuskegee Airmen, the first African American fighter pilots.

"Aim High." That was how I lived my life. That was all I ever did. I wanted to be the best, so I pushed myself hard. I was on my own ass harder than any parent or coach could have ever been. The air force represented a pride and a focus that I hadn't seen anywhere else but on the football field. Any fool could scream, paint his face, and shoot a gun. You didn't even have to leave Texas to find that.

To me, the air force represented the elite. You needed an engineer's smarts to navigate an airplane, plus the body of an athlete to endure flight. I imagined myself in a cockpit, flying fast, feeling the pressures of the g-forces pushing me back in the seat, while the earth rotated forty thousand feet below. While one door had closed on my professional football career, in my mind, it felt as if perhaps another one was opening.

My door opened a short time later, one Saturday afternoon while I was sitting in my room reading an air force recruitment brochure. I heard a loud thump, and a familiar grunt.

"Bitch," I heard my stepfather say.

My stepfather and mother were going at it again. It was happening more often than it used to. I decided right then and there that I had had enough of that bullshit. I wasn't a frightened little boy peeking through the crack of the door anymore. Nor was I a thirteen-year-old who was going to lean back and get choked out. I was seventeen years old now. I played football, and I wasn't afraid of getting hit. I lifted weights; I drank my milk and ate my vegetables. I was strong, I was quick, and I was fast, I ran a four-and-half forty; and it was time someone put this triflin'-ass nigger out of his misery. Yeah, I said nigger. I meant it, too.

I opened the door to see my stepfather jamming my mama up against the wall. He was choking her and throwing her from one side of the hall to the other. He held her off the ground by the neck with her feet dangling in the air. King of the couch potatoes was standing there in only a pair of Fruit of the Loom briefs from Kmart acting like GI Joe. I thought, "Fuck him and his Vietnam nightmares." This shit had to stop and I was going to stop it.

I rushed back into my room, reached down by my bed, and grabbed my homemade nunchakus. Everyone had them back then. The first ninja movies had come out and the late great Bruce Lee was an idol. I ran back into the hallway, lunged at my stepfather with twirling nunchakus, hitting him square in the head with the hard wood.

"GET! OFF! MY! MAMA!"

I hit him so hard that I split his wig and put a knot on his head that protruded at least two inches from his forehead. It would have felled anybody else, but he was in full berserk Vietnam vet mode. He ran into the bedroom. "Mickey...run!" Mama yelled.

I ran out the back door of the house through the patio door and jumped over the hood of the truck parked in our fenceless backyard that faced the end of a cul de sac. My stepfather chased close behind wearing nothing but his underwear and brandishing his .357 magnum. I cowered on the other side of the truck, shaking and terrified he would find me and shoot me to death. I just squatted there, afraid to move or take a breath, praying to God that he would go back in the house. Either that or hoping He would grant me a swift passage into heaven.

To this day, I won't wear Fruit of the Loom underwear. I don't even like the numbers three, five, or seven. I couldn't watch him hurt my mother anymore. One of us had to go. It was going to be me.

Not long after, I sat at the big desk, poised with the pen in my hand, reading over the paperwork one last time.

"You sure, you're ready to do this, son?" the recruiter asked.

"I'm ready," I answered.

"Good. It's the best decision you'll ever make in your life." I looked up at the air force recruiter and then at the posters on the walls of his office—the shots of the F-15 Eagle and the F-16 Fighting Falcon. I imagined myself in the cockpit, flying high...

Twenty-five years later, the terror in the little girl's frightened eyes reminded me of my mother's. The angry man stood there, looking deeply into my own eyes, filled with my teenage rage, as my mind's eye was reliving the painful events from my youth. But just like my stepfather, the angry man saw the steely resolve that said I meant business, and he completely morphed into a gentle middle-aged man right before my eyes. He let go of the little girl's arm, put his head down, slowly turned, and peacefully walked away. The crowd followed him, hurling insults at him, as he walked down the street. Someone threw a rock at him.

Raymond shared what he found out: that the man was possibly the little girl's uncle and was known to be abusive.

I was floored. "What?" I asked. "Does she live with him?"

"No, I don't think so," he said as he got back in the Dodge Ram.

I climbed in on the passenger side. We drove alongside the little girl as she walked off down the road still tightly clutching the band of her underwear where she had stuffed the money for safekeeping. Raymond asked her if she would be okay. She nodded, smiled, and said, "*Tanki!*" which is Mende for "thank you."

Apparently, the man had seen Adisa give her the American dollars and decided he was going to get the money. I turned toward the backseat where Adisa was sitting. "What did I tell you back in the States? Huh? No media liability! Do not *do* or *say* anything that will bring more attention to us than what we already have. Didn't I say that?"

"Yes," he replied.

"Then what the fuck were you thinking? You could have gotten that little girl killed!" I shouted.

"I was just trying to help—"

I exploded, "Just do your fucking job, Adisa! Getting great sound is all I need you to worry about! That's help enough, Okay?"

"I got it, man," he said quietly.

"Good, now let's get the hell out of here, I have a reception to get ready for."

My words fell on deaf ears. Adisa Jones gave money to, hugged, kissed, and tossed in the air every single boy and girl he encountered in Sierra Leone. He couldn't help himself. He absolutely loved the people of Sierra Leone.

That night, the heat and humidity made it hard to smooth out the wrinkles in my suit. I was very nervous. Jackie had worked very hard to put together a group of local businesspeople for the evening. She felt that it was important that Raymond and I know them. Antonio came to my room to check on me. I was running a little late.

When we finally arrived at a neighboring hotel, night had fallen. The room was full of guests and fans. I noticed Antonio walk in and then turn right around and walk back out. I kept pushing forward, making my way through the crowd, shaking as many hands as possible before I sat down to eat. Breton walked up to me and whispered something in my ear. I jumped up and ran to the parking lot just in time to catch Antonio jumping in the car. Breton had revealed Antonio's secret and I now knew the reason for his sudden retreat.

As I approached, he said, "Hey, man, I'm so proud of you tonight and so excited for ya I didn't even notice I had the wrong shoes on." Antonio had put on one black shoe and one brown shoe. We fell out laughing. It was the first real, full-bodied laugh I'd had since arriving in Sierra Leone. I felt the stress and anxiety of the last few days lift off my soul.

Back inside, Raymond and I met Mr. Kalu O. Kalu, a banker, and Mr. Kayode Adeniji of Hewlett-Packard. We all shook hands and pledged to help return the country to its former greatness, to a time like when it was known as the Athens of West Africa because of the quality and number of its universities.

CHAPTER 11

Chief Gondobay Manga

On our third day in Sierra Leone, I hired two boats to take the team to the Bunce Island Slave Castle. I couldn't wait to get there. I finally had the opportunity to meet Professor Opala, who toured Bunce Island with us.

I felt a range of conflicting emotions—anger, hurt, disgust— but at the same time I was very proud about what I saw and heard there. The anger stemmed from my own ignorance. I knew nothing about Bunce Island's history and its connection to the development of the Southern region of the United States. I listened as Professor Opala explained how Bunce Island was built by the British exclusively to process West African slaves with rice-harvesting skills, destined for South Carolina and Georgia. Fifty thousand slaves from Sierra Leone were processed at Bunce Island alone.

We learned of slaves who willed themselves to death while on the island and others, trying to escape, who were killed by sharks in the deep waters surrounding the castle. I stood in the center of a corral where three hundred slaves lived chained together with only a small trough of rice to eat placed between them. I felt hurt by the humiliation they endured. I found myself feeling disgusted as I looked through a display window depicting the castle where the slaveholders sat around sipping wine and spirits as they chose which slaves they wanted to buy or molest.

Somehow, after hearing all of the horrific statistics and facts, I still felt a sense of pride. Yes, the slave castle was designed by the oppressor, but it was built by the oppressed. And it's still, hundreds of years later, standing for the world to see and understand the atrocities that took place there.

As I stood on Bunce Island I felt I was a living testament to the indomitable spirit of my great-great-great-great-great-grandmother. I pledged $25,000 to help Joe Opala complete a CGI rendering of what the Slave Castle may have looked like before its deterioration.

While we were there, a local man approached our group and presented Dr. Panossian with a very sick boy. He had cysts on his back brought on by tuberculosis. Dr. Panossian looked him over and decided to do field surgery to remove the cysts right there on the island. He later told me, after the surgery, that he didn't think the little boy would make it.

Daylight was fading fast. Our boats had no headlamps. I told Sonya to take one of the boats back to the mainland with the group and that I would stay behind to assist Dr. Panossian. We finished the surgery and we got back into the remaining boat. As soon as the sun fell beyond the horizon our boat stalled, the engine burning out as debris strangled its propellers. It was too dark and dangerous for anyone to dive into the murky water and untangle it. We slowly limped back to the mainland with one engine, our boat's captain navigating by the stars.

★   ★   ★

I woke up the next morning feeling grumpy from not sleeping well. I was not very happy up to that point with Guy's camera work. But I chose him, knowing he was inexperienced, so I knew I would have to take the hit. I could see that he was a really nice guy, but I quickly realized that he needed to be directed every step of the way as he would be if we were shooting a movie on a set. That level of direction was impossible here. Sierra Leone was not a controlled environment, to say the least. I couldn't predict what would happen one minute to the next. I couldn't "set up a shot" as I could on a movie set. So, I decided to give him some direction. "Follow me," I said to him.

Guy and I stepped out of the Hotel Barmoi compound and walked about two hundred yards away from where the rest of the team was loading up the Land Rovers. "I want a three-hundred-and-sixty-degree shot just like the famous one François Truffaut used in his film *400 Blows*," I said. I went on to carefully explain exactly what I wanted.

"Yeah, yeah, yeah, I know what you want," he said.

I looked at him and knew full well that he didn't. And sure enough, he fucked up the one directed shot I gave him. From then on, I just told him to keep the camera rolling and just point and shoot until I said, "Cut."

The team piled into the 4x4s for another day of adventure. We drove in a single-file formation. I insisted that the drivers keep a two- to three-second distance from bumper to bumper, something I picked up while in the military. In the military this was a way to be sure we weren't attacked by an unseen enemy. While I wasn't expecting an attack per se, it made me feel safer. I felt responsible for these people; I didn't want anything to happen to them.

We stopped at a local store in downtown Freetown to purchase some bottled water. While some of the team were inside, I got out and looked around to see what I could film. My photographer, Michael, was fast on my heels, camera in hand. He was clicking away as I came upon some little boys gathering water in a ditch from a dirty and broken underground water pipe. The image was just as disturbing to me as the boys' reaction to my approach. They eyed me nervously as I asked them what they were doing. As they answered quietly, their eyes darted back and forth from me to Michael's camera and then back to me.

I couldn't process what I saw. How could it be that we had entered the twenty-first century and these children didn't have clean drinking water? Why were these children forced to live this way? There were a few Sierra Leoneans working with our crew. When I asked them, they explained that this was their reality since the war started and ended. They told me that every year the president said that things would get better in Sierra Leone, and every year things got worse.

I said to myself, "A change is gonna come, one day a change is gonna come."

As we drove away from the scared little boys scavenging in the filthy ditch, I felt something popping in my chest. I clutched the area with my hand and realized that it was my heart... pounding, breaking. Each and every hour of every day I woke up in Sweet Salone it broke a little more. I remained silent and tried to stay poised as our caravan snaked up into the mountain-ous area of Sierra Leone.

I began thinking about my own children and how blessed they were. I began thinking about my experience in Namibia with Craig Matthews. I remembered how hard I watched him work, trying to make things better for the Himba people. I felt something wet running down my face. At first I thought it was a drop of the light rain that had started to fall outside. It wasn't. I was crying. I remembered asking Craig how he could stand to be away from his family for so long. His answer rang in my mind's ear just as it had those many years ago. I heard him say,

"This, Isaiah, is my passion," as if he were there saying it to me at that moment. I turned my face away from my driver, stared out the window, and wiped away my tears.

We arrived at the Bo Hospital on May 27, 2006. I met with Dr. Andrew T. Muana, the physician in charge, and asked Dr. Panossian to interview him. Built in the 1940s, the Bo Hospital was in extremely poor condition. It didn't have clean running water, electricity, sterile instruments, or gloves. The staff washed and reused the rubber gloves they had. Their operating room didn't have any modern instruments. The hospital had no oxygen tank or bottles anywhere on the site for emergencies. They used tall "wooden crucifixes," slats of scrap wood they nailed together, as their IV poles.

The children's malnutrition ward looked like a makeshift refugee camp, and the ICU that housed patients suffering from AIDS was a devastating sight. To say I was floored by what I saw would be an understatement. I walked the darkened corridors lined with empty sockets yearning for lightbulbs, past moaning, dying patients lying on hardwood makeshift beds, standing next to the six-foot-tall makeshift crucifix IV poles. It was as if their eyes were beseeching me, their gazes burning through me asking, "Why has the world forgotten us?" "Why are we left unheard?" "Why are we being left here to rot and die without dignity?"

The hospital staff looked as forlorn and as helpless as their sick and dying patients. The nurses had the "thousand-yard stare," physically their bodies were there in the hospital, but their minds and spirits seemed to have departed. Desperation and hope seemed to be waging a fight for the light, but desperation was winning. I felt so helpless; I didn't know where to even begin to help. I pulled out a copy of Jeffrey Sachs's UN Millennium Project and left it for Dr. Muana. I didn't know what else to do.

I was so overwhelmed that finally I had to walk away from my camera crew. I found a dark and unused room, stepped inside, and just cried. "God," I asked, "why would you bring me here and not be able to do anything? God, *please,* tell me what to do!"

I walked out of the room and picked up a little boy who was lying there alone, suffering from malnutrition. He seemed so determined to live. I felt empowered by his little spirit and immensely humbled by his will to live. As I walked out of the children's ward I heard myself pledging to the doctors and staff that I would help raise awareness of the plight of Sierra Leone and do everything within my power to provide positive and timely improvements for their hospital. Even as I said the words, I knew it would be (and it still is) a Herculean task, but somebody had to let the world know what was going on there.

As the day progressed I became increasingly more agitated. I couldn't recall a time in my life when I ever felt more helpless. What I was feeling was beyond culture shock now. I was feeling completely powerless.

During a meeting with the members of the BO Council, I felt my spirit shift from the despair I had been feeling earlier to something different. In the middle of the meeting I felt compelled to say, "Before I'm inducted as an honorary chief tomorrow, my great-great-great-great-great-grandmother says that she forgives you."

The women in the council dropped their heads. The men sat there staring at me, speechless. Raymond's brother, Alieu Manga, jumped up and shouted, "There were extenuating circumstances, there were extenuating circumstances, there were extenuating circumstances then! What would you have done?" he asked.

I heard myself say, "I would have died before I sold you away."

Alieu stood there with his mouth agape and I watched his body drop back down into his seat as fast as he had stood up. It felt like a poltergeist had flown around the room. I looked at Sonya, who looked as if she wanted to turn and run from the room and keep going until she reached the comfort of an American border. As taboo as the subject was between Africans and African Americans, I am glad that I said it. What I said that night wasn't coming from me, it was coming from my ancestors who, for hundreds of years before me, hadn't had the opportunity to say it. I know I was placed in that situation to speak the truth, my truth, and I was glad I did. The forgiveness was spiritually cleansing. At least for me and the Manga family that karmic chain of guilt was broken. Now my ancestors could rest in peace, and tomorrow we would all move forward together.

I was exhausted from what I had seen and experienced. The next day was going to be a big one for me. I was going to be inducted as a chief. There were preparations being made for a big party in Ngalu afterward. I gave Raymond the $100 needed to cover the costs for the party. I was told they planned to kill a cow on my behalf. I didn't feel too good about that, but it was the culture that I was about to embrace as my own. The one good thing about it, at least two hundred people would eat well that day.

I returned to the hotel and headed straight to bed.

The morning was bright and calm. I wore my "good luck scrubs," because it was hot and everything else I had was dirty. They were the same scrubs I wore for good luck on the days I had to shoot scenes performing surgery. They were given to me while doing research for my TV role. I observed my first open heart surgery in these scrubs, performed by Dr. John Robertson, a cardiothoracic surgeon, at the Saint John's Health Center in Santa Monica, California. He was amazing to watch.

I was excited for the ceremony and what the day might bring. There were children lined up along the road as we drove to Gerihun for the ceremony. It was beautiful to see. Then I suddenly had a strong feeling of recognition, another huge déjà vu moment. Suddenly, I realized, this was it! This is what my dream, "the Rerun," had been about for so many years. I wasn't crazy, well, not totally…my DNA and my dreams had delivered me to this day.

I asked Raymond to stop the SUV. I got out and walked a few yards away and stopped. I had the distinct feeling that I had been on that very spot before. Nearby, there was a tiny bridge. I walked across it and just stood there, quiet, still. A woman and child were bathing in the stream below me. They looked just like the people in my dream. I know it sounds crazy, but I knew this was "the Rerun" playing itself out right there before me; this was my dream actually materializing! It would be impossible for me to try to explain to anyone what I was feeling at that exact moment. To be there, in that moment, after so many years of dreaming about it, the verisimilitude rendered me speechless. I continued to stand there, stock-still, taking in the scene for several minutes. I feared any perceptible movement might disrupt what was taking place, might, like waking up, make it disappear. I was afraid to move.

I turned around and slowly walked back to the SUV and climbed in. I was anxious to continue on to meet with Paramount Chief Demby, Josephine Demby, and Chief Lamin and see what more would unfold. When I got out of the car, I could hear the sound of a horn blowing. It was a magnificent and ancient sound, familiar yet foreign. I soon realized that was meant to signify to everyone that I had arrived.

I was shocked to learn that the plans for the day were to make me a bona fide chief and not just an "honorary" one. I also had no concept of the huge responsibility the title of chief would eventually bring. Nyande Manga, Raymond's mother, was convinced that I would be fulfilling an ancient prophecy for the nation of Sierra Leone and the Manga legacy. I later learned that even Raymond Scott-Manga himself had not been made a chief. Raymond reminded me that Uncle Julius T. Manga and Nyande Manga had based their decision to give me the name Gondobay because Nyande's husband and Raymond's father's Christian name was Joseph Washington Scott-Manga (his tribal name was Komosor Kini Manga). My last name was Raymond's father's middle name. It was another one of those moments that made me certain my destiny was tied to Sierra Leone.

The time had come for the ceremonial horn presentation. It is customary in Sierra Leonean culture for a horn to be carved for every new chief. The carving was simple but magnificent. The chief's horn is used to sound his arrival. "That's hot! It is so beautiful!" I thought to myself.

I was given a tour of the Demby lineage replete with lithographs and photos of past chiefs. I had to wade through a sea of laughing children as I walked. They were gathered around, so close that I was afraid I would step on their little toes. Before I was introduced to Paramount Chief Demby, I was told that he was ill. But when I shook his hand it was huge and strong. His grip did not betray his power. Paramount Chief Demby was the spitting image of the boxer Larry Holmes.

Next I was introduced to Josephine Demby, possibly next in line as chief, which was very rare and a big deal. There had been only one woman chief in the history of the chiefdom, many, many years ago. Josephine took me on a tour of the village. She was elegant and gestured intensely with her hands as she talked. She showed me the river where three hundred women, men, and children were massacred during the war.

I noticed there were railroad tracks along the path we walked and imagined how this village must have thrived years ago. The pride there among the people was palpable. Raymond showed me a gravesite of the former chief who dared to resist the rebels. We stopped in the village of Njala Kendema and a *Ngoboi* dancer, covered in raffia and rags, thrashed about in front of me. In Sierra Leone, the *Ngoboi* is a "spirit masquerade" or "devil masquerade" that emulates the power of nature spirits that live deep in the forest, far from humans. I felt that, and challanged the spirit to a "dance off." I won.

We finally arrived at a house a mile outside of Ngalu. I was asked to remove my clothes and put on the ceremonial dress specially designed for me. As I was getting dressed, Raymond explained to me that the name Gondobay Manga had not been used in his family for centuries. He leaned in close and said, "I just want you to know that there is folklore here that says there will be '*a man from another land*' that will return to Sierra Leone to help rebuild it."

I was then lifted up and put on what looked like a huge hammock (*Boe Mei*) and carried on the shoulders of four men for at least a mile. Two hundred people gathered for the processional. Chief Julius T. Manga of the Wunde Society initiated me. His face looked like my face and his charisma outweighed his body size. He was a small man but he had a very large presence. He walked alongside of me the entire time, making sure that someone was continually fanning me. I felt that I was transcending time and space. I could not find the words to explain what I was feeling. Nothing felt adequate to describe what was happening to my heart, to my soul. All I could do was smile and wave intermittently. The drums and music transformed me. My spirit was at peace. I felt as if I could do anything.

I thought of my mother. I could feel her energy. Once again, I recalled the last words she said to me, "Spread the love, son. Spread the love." The road we traveled down reminded me of the terrain that I rode my bicycle through as a kid. I thought of the weeds and branches that would punish me and scratch my face in retaliation for making a new path for myself. On this day, at this moment, all I could feel on my face was the wind and the sun, and it felt good.

I was guided over to the headstone of Gondobay Manga himself. Gondobay Manga was one of the warrior leaders who defended the Ngalu village while his father and his brother, Chief Manga, in Kono went east to help defend and fight against northern raiders of Arab extraction from Guinea. Gondobay was subsequently killed in Ngalu when he was betrayed by other Mende families who feared the vast power of the Manga family. The Manga clan did not serve as a "good host" to the British colonists, especially when the Brits tried to outlaw "moon shining," something the Manga clan was well known for. As a result, many of the Mangas ended up in prison on Bunce Island, their power undermined by the Brits.

The Brits subsequently tried to make their own chiefs from those who were loyal to them. But the people always knew who the real ruling and land-holding families were. The Manga family lay low for many years and multiplied in the Bo and Kono region, sending many of their offspring overseas. These are the stories that have been passed down from generation to generation. But most of the time line can be verified by matching British records of their activities on the coast of West Africa.

I vaguely remember Uncle Julius pouring libation with some rum and kneeling down to pray and kissing the headstone. The next thing I knew I had my *Tikpoi* (staff) raised high over my head and heard the cheers of the villagers. I was officially a chief. It was as if I had left my body. The experience was surreal. I was standing there, in the middle of Sierra Leone, and I had just been officially made a chief. Life is truly amazing; we never know where its path might lead.

Everywhere I went as a young man Africans asked me, "What part of Africa are you from?" Here, at eighteen months old, I already looked African.

At four years old I already knew what to do in front of a camera.

With my beloved grandmother "Muh Dear." Cycling would soon play a key role in my unusual childhood dreams of my African destiny.

In the company of Uamahuno, the beautiful Himba woman I met on my first trip to Africa to play the lead in the film *Kin,* shot entirely on location in Namibia.

I had the privilege of working with John Amos—in the role of Troy Maxson and me as Cory Maxson—in August Wilson's *Fences* at the Capital Repertory Theatre in Albany, NY.

With my mother, Faye Marie McKee, who took me to a party where I first met a man who had African locks (dreadlocks)—an encounter that left an indelible impression on me.

With my lovely wife, Jenisa Washington, who reminded me of the beautiful woman I'd dreamed about after seeing Marie-Guillemine Benoist's seventeenth–century painting *(left)* Portrait of a Negress.

While I was at Howard University, I told people I wanted to be an actor and had a ten-year plan to work with Spike Lee, who was then a new director—folks wrote off my vision.

In my bearded phase with Moza Cooper, Melvin Van Peebles, and Jenisa, attending the Pan African Film Festival in Los Angeles, February 2004.

I was honored to receive the 2005 Canada Lee Award. Lee was among the most respected African American actors of the 1940s and a tireless Civil Rights activist. With me are photographer Bill Jones of *JET* magazine; actress Vanessa Williams of *New Jack City, Melrose Place,* and the Showtime hit *Soul Food*; and Congresswoman Diane Watson.

My team on the May 2006 trip to Sierra Leone *(left to right)*: Guy Livneh (my cameraman), Dr. Andre Panossian (my doctor), Antonio K. Hubbard (my security), Raymond Scott-Manga (my tribal brother), me with my bodyguard standing behind me, Breton F. Washington (my architect), Crispian Kirk (my human rights attorney), and Adisa Jones (my soundman). The man in African dress was a guest at the reception whom we welcomed into the photo.

Before leaving the mainland of Sierra Leone, I gave thanks!

Wearing my *Oprah* T-shirt helped smooth the way with Sierra Leone's customs officials.

I'm laughing with joy
at becoming Chief
Gondobay Manga II.

A newly crowned chief, I walked in a chief ceremony with local villagers.

Chief Gondobay Manga II examines the chief's Tikpoi *(left)* and pours libation *(below)*.

The ceremony involves carrying the chief in a hammock–like throne and shielding him from the sun. Uncle Julius T. Manga is at my side during the procession *(above)* and strong young men carry me as the entire village surrounds us *(below)*.

Primary school students at Ngalu joined the procession *(above)*. The procession ended *(below)* at Chief Gondobay Manga I's burial site, where I bowed down to honor my namesake warrior-leader who had defended the Ngalu village.

I raised my Tikpoi in triumph after becoming Chief Gondobay Manga II.

The Moorish Chief by Eduard Charlemont. My mentor taught me that if you want something, get a photo of it, hang it on your wall, and meditate on it every day. I connected with this painting and began to see my spirit-self in this image.

From Freetown Airport, I journeyed back to the U.S. feeling fully African American! I was determined to give back to Africa by building a school in Sierra Leone.

At the Foday Golia Memorial School students are lined up for classes.

In front of the new building, the entire student body cheers!

The headmaster, Mr. Paul S. Moore, and his students at the school in Njala Kendema.

My work lobbying on behalf of Sierra Leone often took me to Capitol Hill and to the United Nations. I met with Senator Kempthorne (R– ID) and Alphonso Jackson, former HUD secretary *(above)*, and received a United Nations ID Badge *(below)*.

After my induction ceremony I asked Raymond what I could do to show my commitment to the villagers and the country. He mentioned that the former chief of Njala Kendema, Chief Foday Golia, dreamed of having a strong school built for the children. He prayed for one on his deathbed. Within minutes, I heard myself pledging to help finance the construction of a school in the Bagbwe chiefdom village of Njala Kendema. Afterward, I paused and thought to myself, "What the hell did I just do?"

While we were in the village of Ngalu, Dr. Panossian examined at least one hundred children. Women and children were lined up around the house. It was hot and at least ten degrees hotter inside the house. I noticed a little boy standing outside, his head bleeding profusely. I motioned for him to come inside. I put on some rubber gloves, thinking he would need stitches. His mother explained he had been hit with a rock while playing. I thought, "The rock-throwing game was my favorite game too as a child, until someone got hit!"

As I cleaned away the blood with a towel I realized the little boy's wound wasn't as bad as I had first thought. "He's just a bleeder," I said.

Andre said, "No stitches?"

"Naw, it's just a scratch." Eventually, we ran out of the Children's Tylenol we had brought along with us and started to pack up to go. As we were leaving Njala Kendema, Dr. Panossian walked up to me and whispered, "We have a problem here that I think I can fix."

"What is it?" I asked.

He walked away and disappeared around a house that stood nearby. A few minutes later, he returned with a little boy in tow. The boy's name was Ambrose Wudie. Dr. Panossian explained to me that the boy had been ostracized by his village because a stick injury to his face had resulted in an outgrowth of flesh on his cheek as the skin tried to heal itself around the piece of stick. Andre called it a granuloma. He decided to operate on little Ambrose right there.

I asked, "Are you sure? Is it life threatening?"

"I'm a plastic surgeon," he said, "and this kid is being treated poorly because of this thing. I can remove it and give him a chance to smile again."

"Cool, what do you want me to do?"

"You can assist me."

"Let's do it."

The surgery was a success. Afterward we all piled into the SUVs and headed back to the hotel. I said, "Andre, I think you are the first Armenian doctor to do two successful field surgeries in all of Sierra Leone. You're my 'Top Gun,' baby!"

"Thanks, Chief!" he replied.

My team and I were having lunch, reviewing the agenda for the day's journey, when all of a sudden I heard screams and chaos outside of the restaurant. I instinctively gripped my case knife in my right hand.

"Are those screams?" I asked. Several hotel groundskeepers quickly ran past our table. I jumped up, heading in the direction of the screams, barking an order for Guy to grab his camera and follow me. I noticed him fumbling with the lens as he followed.

"Humidity!" he said, running behind me.

We both ran onto the catwalk connecting the upper pool area to the rooms. As we reached the site of the commotion, I could see dark smoke filling the hallway. I instinctively yanked a fire extinguisher from the wall and continued running, never looking at it until I lifted it up to aim it toward the open door in front of me. A man ran out, covering his mouth with his hand.

I glanced behind me, Guy was there, but I thought too far

away. "Come closer," I yelled, "I need you to film this!" Entering the room, I bent over as low as I could to get below the smoke. I popped the plastic tie on the fire extinguisher, frantically looking left and then right, trying to locate the source of the fire. I made my way through the smoke and onto a balcony.

I saw Antonio, in his swim trunks and shirtless, standing in the middle of the pool below me. I shouted, "Can you see where the fire is coming from?" He coolly pointed up and to my right. I followed his eyes and then saw what he saw, an air conditioner on fire on the balcony next door.

"Damn, I'm in the wrong room!" The fire was burning faster now and smoke was billowing from the balcony. I broke into a sprint and ran headlong into the adjacent room. I was immediately hit in the face and lungs with thick, dark smoke. The smell of melting plastic and electrical wires stung my nostrils and eyes. Completely blinded, I ran toward the glass balcony door, yanked it open, and hit the air conditioner with three short bursts from the fire extinguisher. Closing the door, I dived down to the floor and took a few gasps of air. Then I jumped up and repeated the action again, but this time I could not close the glass door, something was blocking it.

There was a wall of white powder mixed in with the smoke. I couldn't really make out what it was. I released another long burst from the fire extinguisher directly at it until I saw the flames had completely died out. Suddenly the white powder and smoke began to move! It started advancing toward me, grabbing desperately at my legs. I tried to focus wondering if I was now on fire. I blinked a few times trying to clear my eyes. I realized there were hands pulling at my legs! I stepped back and realized what was holding the glass door open, it was a man covered completely from head to toe in white. He was trying to pull himself upright. He looked like someone who had been frozen in a blizzard, completely snow white. The only other color I could see was the dark brown of his eyes.

"Oh my God!" I thought. "He must have been on the balcony trying to fight the fire too!" Apparently he had become overwhelmed by the smoke and dropped to the balcony floor, trying to crawl out. That's why I could not close the glass door. He was trying to crawl back into the room!

He ran by me in horror. I walked back out onto the balcony and assessed the damage. Dr. Kamara was very, very lucky. He was the only African who owned a hotel in Sierra Leone at that time. The only thing damaged from the fire in his hotel was the air conditioner itself.

I walked out of the room and looked for Guy. He was standing fifty feet away from the door, holding his camera.

"Hey!" I said. "Did you get that on film?"

He walked over and replied, "No, it was too much smoke, I couldn't see anything."

"Yeah, right!" I said, and walked past him, back to the restaurant to finish my lunch. Then a very familiar face appeared. Award-winning actor Jeffrey Wright had walked in. Jeffrey is an example of someone who has taken the initiative to make an immediate impact on global problems. After seeing *Cry Freetown (2000)*, a documentary film depicting the victims of civil war in Sierra Leone, Wright was inspired to learn more about issues in Africa. He took his first trip to Sierra Leone in 2001 and, since then, has made twelve visits to the country, concentrating on sustainable development. I was shocked to see him standing there. "How did you know I was here?" I asked.

"Isaiah." Jeffrey smiled. "It's Sierra Leone, the whole country knows that you are here."

"Yes, but how did you know where to find me?"

"Isaiah, I can find anyone here," he replied. "You need any security?"

"No, I'm good. I have a special agent and the U.S. embassy watching my back."

"Well, if you need anything, just let me know. I am very well connected here."

"That's good to know, you hungry? You want something to eat?"

"No, I was just stopping by to say hello. I've got some business meetings to attend. Be safe out there."

"I think I'm okay, brother, be well."

And with that Jeffrey turned around and walked out of the restaurant.

After lunch, we traveled to the Bo School. The school has a national reputation for graduating the best and the brightest students in Sierra Leone. We handed out a few pairs of NIKE sneakers and dropped off seven soccer balls, nearly causing a riot. Two hundred Bo School boys went crazy, all trying to get a ball. The school's headmaster was able to calm them down, but I was a little embarrassed. I wished we had more to give them.

I explained to them who I was, why I was there, and why I was so proud to know them. One boy, who couldn't have been more than twelve years old but stood at about five foot ten, asked me if I could bring a basketball the next time I came. Some of the other boys snickered at his request. I promised him that I would personally bring him a basketball when I returned. He smiled and ran away.

I signed some autographs. Then we piled back into the SUVs and drove away. I will never forget the sight of all of those brilliant young men, all dressed in white shirts and white pants, smiling. Raymond seemed to be very proud to witness our meet and greet at the school. He said that being there brought back memories of when he attended Bo School as a young boy.

★   ★   ★

Mohamed Kamara was our driver for the day. He was an extremely quiet and resourceful young man with strong ties to his mother and brothers. He was taken by the rebels during the war but managed to escape, hiding in the jungles to survive. He worked very hard as a guide and driver for tourists to provide money for his younger brother's education.

Later, when it was time to build the school in Njala Kendema, I made him project manager. After watching how diligently he worked, I began to bond with him, knowing that I could trust him implicitly.

I took the opportunity to walk over to a kiosk and buy myself some homemade "cigarettes" before we headed off, through some pretty rugged terrain, to our next destination, the Majestic Mining Company at the Sewa River. As we drove, Raymond talked in great detail about how important diamonds were to the economy of Sierra Leone as well as most of Africa.

A few minutes later, I found myself hanging off the hood of one of the Land Rovers with a camera. I had relieved Guy of his camera duties, deciding to take matters into my own hands to get the shots I needed. I thought some high-speed "action shots" would spice up my documentary.

Sonya insisted that Mohamed stop the truck. She got out and proceeded to tersely remind me of my three children and wife at home. I reluctantly got off the hood and slipped into a "heart of darkness." I wondered if this was what Francis Ford Coppola meant when he talked about what he went through psychologically when he filmed the classic *Apocalypse Now*. Then I wondered what in the hell was in those cigarettes.

Mohamed continued to maneuver the very winding and demanding roads through tall, lush green grass. The grassy walls that had accompanied us for miles began to widen and eventually disappeared. I could see a clearing up ahead that grew larger and larger, finally revealing the most expansive and cavernous land mass I had ever seen. It looked much like the Grand Canyon, except these chasms were manmade.

Upon our arrival, Mr. Joe Demby, of Aureol Investments, introduced himself and proudly gave me the tour of the Majestic Mining Company. It was here that I saw up close and personal how the diamond business worked.

I couldn't help but think back to what I had read about how much the conflict over diamonds had cost Sierra Leone. The country suffered horrifically, both socially and economically, under the reign of the terrorizing RUF, the civil war, and the fight over diamond control. Economically, the country was cheated out of millions of dollars by illegal diamond trafficking. But the social effects were equally devastating. From 1991 to 2001 the civil war had claimed more than seventy-five thousand lives and turned a half million Sierra Leoneans into refugees, not to mention the millions who stayed but were displaced from their homes.

As part of the tour, Mr. Demby showed me huge barrels of oil that were used for disciplinary purposes. He explained that if a worker was suspected of or caught swallowing diamonds to smuggle off-site, the oil was poured down the suspect's throat. The diamonds were retrieved once they exited the worker's body either through vomiting or the more "southerly orifice." The practice seemed so barbaric to me I couldn't manage to comment.

I was amazed by everything I saw at Majestic Mining. The raw diamonds sifted straight out the "sluice box," huge holes dug into the ground. Yellow earth movers with Caterpillar in big black letters stenciled on the side just kept digging, digging, digging.

Chapter 12

A Changed Man

We were on our way to Kono as darkness fell. For hours we followed behind our guide, Thani, who resembled the football player Terrell Owens, on his motorcycle. The fatigue, heat, culture shock, sangria, and local cigarettes were all taking their toll on my psyche. Michael, Raymond, and I played a CD by the R&B group P-Square over and over again. Our air conditioner had blown out and it was too hot to keep the windows up. I applied Vicks VapoRub to my neck and arms to protect me from mosquitoes that were particularly vicious at night. I listened to music, breathed in the eucalyptus of the Vicks, and stared at the tiny red brake light on the back of Thani's motorcycle peeping in the night ahead of us. The tiny light seemed to float, suspended in midair. Up and down, up and down, up and down, we rode along the endless bumpy road into the ominous pitch-black darkness.

This was not the place or time to become stranded on the road. For the first time since arriving in Sierra Leone, Raymond drove in complete silence.

He had solemnly explained that this area was the battle-ground for much of the heavy fighting during the war. I could feel the spirits of dead people wandering around the densely wooded areas surrounding us, those who had been tortured and murdered in the civil war. It was as if you could reach out and touch the malice that ran rampant and unchecked for eleven years. Evil was in the air.

Thani's brake light suddenly glowed even brighter and was getting larger and larger. I realized he had stopped in the middle of the road. As we drove closer, I could see that Thani was talking to a tall, thin man. When I looked just past him, it became clear why he had stopped. A huge cargo truck was overturned and lying in the middle of the road, blocking our path. Two other men sat very quietly off to the side of the road by a small fire. They didn't look very happy about our sudden arrival.

I asked Raymond to find out if they needed any help getting the truck right side up. I took out my flashlight and shone it on the vehicle, illuminating three huge chains wrapped around the truck's chassis that branched off in different directions into the dark weeds. Someone from a high point alongside the road had already been trying to upright the truck.

"You think we can use our Land Rovers to help get this thing back on its wheels?" I asked Raymond. He assessed the situation while the two men sat completely still, carefully watching us. Suddenly it dawned on me, the truck had been vandalized. The doors, windshield, cargo, and seats were all gone.

I looked at the two men. They looked away and put their heads down. I could see the edge of a jack handle one of the men had under his leg. Help was the last thing these guys wanted. They wanted us to turn off our lights and leave them the hell alone so they could get back to the business of picking the truck apart. This truck would be nothing but a skeleton of itself before sunrise.

I decided to prolong the thieves' discomfort for a little longer. "Breton," I shouted, "get over here! You are an architect!" Breton sheepishly walked over, probably thinking I'd lost my mind. I looked up on the hill directly above us and spotted six to ten villagers lurking in the tall, dense grass. I had no idea if they were watching out of curiosity, or if they were sizing us up as potential robbery victims. I saw Raymond notice the "guests" skulking up above us too. He strongly suggested that we mount up and leave.

But I stubbornly said, "No, no, nooo. We are here to *help*. Let's help these good men!" Everyone looked at me as if I was crazy. Breton and I investigated all the possible angles and places we could hook chains to get the proper leverage to upright the truck. I didn't let anyone in on my private joke on the thieves; I acted as if I was quite serious about helping them.

"Isaiah! Come on, man," I heard Adisa say. "Let's get out of here, brother. This shit doesn't feel right."

I glanced over at him and realized he wasn't wearing his sound gear. Adisa *never* takes his gear off. I looked back up the hill and could now see more villagers had arrived, taking in the scene. I decided not to push our luck any further.

"Okay, kids," I said, "mount up!" We piled back into the SUV and drove behind Thani up onto the very hill where the villagers were watching. We found a new path to take and drove slowly through the high grass until we cleared the wreckage. Raymond navigated the Dodge Ram back onto the road and we continued on, driving into the darkness.

When we finally arrived in Kono, there was a youth organization waiting to greet us. The kids were holding up a huge banner with my name on it. Raymond said, "They have been out here waiting for us since twelve noon." It was after midnight.

The team assembled in the hotel restaurant and the youth organizers began to lay out their concerns and needs. I listened, took notes on their requests, and told them I would do what I could do. This was just my first trip to Sierra Leone, I had been here but a few days, and already I had pledged to help finance the construction of a much needed school in the village of Njala Kendema and a CGI of the Slave Castle at Bunce Island, and taken on the Herculean task of raising the world's awareness of the serious problems plaguing Sierra Leone, and helping to return the country to its former greatness. I quickly remembered and understood the advice Eric Nonacs shared during our meeting at the Clinton Foundation. He told me to make sure that I did not promise anything that I could not deliver.

The meeting adjourned and the youth organization left. It was close to 2:00 a.m. I wasn't tired, so I stayed in the restaurant area and asked for a mango to eat. Dr. Panossian was wired too, so he joined me, as did Thani, who also worked for a diamond company in the area. He was supposed to be in Kono to enforce the Kimberley Process, which, according to its Web site, is a "joint government, industry and civil society initiative to stem the flow of conflict diamonds—rough diamonds used by rebel movements to finance wars against legitimate governments."[7]

To my surprise, he reached over and tried to hand me some gold dust and raw diamonds to smuggle back to America for him. He wanted me to sell them and purchase a computer and another motorcycle for him. He said the motorcycle he had was always breaking down. When I declined his offer, Thani looked at me as if I was crazy.

"You don't like money?" he said in his deep raspy voice.

"I like money," I replied, "but this is not what I came here for. I came here to help you. I came here to see how I can help you farm your land, not have you displaced for diamond mining. Isn't that what you told me your villagers needed? Shovels for food and not shovels for diamonds?"

"Hmmm. You are a man of your word, I see," he said.

"Yes, I am," I said.

"Be careful," he warned, "men have died here trying to keep their word."

"If I die here, keeping my word, that can only mean I will be in better company than I am now," I answered back.

Thani smiled at me, stood up, and walked away.

I sat there for a moment, then pulled my Karambit knife out of my pocket and slowly carved the skin off of my mango.

If there is a hell on earth, it was here in Kono. There was no electricity, and the darkness was filled with the pain of the past. The Kono district is where the most intense fighting for control of the diamond mines took place. Everything looked exactly as it did during the conflict. It was as if time had stopped. Everywhere I looked there were war-torn buildings that bore the pockmarks of heavy artillery and large bullets. Under other circumstances, I would have thought I was on a war movie set.

Among the most damning things I saw was a huge, sand-colored artillery cannon. It sat right in the middle of the street. It had a sign hanging from its muzzle that read War Don Don (meaning war is over), We Love Peace.

The next day we were escorted by the Kono police. They took us to an artisanal mining ground. When the workers caught sight of us, they dropped their shovels and began to run away. The policeman yelled, "Hey! Stop running! We are not going to arrest you today! This man from America wants to talk to you!"

Wearing no protective covering or rubber boots, the workers dug all day in the hot sun, through mud filled with piss, vomit, and feces, hoping to find a diamond. In return they received two cups of rice as pay.

We drove over to the Tongo Fields clinic, thinking we might find someone who could use our extra medicine. The nurse we met there had lost her baby that night. She was nine months pregnant.

This place was full of evil. I felt as if I were surrounded by despair and deceit at every turn. I started to have a meltdown. Alone in my room that night, I prayed, "God make it stop. Make it stop. I want to go home now. All I'm doing is handing out fucking soccer balls." I silently screamed. "I just told these people that I will be back. I will be back? I sound like, like fucking Arnold Schwarzenegger. I feel like a fraud!" I felt so helpless. *I wish I could have done more.*" That's what Bill Clinton told me on the phone the day we talked. Now I understood what he meant.

The VP fell asleep. Jackie and I brought him gifts—a bottle of Johnnie Walker Blue scotch and a beautiful cigar box—and he literally fell asleep. There was speculation that the good vice president of Sierra Leone suffered from the effects of the bite from the dreaded tsetse fly. So for falling asleep I excused him. However, I was still unclear as to exactly what his position was on the issues of the day. I wondered how he could deal with so much extreme poverty in Sierra Leone and not do anything about it. But I guess his falling asleep was my answer; it really spoke for itself. The negligence by the government was evidenced by the neglect of the impoverished people of Sierra Leone that I witnessed wherever I went.

Halfway through our conversation, he said, "Isaiah, just do it, I will not interfere. Just do whatever it is you want for this good country. The Chinese, they don't talk, they do. You are welcome here."

I asked him point-blank about the rampant graft and corruption. "Sierra Leone is not the only country that suffers from corruption," he said. "You have lots of corruption in the United States and Britain. We have policies in place to fight corruption just like anywhere else in the world." He looked at me with his sleepy eyes and smiled.

"That's a good point, sir," I responded, "but the United States and Britain are not the poorest countries in the world." My team, all sitting around the table with us, dropped their heads. It was as if they were saying, "Oh shit, why did he say that? We are dead." I continued, "Thank you, Mr. Vice President, for your time. It's truly appreciated. I don't know what my next steps are and I don't know how I'm going to do it, but I will return to Sierra Leone and I will make sure the world knows the good that is here."

After a three-hour drive, we finally arrived back in Freetown. It was May 31, 2006, and we were about to conduct our final interview of the trip with U.S. ambassador Thomas Hull. During our discussion, something he said really stood out for me. "Isaiah," he began, "I think that most African Americans in North America today will find that they have ancestry here in Sierra Leone. I feel that Bunce Island is the Auschwitz for African Americans. I hope that there are more of you who will come and see this beautiful country. It is my hope that you will all help restore Sierra Leone to its former greatness."

With that, I stood up and shook his hand. We left the U.S. embassy and drove toward Hotel Barmoi. As we drove past a small beach, I asked my driver to pull over. I got out, walked over, and collapsed down on the sand. I just sat there, in a lotus position, watching the sun disappear beyond the horizon.

As I hate good-byes, I work to avoid them at all costs. When Raymond dropped us off at the airport, I gave him a quick hug and said, "I will see you again soon." I had come to Sierra Leone as Isaiah Washington, but I left as Chief Gondobay Manga II. And if I had any doubts about what that meant, I was about to learn. While we waited for our flight, a man stole some money from Sonya. She pointed him out to the police, and they caught him and brought him over and presented him to me. He gave Sonya the money back, but the airport police saw my *Tikpoi* (staff) and requested that I follow them into the men's room. When I stepped inside, the thief was lying on the floor; they had roughed him up pretty good.

One of the policemen asked menacingly, "What would you like us to do with him, Chief?"

"Nothing," I said. Sonya had her money back, I didn't understand the question. But danger quickly cut through my naïveté. The policemen looked at each other, confused, and then back at me with complete disdain on their faces. Clearly "nothing" was not the right answer.

I realized what they wanted and started yelling. "Don't you ever steal from me again, motherfucker. Do you understand me!"

The policemen stepped back a little, now excited by my angry words and reaction. The frightened man reached for my *Tikpoi* and tried to kiss it. I stepped in closer and stomped my foot near his head to make my point. The thief started kissing my feet and begging for forgiveness. I continued, "Look at me. Look at me! You steal from me, you steal from yourself!"

That seemed to satisfy the policemen. One of them violently kicked the thief in the head, stunning him for a few seconds. Then the policemen lifted him up by his arms and dragged the miscreant outside. They violently and loudly chastised him more, and then ceremoniously tossed him hard onto the street outside the airport. I stood there in the men's room for a second, trying to digest what just happened. I slowly walked out of the door and rejoined my team, as Chief Gondobay Manga II, a changed man. My team and I were escorted to the VIP room to wait. Sonya informed me that our Astraeus Airlines flight would have a long delay. We all settled down to wait. Jackie leaned over and whispered something to me about a woman quietly sitting across from us. "That's Mrs. Zainab Bangura," she said quietly. "She is someone you need to know."

"Really? Why?" I asked.

Jackie continued, "She is arguably Sierra Leone's best-known female politician and civil society activist. She made headlines in the 1990s as a vocal woman denouncing corruption. In 1996, when the first civilian government was elected after years and years of one-party rule and military coups, she founded the Campaign for Good Governance. The CGG is a civil society organization that advocates democracy, human rights, women's empowerment, and good governance. In six years, the CGG has become a strong civil society organization and known as a reliable source for donors to measure good governance."

I gave a quick glance toward Zainab Bangura and whispered to Jackie, "Damn. She's a bad lady."

Jackie said, "Iron Lady."

"What?" I asked.

"Her nickname is Iron Lady," she explained. "In 2002, Zainab formed her own political party, the Movement for Change, and ran for president on a platform of fighting graft, guaranteeing women equal rights, and ending poverty. She became the first woman to run for the presidency here."

"Well, she clearly lost," I said. "It must have been intense for her, right?"

"Her opponents attacked her mercilessly and claimed that she wanted to ban female genital mutilation, which is a valued element of the cultural heritage here. Overnight she became a traitor to tradition. The women of the Bundy societies turned against her."

"What is she doing now?" I asked.

"In 2005, she joined the United Nations Mission in Liberia as chief of civil affairs. There, she was again in contact with the person she most admires in the world, Ellen Sirleaf-Johnson, Liberia's president and Africa's first female head of state," whom she knew from her activist days," said Jackie.

"Got it," I said. I stood up, walked over to Zainab Bangura, and introduced myself. "Excuse me," I said, "I don't mean to bother you but—"

Before I could finish my sentence she cut me off, but with a smile. "I know who you are, please have a seat." I was not at all offended. What you may interpret as rude is not always interpreted that way in African countries. She was not being rude, she was being strong.

"I've been here to learn as much about Sierra Leone as I can," I told her. "I took a DNA test that says I'm Mende and Temne, read everything I could about this country, and this is my team. Jackie Coker, over there is Sonya Gay Bourn, Breton Washington, Michael Caulfield, and Dr. Andre Panossian."

Zainab graciously nodded as she addressed everyone with a soft smile. I sensed that her soul was weary, but in no way did she appear tired. "It is my pleasure to meet all of you, I hope your trip was a successful one," she said.

"Yes, it was," I continued. "We covered a lot of ground. Do you know Joe Opala?"

Her face lit up. "You know Joe Opala? Oh yes, Joe Opala and I have known each other for many years." Zainab shared a story about her heartache during the war, how she became a refugee, having to flee to Guinea for her safety. I listened intently as she spoke. I was transfixed and hanging on her every word. When Zainab finished her story, Sonya asked, "Ms. Bangura, is there a way we can reach you? We would love to be able to keep in touch."

"Oh, of course," she said as she gave us her number and asked that we call her. "I'm in the U.S. all the time," she explained. I thanked Zainab for her time and left her alone to relax. I knew I would see this lady again soon. I could feel it. I also knew that I myself would soon become a voice for the people of Sierra Leone...people who had no voice.

CHAPTER 13

"A Diamond Is Forever"

I was driving down the 405, lost in thought, when Kanye West's Grammy Award–winning rap song "Diamonds from Sierra Leone" started playing on the radio. I had never really listened to the lyrics so attentively. Bobbing my head to the beat, I looked down at the dashboard and realized I was going nearly one hundred miles per hour! The song ended. I backed off the gas pedal and switched the dial to KPFK 90.7 FM, the NPR station.

There was more bad news from Iraq, there were more soldiers dying, there were more bombings and more bloodshed. I reached down and pressed the mute button. Up ahead of me was a line of cars for as far as the eyes could see. I began negotiating the traffic like a star running back evading his defenders on the field. I slipped effortlessly between other cars, in and out, switching from lane to lane, as my mind drifted further away from Los Angeles and back to Sierra Leone. This happened often since I had returned. I had spent only two weeks there, but I felt as if I had a lifetime of experiences. A scene from Kono replayed in my mind....

I remembered Thani's deep voice as we sat at the table in the early-morning hours in the restaurant in Kono as I declined his offer to smuggle raw diamonds to the United States. "You don't like money?" he had said, smirking, as he mocked my sincere desire to help the Sierra Leonean people.

Then another thought started to pulse through my mind. My lips began to move, forming the words from Chinua Achebe's *Anthills of the Savannah:*

> *The worst threat from men of hell*
> *May not be their actions cruel*
> *Far worse that we may learn.*
> *And behave more fierce than they.*

I continued to reflect on my time in Sierra Leone, still unable to understand what had happened to the people there. How could some small pieces of carbon, with no great intrinsic value on their own, be the cause of such widespread death, deception, destruction, and misery for over a decade?

In my mind, someone had to be responsible. Three days after I arrived back home, I knew exactly what I had to do next. My inexorable dream, "the Rerun," had become self-evident the day of my induction. It was up to me to help the people in the dream.

I couldn't get "A Diamond Is Forever," the De Beers slogan, out of my thoughts. I wanted to know the people who created the words at the center of so much of the death and pain in my homeland.

So as I always did when I was curious about something, I did some research. Legend says the slogan was created late one night in 1947 by a Frances Gerety, an N. W. Ayer Advertising Agency copywriter working against a deadline on a De Beers campaign. Dog-tired, she is said to have put her head down and said, "Please, God, send me a line." She wrote down, "A Diamond Is Forever." The next morning Gerety knew she had "something good." And indeed she did.

Ayer's copywriters caught perfectly the powerful double meaning of Gerety's slogan in a 1950 ad with the following headline: "May Your Happiness Last as Long as Your Diamond." This ad combined three components that were characteristic of ads of the period: first, a painting of an idealized romantic setting by a famous modern artist; second, a poem that positions the engagement diamond as the symbol of undying love; and, third, a section devoted to practical advice about selecting a diamond.

The combination of poetry and practicality was meant to "help motivate people to want diamonds and overcome any barriers to actual purchase." It worked.

By the 1960s De Beers had successfully instilled the idea that giving a diamond was the best expression of one's love and commitment. As part of its mystique the diamond now had a formal ceremonial significance that was exclusive to this gem. In the 1970s, De Beers kept the gem's appeal equally vibrant for traditionalists and nontraditionalists alike. And from then on, its ads remained mindful of constantly shifting cultural and social norms.

"A Diamond Is Forever." In those four words are concentrated all of the emotional and physical properties of the diamond. The slogan became the cornerstone of the company's global-marketing program for diamonds and was translated into twenty-nine languages. Amazingly, the slogan's impact has been as powerful in every language.

I figured that it was high time that the people of Sierra Leone began to experience some of the "happiness," and share in the love and the commitment their diamonds represented.

It is impossible to fathom the trillions of dollars' worth of Sierra Leonean diamonds that have been sold around the world since their discovery. It was mind-boggling to me that such atrocities could be allowed to prevail for as long as they had. The reason had to be about much more than tribalism. As I continued to do my research, I began to run into some inscrutable verbiage on the Internet regarding De Beers's stance on the economic development of Sierra Leone. It was information that would lead one to believe that De Beers was socially active in Sierra Leone.

Judging by what I saw on the ground there, in places like the Majestic Mining Company, I wasn't convinced. I needed to find out what was really going on for myself. The more I researched, the more I found it extremely difficult to believe that in 1984 De Beers simply walked away from such a lucrative resource. There had to be a reason for this "indirect" relationship with Sierra Leone, some justifiable cause to allow Sierra Leone to deteriorate in the years that followed. It all just seemed too inhumane and too unjust to comprehend. I needed to see and hear exactly what De Beers was willing to do for a country that had enriched it.

I found the name of Joan Parker. In 2006, Joan was the De Beers Group U.S. Public Relations Manager. She spearheaded the marketing strategy to brand the De Beers Louis Vuitton Möet Hennessy joint venture, making De Beers LVMH a household name. I had no idea how to reach her until I *happened* to see a photograph of her on a wireimage.com Web site. Luckily for me, the young photographer who had taken her picture was a colleague of mine, Jeff Vespa. I called Jeff and he confirmed that he had indeed taken the picture and that he knew Joan Parker personally.

"Isaiah, Joan Parker is one of my dearest friends," he said.

"No way! She is a friend of yours? Small world!"

I explained to Jeff that I had just returned from Sierra Leone and that I wanted to reach out to a representative at De Beers and see if I could persuade De Beers to invest in a few projects. I had the idea that it could rebuild the Bo Hospital and build clean water systems and primary schools in the country. I told him that I would love to be a spokesperson for a De Beers–funded initiative. Jeff thought I had a good idea and that my experiences in Sierra Leone would intrigue Ms. Parker. He agreed to make the introduction.

Less than twenty-four hours later, Joan Parker and I had an hour-long phone conversation. After hearing my passion and vision for Sierra Leone she agreed to set up a lunch meeting with me and the De Beers Director for External Affairs, Mr. Rory More O'Ferrall.

A week later, I was in New York. Joan asked me to meet her before our meeting at the De Beers store on Fifth Avenue, one of the world's most exclusive shopping corridors. I stepped off the busy street through a tall, shiny glass and metal door, and Joan appeared as if on cue. She gave me a brief tour of the store, taking me past the elegant see-through display cases filled with shimmering diamonds of all shapes and sizes.

"Oh my, we have to hurry!" she exclaimed as she glanced down at her Chopard Happy Diamonds watch. We headed across the street to the Peninsula Hotel, where we were to have lunch with Mr. O'Ferrall. A well-dressed gentleman was already sitting at the table when we arrived. "Hellooooo, Rorrrrry!" Joan said as we approached. "How have you been? I hope you haven't been waiting long. I want you to meet Isaiah Washington."

"Hello, Mr. O'Ferrall. It's a pleasure to meet you, sir," I said.

"Rory, please," he said, "please call me Rory."

He gestured for us all to sit down. I remained standing, assisting Joan with her seat, unbuttoning my suit coat, and making sure that Rory was seated before I slowly eased down into my chair.

"Rory, thank you so much for coming out today," Joan began. "I know you have a hectic schedule." Rory said he was delighted to be there.

"So, Joan here tells me you are doing some good things in Sierra Leone," he said to me.

"Yes, sir," I replied. "As you know, Sierra Leone has had severe difficulty recovering from the war. While I was there I pledged to return to the United States and let everyone know about the good things that I saw. I want to support the indomitable spirit of the people and their willingness to better themselves and their country. I drove from Freetown, to Bo, Kono, and Mekeni and back to Freetown, asking what top five things the people would change right away if they could. The number one issue was corruption."

Rory replied that he was very familiar with the problems in Sierra Leone. "As a matter of fact," he said, "I personally supported a village there before and during the war. It's tragic. It was just tragic what happened there."

I assured him I couldn't agree with him more. I went on, "I was wondering where De Beers stood regarding the plight of the people of Sierra Leone today. I mean, I am well aware of De Beers's history with the country—"

Rory interrupted, "De Beers hasn't done any business in Sierra Leone since 1984."

"Directly," I said.

"I beg your pardon?" Rory said.

I continued, "I discovered in my research that De Beers controls over two-thirds of the world's diamond supply."

"De Beers has founded and funded the Diamond Development Initiative to address many of the issues arising from diamond mining in several countries," he said. "Here, I brought some brochures for you."

I quickly read through a brochure that explained De Beers's

global involvement with the Diamond Development Initiative (DDI) and the Kimberley Process. The DDI, according to De Beers's Web site, "brings non-governmental organizations, governments, and the private sector together in a common effort that aims to convert diamonds into an engine for development, and to formalize the economies surrounding artisanal diamond mines."[8] The Kimberley Process, which I'd heard about in Kono from our guide, Thani, created a certification and regulatory system for diamond mining in several African countries.

I looked up at Rory and asked, "Thank you, sir, but what about Sierra Leone?" He paused and looked at Joan as if to say, "Help." Joan looked at him and smiled.

I pressed on, "Sir, if I may, De Beers has made trillions of dollars from diamonds extracted out of Sierra Leone since 1935. I am aware of the poor governance since Sierra Leone's independence in 1961. I am aware of the endemic graft and corruption that is sustaining the present condition of Sierra Leone. I am also aware that none of this is the people's fault. I am aware that eight out of nine people in Kono would rather use their shovels for farming than for diamond mining to provide for themselves and their families. The innocent children who are dying as we speak deserve a chance, sir. *They* deserve to have a stake in their own country's resources. *They* deserve to benefit from the diamonds mined in their country. I have been there and it's just not happening. How can a country so rich in resources be the poorest country in the world? I'm asking you if you think De Beers would join forces with me to ensure that the people get the help they deserve."

"Isaiah," he said, "your passion and vision for Sierra Leone is not wasted on me. As I mentioned before, I am well aware of the issues regarding Sierra Leone. If you need me to answer any questions regarding DDI or would like to see what we are accomplishing in Botswana, I would be more than happy to facilitate that."

I looked at Rory's face, at his rose-colored cheeks and deeply compassionate eyes behind his gold-rimmed glasses. "Yes, sir," I said. "I understand. I will call you if I have any more questions."

Joan, Rory, and I finished our lunch mostly in silence. Joan commented on the great weather in New York, and Rory and I agreed. It was in fact a beautiful summer day in New York. I returned to Los Angeles and received a message from Rory, calling from London. He asked me to call him as soon as possible.

When I dialed the number he left, Rory picked up. "Isaiah, it's so nice of you to call. I wanted to tell you that it was a pleasure to meet you. I really respect what you are doing for Sierra Leone. I just wanted to let you know that I am retiring soon and that I want you to know the wonderful woman who will be taking over. Her name is Rosalind Kainyah. She will be Director of Public Affairs at the De Beers Group in the States. She is a very talented woman. She will be your contact here at De Beers effective immediately and she is expecting your call. I wish you all the best, Isaiah."

I thanked him. He told me if I was ever in London that I should not hesitate to call him. "Cheers!" he said, and hung up.

"Okay," I said out loud, "Ms. Rosalind Kainyah. What can you do for Sierra Leone?"

I checked another voice mail. It was a message from the office of Sally Morrison, director of the Diamond Information Center (DIC). I called her office number.

"Hello, Sally Morrison, this is Isaiah Washington calling."

"Isaiah, it's a pleasure to meet you," she said. "I hear you're doing work in Sierra Leone."

I confirmed that I was.

"That's great," she continued. "I'm told you visited some diamond mines there."

"Yes, I did."

"You took a lot of pictures I'm sure."

"Yes, I was there documenting the horrible conditions all over the country."

"That's fantastic. What are you going to do with the pictures?"

I paused for a moment, not sure where the conversation was going. "Nothing, they're for my Web site. Why do you ask?"

"I was just curious," she said. "I participate in a lot of fundraisers and I thought maybe you could come to one of my events and see what we do."

I told her I would love to.

"This is great," Sally continued. "I will put your name on our invitation list. I have to take another call, but the next time I'm in Los Angeles, let's grab some lunch or a coffee, okay?"

"That would be great!" I told her.

We hung up. In August, Rosalind Kainyah returned my phone call and told me she was still settling in to her new role at De Beers, but that she would be traveling to Los Angeles in September.

CHAPTER 14

Lobbying to Save Lives

On June 21, 2006, Crispian met me at the Hotel George in DC. In his capacity as NAACP human rights attorney, he was able to arrange some meetings with various "key" politicians he thought would be able to help support my efforts in Sierra Leone. Or at the very least, people he thought would hear me out. I knew as well as he did that trying to convince U.S. politicians that Sierra Leone deserved a second, third, or fourth chance from the American government would be a difficult task. The last forty-five years of Sierra Leone's leadership—or lack of it—had contributed to bringing the country to its knees, and its ultimately becoming a failed state.

My team was scheduled to meet in my hotel room. There was a knock on the door. Sonya opened it and Jessica Peetoom from Congressman Kevin Brady's office, Dr. Andre Panossian, Jackie Coker, and my new cameraman, Gonzalo Accame, all walked in.

Gonzalo and his assistant began setting up their equipment.

I carefully went through my notes on the agenda for the day as Crispian explained whom we would be meeting with. He passed out some sheets of paper and said, "In your hands are the list of representatives that Isaiah will meet today: Senator Sam Brownback, Senator Barack Obama, Senator Arlen Specter, Senator Tom Coburn, Senator John Thune, Congressman Tom Tancredo, Congressman Kevin Brady, Congressman John Conyers Jr., Congressman Donald Payne, Congresswoman Barbara Lee, and Congressman Russ Carnahan.

"Keep in mind that many of these representatives will be on the floor voting, so timing is critical. You will understand later." I stood up, got in front of everyone, and said, "This will be our theme song for the day." The song "Crazy" by Gnarls Barkley was playing on the room's CD player, I turned up the volume. Sonya's phone rang, but I continued to groove with the song until it was over, trying to make myself and my team relax and laugh a little before we headed out.

Sonya pulled me aside, "I just got a call from a friend of Adisa's. He's in the hospital."

"What?" I said. "What is he in the hospital for?"

"The doctor thinks it's Lassa fever," Sonya answered.

"Lassa fever! Oh my God. What the hell is that? Andre!" I said, turning to Dr. Panossian. He asked Sonya what hospital Adisa was in and proceeded to make a call. My head started to spin. "This is not good. What do I do? I can't cancel these meetings today. Think! What do I do?"

I made a general announcement to the team about my former sound designer, Adisa Jones. "Dr. Panossian is on the phone right now with Daniel Freeman Memorial Hospital," I said. "We have a man down, but we will take the scheduled meetings as planned. This is for Sierra Leone. Adisa loves the children there. He would want us to press on."

With that, I instructed the team to gather their things. We

were going to Capitol Hill. I gave Sonya a number to call. "Sonya, get Clinton's office on the phone," I said. "Ask for Jay Carson or Eric Nonacs. Tell them about Adisa." Gonzalo put a microphone on me then I grabbed my suit coat and headed out the door. I was a very determined man. Adisa's illness gave me even further incentive to make my trip to Sierra Leone mean something. Our three black SUVs rolled down Pennsylvania Avenue in the same single-file formation we used in Sierra Leone. I sat in the front seat blasting "Crazy."

I couldn't believe what had happened to Adisa. I thought about seeing him not long before in Los Angeles. When we talked, he told me how happy he was about what we accomplished together in Sierra Leone. He teased me about my "No Media Liability" speeches while we were there. We were both at the same fund-raiser for Tiffany Persons and her Shine On Sierra Leone Foundation. I was invited because I had donated $5,000 to the organization. I remembered saying to him that he looked great but commented that he was sweating profusely. "Sweatin' is good for the skin, my brother!" He smiled his trademark smile highlighted by his manicured and trimmed mustache and then he happily walked away. That was the last time I had seen him.

"Lassa fever? How did he get that?" I wondered.

We pulled up in front of our destination, the United States Capitol building. As we proceeded through security, I looked up and immediately saw the *Apotheosis of Washington* painted by Constantino Brumidi in 1865. I literally had to catch my breath. It was the first time I had stood in the Rotunda. Even the most cynical and apolitical person would have to agree that the Capitol Rotunda is one of the most serene, powerful, and beautiful places in the world.

Crispian tugged at my arm. "I know," he said, "but we gotta keep it moving."

Our first meeting was in the House of Representatives. I was scheduled to meet with Congressman Tom Tancredo. Together, he and I watched in its entirety the one-hour video presentation I brought. Los Angeles–based filmmaker Abdul Malik Abbott and I had worked together editing forty-three hours of footage from my trip to Sierra Leone into a one-hour presentation. We had worked on it for twenty-four hours straight without any sleep. I am extremely grateful to Abdul for his commitment to my project as well as to Congressman Tancredo, who was kind and generous with very good suggestions about whom I should reach out to in Colorado regarding getting aid for Sierra Leone.

The next stop was Congressman Kevin Brady's office. Congressman Brady was his usual affable self. I introduced him to the team as we all gathered around the huge mahogany table in his conference room. Congressman Brady sat attentively as he watched my one-hour video presentation. Noticing the University of Texas T-shirt that I wore in one of the scenes, he said, "I recognize that school T-shirt. It looks good on you." We all laughed.

"Isaiah," he said, "do you know about the Norman Borlaug Institute for International Agriculture over at Texas A&M?" I didn't. "Well, those guys over there run a great organization," he explained. "They are doing some great things around the world. I think you need to get to know them. They do a lot of good in Africa." He asked how soon I could get to Houston and agreed to set something up. "I really like what you are doing with your celebrity. We need more like you," he said.

The next meeting was to be with Congressman Donald Payne, chairman of the House Committee on Foreign Affairs Subcommittee on Africa and Global Health. His staff director Noelle LuSane greeted us and told us that the congressman would be with us shortly. While we waited, Congresswoman Barbara Lee walked in and introduced herself. She informed us that she too shared ancestry with the people of Sierra Leone and had also taken the DNA test by African Ancestry. "I'm Mende!" she announced proudly.

"Wow, that's amazing!" I responded. "It's my pleasure to meet you."

Just then, Congressman Payne walked out of his office and jokingly asked, "Who's creating all this commotion out here? Ohhh, you must be that guy from that TV show that my staff keeps talking about. Well, come on in, they all want to take a picture with you."

Several women ran into his office, buzzing around us. Congressman Payne said, "Man, you're better than an American Express card, I need to take you out with me." After we took a photo together, he invited me to sit down.

Congresswoman Lee joined us and later Congressman William Jefferson stepped in and sat on the arm of Congressman Payne's huge leather chair. I explained what I had seen in Sierra Leone and why I thought it was important to have Americans, especially African Americans, engage and invest in the betterment of the country.

After we watched the video, Congressman Payne told me that the Congressional Black Caucus Foundation could be of service. He thanked me for my passion and interest in Africa and stated that he wished he could see more African American celebrities involved in the issues of Africa.

I looked over my shoulder at Crispian, and he pointed at his watch. I stood up and thanked Congresswoman Lee and Congressmen Payne and Jefferson for their time and headed out the door. Because our meeting with Congressman Payne had run long, Crispian rescheduled Congressman John Conyers Jr.

We went speedily down the hall to Congressman Carnahan's office. As I waited, something caught my eye. It was a photograph of A. S. J. Carnahan, Congressman Russ Carnahan's grandfather. A. S. J. Carnahan was appointed as the first American ambassador to the Republic of Sierra Leone in 1961 by President John F. Kennedy. A.S.J. retired his post in 1963.

I had a copy of a letter in my binder that was written to President Harry S. Truman citing what needed to be done to strengthen Sierra Leone. Congressman Carnahan had a framed copy of the very same letter on his wall! It was chilling. I was so transfixed by the framed letter that I barely heard the congressman come in. "You familiar with my grandfather?" he asked.

"Yes," I answered, turning to see him standing there, "very much so. I have a copy of your grandfather's letter in my binder. I'm using it as the blueprint for what I am trying to do to help Sierra Leone."

"How fortuitous," he said. Crispian walked in and apologized for cutting our meeting short, but he told the congressman that we were running behind schedule and had to get over to the Senate building. "Hopefully we can meet again when there is more time," I said, shaking the congressman's hand. Crispian and I took a subway that delivered us to the Senate side of the Capitol, where our first meeting was with Senator Arlen Specter. Upon arriving we were told the senator was on the floor voting. The senator's staff director offered to take me to the Senate floor. I was thrilled. While we waited, I grabbed Dr. Panossian and went out into the hallway. "Okay, what do we know about Adisa?"

"I called the hospital and talked to a Dr. Yoo, a specialist in tropical diseases. He said that they have run tests. Adisa is hemorrhaging internally. Dr. Yoo says that it appears like it is Lassa fever, but it's inconclusive until they receive the tests from the CDC."

I could feel my blood pressure rising and started to feel hot. "Okay," I said to Dr. Panossian, "do you know anyone in the CDC? We need to get Adisa's test fast-tracked." Sonya came out and said that she had spoken to Eric Nonacs and that he told her that the only antidote for Lassa fever is a medicine called Ribavirin.

"Great," I said, "Where do we get it?"

"According to Eric," she continued "it's only available on military installations."

"This is Adisa's life we are talking about," I said. I felt deeply responsible for delivering him to and from Sierra Leone safely. "Now I'm responsible for trying to save his life. Get Eric Nonacs on the phone." Sonya dialed Eric's number. In the meantime, I called Bill Clinton's assistant. I knew this was a risk, it was a big call, you don't just call the office of a former president of the United States of America and casually ask for a favor, but this was Adisa, and I felt he was worth it.

The phone rang a few times. "It's Isaiah," I said when his assistant answered. "Is the big man around? I have a serious problem." I could feel him tense up over the phone.

"Really? What kind of problem?"

"Well, I have a man down. He was my soundman while I was in Sierra Leone and he has fallen ill. He's in Los Angeles at the Daniel Freeman Memorial Hospital. They think he has Lassa fever."

I told him that Eric had explained that the antidote could be acquired only on a military installation. "I was wondering if President Clinton could help us out with this," I said. He explained that Clinton was in a meeting but gave me the number of his personal physician. "He may be able to help you. Call him," he said.

I called and spoke briefly with the President's doctor. The good doctor explained to me that he was in the middle of a family emergency and was not available to engage. I thanked him for his time and wished him well. Just as I hung up, Senator Specter's staff director walked over and said, "Are you ready?"

"Yes, of course," I said, "let's go."

We walked through the Hart Building on our way to the Senate floor. As we passed the office of Senator Barack H. Obama I stopped and thought for a minute. Ashley Tate-Gilmore, whom I had met at the Correspondents' Dinner, was going to try to facilitate a meeting with the senator that day. I figured it didn't hurt to pop my head in. I walked in and introduced myself to the receptionist. "May I help you?" she asked, looking at me quizzically. I could tell by the look on her face that she didn't have a clue who I was.

"Yes, my name is Isaiah Washington," I told her. "I was wondering if Senator Barack Obama was in."

Sonya stuck her head in the door and chimed, "Come on, mister, we are on a tight schedule, remember?"

"Hey I just want to meet the man. I'm a fan."

"He's on the Senate floor voting. Let's go!"

I took one of his business cards, thanked the receptionist, and left.

We continued on our way. It was a long walk through the bowels of the Senate. The heels of our shoes clicked on the marble floor and echoed quietly down the corridor. When we finally arrived, the security guards made us turn off our cameras. Senator Specter's staff director said, "Wait here a minute, I will see if I can get Senator Obama over to meet you."

"He's here?" I said. I was excited to meet the man, the African American man people were saying was the future forty-fourth president of the United States.

Within minutes Senator Barack Obama walked through the huge doors and said, "Hey, man, I've heard a lot about you. What are you doing on the Hill?"

I shook his hand and said, "Hill Harper speaks highly of you." Hill and I had done *Get on the Bus* together and he had told me about his experience with Senator Obama.

He said, "Hill's a great guy."

The senator smelled of cigarettes. I found myself thinking, "Oh my God, this guy is killing himself! Please, God, don't let anything happen to this man. We need him."

He asked if I had a card. "I'm here to raise awareness about the plight of the people in Sierra Leone," I said, and told him my story.

"That's good; Africa needs a lot of help. Keep up the good work. I'll see you at the crossroads. Hey, look, I gotta get back on the floor. I'm trying to get this Voting Rights Act signed. See you around."

With that, Senator Obama disappeared through the huge wooden doors leading to the Senate floor. "That was cool," said Sonya. I had no time to process meeting Barack Obama, because just then Senator Specter walked over and I introduced myself. The staff director gestured for all of us to sit at a nearby table. I gave the senator my spiel. He nodded and said, "Well, you seem to have vision and passion for Sierra Leone, young man." He asked if we had any current information on the country he could look at.

"No, sir," I said, but I offered to leave him the video of our trip. The senator smiled, saying, "I see you came prepared."

"Yes, sir, and with what I've discovered in my research about Pennsylvania and its connection to reform and Africa, I'm surprised that you are not a Democrat."

Senator Specter laughed a good while and said, "Oh no, I'm going to be a Republican for a long time." We finished up our meeting and headed off to the next meeting on our schedule, Senator Tom Coburn.

Senator Coburn's staff director was waiting in the hallway for us. He told us that the senator was on the Senate floor where we had just come from. Our little group did a U-turn and headed back to the Senate floor. We met Senator Coburn in a corridor just outside it. Since the senator was an MD, I suggested that

Dr. Panossian lead the discussion. The two doctors discussed the horrible medical conditions in Sierra Leone in hushed voices while I stood pressed against the corridor's wall listening to Senator Obama as he eloquently debated the Republicans over the twenty-five-year extension for the National Voting Rights Act of 1965. I kept thinking, "I feel like Forrest Gump right now." Just like Tom Hanks's character in the movie, I was having one amazing experience after the next. I was just following my heart as Forrest did in the movie, and it was leading me to some extraordinary places. Here I was standing outside the door of the United States Senate, listening to Barack Obama debate a vital piece of legislation. Instead of an official meeting, I met him on the Senate floor—working! Life was suddenly moving at lightning speed.

Crispian walked us by Senator John Thune's office, but he wasn't there. It was getting late, so we hustled over to our final meeting, with Senator Sam Brownback. Senator Brownback's receptionist demanded that I take a picture with her before she would let us in. She then walked us into the senator's conference room and said he would be with us shortly. I asked Sonya to call Daniel Freeman Memorial Hospital for an update on Adisa. It wasn't good. Apparently, his internal organs were failing. He had had to be revived twice.

A knot started growing in my stomach and I wanted to throw up. But I had to steel myself and press on. I asked Sonya to load the video and cue it up to the middle. By this time I realized the hour-long presentation was too lengthy to sit through for each meeting.

Senator Brownback walked in. "What can I do for you?" he asked after we shook hands and sat down.

I told him, "I've just returned from Sierra Leone and am here to raise awareness of the good things I've seen there and why I think Sierra Leone deserves another chance in the world."

"Well, Sierra Leone doesn't have a very good reputation in this town," the senator said.

"Yes, sir," I responded, "I realize that, but the children are suffering for what adults have done."

"Good point," he said, "but the U.S. government isn't going to give you any money for Sierra Leone."

I explained I wasn't there for money. I was there to find out if he would support me if I could get some things done on my own. "I was hoping that I could come to you for support once I achieve my goals."

"How are you going to do that?"

"I am going to build a school," I said.

"That's great; now tell me about the child soldiers." I blinked in miscomprehension and looked around the room. "I'm sorry?"

He repeated, "I know how bad things are in Africa. What I want to know is what's going on with the child soldiers there."

"Senator, the war has been over for four years now, there are no child soldiers anymore."

He adjusted his tie. "When are you going back?"

"As soon as I can," I told him. "I have a 365-Day Plan put together with some of my goals."

"That's good. Well, I wish you the best of luck. Let's keep in touch."

I thanked him for his time, we shook hands, and my team and I left.

Gonzalo took a shot of me, Crispian, and Dr. Panossian with the Capitol in the background. It was a beautiful shot and a great day of lobbying for Sierra Leone on the Hill.

We drove back to the Hotel George. Dr. Panossian and I walked into the Bistro Bis and I ordered a scotch on the rocks. I turned to him and said, "Andre, I need to know what the fuck is going on with Adisa. If it is Lassa fever, the CDC is going to quarantine Adisa and the Daniel Freeman Memorial Hospital, right?"

"It could happen," he said.

"Do you think Adisa is going to make it?" I asked.

"He is really, really sick, Isaiah. I ran a check on this Dr. Yoo and he knows his stuff."

"You didn't answer my question." I pulled out my mobile phone and called Dr. Keith Black at Cedars-Sinai. I dragged Dr. Panossian into the coat check closet where it was quiet and put him on the phone. He explained what he knew about Adisa's case and handed the phone back to me.

"Keith," I said, "who is the best internist you know? I need the best man ASAP!"

"Calm down, Isaiah," he said. "Let me make a few calls and I will get back to you, okay?"

Dr. Panossian looked at me dumbfounded. "Was that *the* Dr. Keith Black?" When I confirmed that it was, he said, "Wow. I just talked to *Dr. Keith Black*." I guess we were all having extraordinary experiences that day.

"I need a stiff drink," I said.

We walked out of the coat check closet and back to the bar. A waiter saw us emerge and jokingly said, "Get a room, guys."

I knew that I would become a voice for a people that had no voice. That's the pledge I made to myself and the people of Sierra Leone on the day I left Freetown. On July 20, 2006, the NAACP National Convention took place in Washington, DC. NAACP President Bruce Gordon invited me to speak at what was to be the first NAACP convention appearance of President George W. Bush's presidency.

The auditorium was crackling with anticipation as high-profile guests such as Jesse Jackson and Condoleezza Rice walked in and took their seats. I was one of a cadre of special guest speakers scheduled to appear. I was supposed to speak after the President, but he was running late, so I was asked to begin my speech earlier than planned.

I stepped up to the podium, a little intimidated by the huge crowd of civil rights leaders and political elites. I was about one minute into my address when the event organizer came over and whispered for me to inform the audience that President Bush had arrived.

I took my seat and watched as the President strolled to the podium to thunderous applause. I couldn't help but notice how intensely charismatic he was in person. I sat on the dais a mere ten feet from him. I noticed, as he delivered what I thought was a brilliant and heartfelt speech, that his left foot was crossed behind his right one in a very relaxed manner.

The parts of his speech that stood out for me most as later quoted on the *New York Times* Web site were this:

> For nearly 200 years, our nation failed the test of extend-ing the blessings of liberty to African Americans. Slavery was legal for nearly a hundred years, and discrimination legal in many places for nearly a hundred years more. Taken together, the record placed a stain on America's founding, a stain that we have not yet wiped clean.
>
> When people talk about America's founders they mention the likes of Washington and Jefferson and Franklin and Adams. Too often they ignore another group of founders—men and women and children who did not come to America of their free will, but in chains. These founders literally helped build our country. They chopped the wood, they built the homes, they tilled the fields, and they reaped the harvest. They raised children of others, even though their own children had been ripped away and sold to strangers. These founders were denied the most basic birthright, and that's freedom.

Yet, through captivity and oppression, they kept the faith. They carved a great nation out of the wilderness, and later, their descendants led a people out of the wilderness of bigotry. Nearly 200 years into our history as a nation, America experienced a second founding: the Civil Rights movement. Some of those leaders are here. These second founders, led by the likes of Thurgood Marshall and Martin Luther King, Jr., believed in the constitutional guarantees of liberty and equality. They trusted fellow Americans to join them in doing the right thing. They were leaders. They toppled Jim Crow through simple deeds: boarding a bus, walking along the road, showing up peacefully at courthouses or joining in prayer and song. Despite the sheriff's dogs, and the jailer's scorn, and the hangman's noose, and the assassin's bullets, they prevailed.

And this:

We're leading the world when it comes to providing medications and help. Today more than 40 million people around the world are living with HIV/AIDS; 26 million of those live in Sub Sahara Africa, including 2 million children under the age of 15. We're calling people together. We pledged $15 billion to provide medicine and help. We launched the emergency plan for AIDS relief. Before this AIDS emergency plan was passed, only 50,000 in Sub Sahara Africa were getting medicine. Today, that number has grown to more than 560,000 people, and more are getting help every day. By working together we can turn the tide of this struggle against HIV/AIDS and bring new hope to millions of people.[9]

As the President finished his speech and made his way through the elated crowd, I thought to myself, "How the hell do I follow that?" I stepped back up to the podium and noticed that Jesse and Condi had left the room. I knew the only reason 50 percent of the audience was there was to hear the President. I took a deep breath and explained why I was invited. I spoke about my DNA test and what it revealed to me. I talked about the plight of Sierra Leone and its children. I told the audience about what it would be like if all African Americans knew where they came from. I talked about what Paul Robeson, Langston Hughes, W. E. B. DuBois, Malcolm X, and Martin Luther King Jr. would have done if they had known *their* African ancestry. I spoke about who Gondobay Manga was and why I was made Chief Gondobay Manga II. I told them about what it would be like to finally bridge the gap between African Americans and Africans, and what it would be like if we could all work together to create a strong economic base for ourselves in Africa.

I spoke from my heart. When I was done, the crowd responded with a wonderful round of applause. I thanked the audience for listening on behalf of the Sierra Leonean people and returned to my seat. It was done. The voice of Sierra Leone was heard that day. And this was just the beginning.

CHAPTER 15

The Gondobay Manga Foundation Is Born Amid Crisis

I flipped open my laptop and began checking e-mails. There was one from Jeffrey Sachs. I jumped up and literally started dancing around my trailer, causing it to rock from side to side. There was a knock on the door. "It's open!" I shouted.

The second assistant director on my TV show peeked her head in. "You okay in here?"

"Yes!" I answered. "I just got the greatest e-mail EVER! You wanna read it?"

"Wow," she said, "it must be really good."

"It's from Jeffrey Sachs!"

She just stood there, looking puzzled and confused, not having the first idea who Jeffrey Sachs was. "Never mind," I said, deciding not to interrupt my good feelings by stopping to explain.

"They just called on the radio," she said. "They need you in makeup."

"Great. I just have to read this e-mail one more time."

Subject: RE: Per *Isaiah Washington*
Date: Tue, 29 Aug 2006 16:30:38–0400
Dear Sonya,

Great! I'm eager to get some of my team over to Ngalu.
Can you give me the coordinates of the village? When might
be a good time for a visit?

My group is based mainly in Bamako, so it should be
feasible to get them to Ngalu sometime within the next few
weeks.
Best,
Jeff Sachs

Jeffrey D. Sachs
Director, The Earth Institute at Columbia University

I knew that this wasn't an official commitment from Jeffrey Sachs to make my village one of his Millennium Villages, to make it sustainable through his organization. The important thing was that the very village where I was made Chief Gondobay Manga II was now on his radar.

I officially opened my office for the Gondobay Manga Foundation (TGMF) on September 1, 2006. I made Sonya Gay Bourn the president; Dr. Andre Panossian, Jackie Coker, Breton F. Washington, and my lovely wife, Jenisa M. Washington, became my board of directors. I took on the role of chairman.

The first official TGMF meeting took place during a one-hour lunch break in my trailer, with Rosalind Kainyah from De Beers and Jamie Cadwell from the Diamond Information Center. I passed around a bottle of Yellowtail merlot and discussed how TGMF, De Beers, and the Diamond Information Center could work together.

"Rosalind, is De Beers prepared to write a check to rebuild the Bo Hospital in Sierra Leone?" I bluntly asked. "The hospital is supposed to serve a population of close to one million people and it doesn't even have an oxygen bottle or any rubber gloves."

"You're not African, so why are you so interested in Africa?" she responded.

"Rosalind," I explained, "that is no reason for me to not care about the people I share DNA with. Unlike you, I had no knowledge of where I was from in Africa or who my ancestors were, and now I do. I care because I can afford to care. So, are you asking me that question because I'm African American or are you asking me because you are Ghanaian?"

"I'm asking because I want to know why *you* want to change things in Sierra Leone," she said. "The conditions are horrible there, but they are horrible all over Africa. You want to rebuild Sierra Leone, I get that, but how do you intend to pay for it?"

"*I'm* paying for it for now," I explained, "but I need sponsorships, partnerships. I need De Beers!"

"Isaiah," she said emphatically, "De Beers is not going to give you any money."

I looked at Sonya. "Sonya," I asked, "does Rosalind have a copy of our 365-Day Plan?"

"She sure does," Sonya answered.

"Jamie, how much is the Diamond Information Center willing to donate?"

Jamie looked at Rosalind. "The Diamond Information Center isn't prepared to donate any money," she explained, "but we can offer you our Rolodex and put on a fund-raiser for TGMF."

The wine was starting to make my head feel tight. "Wait a minute," I said, "you two flew all the way to Los Angeles. I sent a car to bring both of you here to meet me. You drink my wine and now you're telling me you both came here empty-handed? Sierra Leone is the poorest country in the world. De Beers and DIC owe Sierra Leone a great deal."

Sonya piped in, "Ms. Kainyah, Isaiah is very passionate about

Sierra Leone, as you can see. He's put a lot of pressure on himself and probably should not have *any more wine*—"

I interrupted, "Why are you talking like I'm not sitting here, Sonya? I'm sitting right here! Come on, guys, people are dying in Sierra Leone as we speak and we are here wasting time. You know what? I think this meeting is over. Ms. Kainyah has eaten and had her wine and I gotta get back to work. Oh by the way, do we have to pay for the car to drive them to their next meeting?"

"Isaiah!" Sonya exclaimed.

"No, Sonya, what are we doing here? I'm tired of friendly meetings that end up being just a bunch of bullshit. Look, if I had twenty million dollars in the bank, then I would do what I need to do in Sierra Leone myself. But I don't, and the clock is ticking. So Ms. Kainyah, Ms. Cadwell, I'm sorry if I'm offending you."

"I'm not offended by you," Rosalind said. "You are passionate and I know someone who could help you. In fact, your passion reminds me a lot of him."

I started to calm down a little. "Oh really…and who would that be?"

"President Festus Mogae of Botswana," she said.

"Why is that?" I asked, not sure why the president of Botswana would care about helping me or Sierra Leone.

She continued, "He believes the same thing about Botswana. He feels that the natural resources should be owned by, controlled by, and benefit the people. He's done it. I think you and President Mogae should meet."

Three weeks later I received an official letter from the Republic of Botswana.

Dear Mr. Washington,
    At the end of this month my country, Botswana, will be celebrating its 40th Anniversary of Independence.

In this context we are extremely proud of our unique record over the period as Africa's oldest multi-party democracy, and fastest growing economy. A pillar of our progress has been prudent management of our natural resources, and in particular our diamond revenues.

Today Botswana is the world's largest producer of diamonds by value. For our citizens this has resulted in better quality of life. Notwithstanding the fact that our country is prone to drought, nutritional levels have steadily risen over the past decades, in part due to our provision of free food for school children, the destitute and others with special needs. We are especially proud that even during the most severe droughts, not a single Botswana citizen died from hunger.

Diamond revenues have enabled us to provide free education to all, with the result that today close to 90% of our population below 40 is literate, whereas our literacy rate in 1966 was only about 10%. Other social indicators such as children's immunization, Infant Mortality rate and Life Expectancy at birth have improved significantly even though lately, they have been adversely affected by the HIV/AIDS pandemic. Botswana was one of the first countries to introduce Prevention of Mother-to-Child Transmission Programmes of HIV/AIDS. All the initiatives directed at children are in recognition of the need to facilitate smooth childhood development in order to lay the basis for a stable and secure nation. Any nation that places its children in peril, places its own existence in danger.

Indeed, forty years ago I was one of the very few people in my country to have been exposed to a University education. I can still remember the names of my colleagues from back then. Today, tens of thousands of Botswana citizens are studying at tertiary institutions. Included among these are those living in our most remote and marginalized communities, such as those commonly known outside of our country as the "Bushmen." The prudent management of our mineral wealth, especially diamonds, has also allowed us to provide nearly universal access to free health care, with the vast majority of our citizens now living within 15km of a public health facility. All this has been made possible by the fact that education, followed by health, has each year received the largest share of public expenditure.

We recognize that human capital is key to sustainable economic development. Having noted some of our achievements I also wish to acknowledge that we remain as a developing country facing many challenges including the specific challenge of being one of the nations most affected by HIV/AIDS. In this respect, we have at least been fortunate in having the public resources to confront this scourge through such measures as our commitment to prevention, provision of free anti-retroviral drugs as well as support programmes to allow the infected and affected to lead productive lives for as long as possible. In particular, we have extensive orphan care programmes. People from outside our country sometimes ask me why our diamonds have been such a blessing to us. An important part of the answer I believe has been the decision we took at independence to entrust ultimate ownership of the minerals and other natural resources of our country through the state to the nation as a whole, irrespective of who owns the land on which such wealth might be discovered.

This has ensured that all of our citizens—irrespective of their ethnic or regional affiliation—have a collective stake and enjoy common benefits, rather than just those few who by a chance might find themselves sitting on nature's gifts. We have avoided the interethnic conflicts over resources, which have plagued some societies. Indeed a World Bank study released this month ranked us as being among the most peaceful, politically and socially stable, as well as democratic nations not just in Africa but in the world.

Why am I sharing my positive perspective with you? Quite frankly, I am concerned about the growing perception in some quarters that the mining of minerals, and more especially diamonds, throughout Africa is a greater cause of conflict, rather than national construction and shared future. In my country diamonds have been a source of life, hope and future prosperity. To ensure that this continues to be the case Botswana has joined together with other leading diamond producers in the world in something called the Kimberley Process that today ensures that the 99% of the world's diamonds that come from areas free of conflict, like Botswana, can be traced to their point of origin. In other words, we abhor conflict and are active participants in isolating diamonds that are used to promote conflict.

The Kimberley Process provides objective verification that the source of diamonds is not in any way connected with conflict. Thus when you buy diamonds from Botswana and other Kimberley Process countries you can wear them in full knowledge that you have paid for a child's immunization, education as well as overall development and helped the sick secure treatment. The joy diamonds bring to you is also our joy. Our diamonds play a critical part in poverty reduction and sustaining human life. And it is also our earnest hope that those that use diamonds for evil will soon begin to realize the immense potential they can make to the development of their nations. All of humanity stands to benefit from global peace, stability, understanding and co-operation.

I would therefore, be most grateful if you could carry this message of hope to all you encounter.

Festus Mogae
PRESIDENT OF THE REPUBLIC OF BOTSWANA

After I finished reading the letter from President Mogae, I was feeling honored and numb at the same time. I sat in my office chair, staring at the paper in my hands, intensely thinking, "Why are so many people talking to me about these damned diamonds!"

I was desperately trying to figure out what my next move would be. I just didn't know what to think or what any of this meant. I started to feel as I did when I was a little boy witnessing it raining hard on one side of the street while the sun remained high in the sky shining brightly on the other side. It was a conundrum, it didn't make sense. "The devil must be beating his wife," I said aloud.

At that moment the phone rang; it was my publicist, Cynthia Snyder. "Hey you," she said, "why haven't you called me back, aren't you excited?"

"Excited about what?" I asked.

"Have you been checking your e-mails?"

I hadn't.

"I sent the news in an e-mail a week ago! Congratulations, you're number one in adult ratings eighteen to forty-nine! You beat *CSI* last week in the Thursday night slot." This meant that my television show was the most watched by adults ages eighteen to forty-nine.

"Well, God," I said aloud, "now Africa and America know my name. Thanks for another dream come true."

A little more than two weeks later, on October 9, 2006, the actor Patrick Dempsey and I clashed on the set of our TV show. Within hours "reports" of the incident hit the tabloids and the entire world seemed to be talking about me. I had wanted to become a household name for years, but this wasn't what I had in mind. There's little more I can write about it that hasn't already been written.

It was by far a total nightmare, an experience that I wouldn't wish on my worst enemy. I recall walking into my TGMF office feeling that the world had changed and that I was never going to be the same again. Sonya was there. "Patrick and I almost had a fight. We had a horrible argument." I sat down across from Sonya. She just sat there staring at me. For a few minutes, I just sat there too. My thoughts drifted back to Muh' Dear and the fight with the Frazier sisters.

The ring of my mobile phone startled me back to the present. It was a reporter from *People* magazine. Her questions weren't questions. She was condemning me, chastising me even. I listened to her talk because I knew her and I thought she knew me. We had recently discussed doing a story on my work in Sierra Leone.

"Isaiah, this is horrible, but I have to do my job," she said. "You have to tell me what happened. My editors want to know. We put you in our magazine. You're on one of the biggest TV shows in the country. Isaiah...Isaiah? Isaiah, are you there?"

I hung up and walked into my office, closed the door behind me, and slumped down into the chair. Within a few minutes the phone was ringing off the hook. It would not stop ringing. I closed my eyes and took a deep breath.

My ringing phone snapped me back to reality. It was my assistant director. "Isaiah," he said, "we're back in. Your scene is first up."

"Okay, I'm on my way," I said.

As I hung up the phone, I remembered the conversation I had had with John Amos when he asked me if I could be servile: humbly submissive.

"Can you be obsequious?" he had asked me.

I didn't get it then, but I sure as hell got it now. Before I left the TGMF office I checked my e-mails one last time. To my surprise there was an e-mail from Adisa. I had not heard from him since July. I was at the Daniel Freeman Memorial Hospital the day he was released. He didn't have Lassa fever as we had feared; he had contracted hantavirus, a hemorrhagic disease, equally as deadly.

This is an excerpt from that e-mail that he sent to family and friends:

> While in the hospital I can remember crying when I thought of my 85-year-old father. The thought of him having to possibly bury me made me very emotional. My faith was tested immeasurably and being on a ventilator meant death was a real possibility, and although I didn't dwell in fear, I knew the reality of my situation. It is because of this that I am grateful to my mother, my Godmother, family members and close friends who stayed near my bedside during my time of distress and challenge. When my faith weakened and I grew weary, I leaned on theirs. Their never ending hope, enlightened eyes, courage, smiles and presence gave me the strength to keep going.
>
> Once cleared of the virus, my 5 foot 9 inch, 170lb muscular body was reduced to a buck 35 not to mention the fact that my body had atrophied badly during those two

weeks. I couldn't walk, nor could I hold my tiny cell phone, which seemed to weigh a ton. But the rebuilding process had begun. Every day I made small gains. I even told the hospital staff that I was Cassius Clay. I may have come off a bit crazy, but it was all designed to motivate me. During this time, more than one nurse or doctor walked into my room and proclaimed me a miracle. I do believe that there was a great divine force calling for my life to play out this way and that God and the Universe have given me a great opportunity to grow, and gain insight with regard to my purpose on the planet.

I often laugh and joke with Isaiah about the ethnic group to which he belongs—the Mende of Sierra Leone. I tell him that if I had known ahead of time that the initiation process for his group required confronting death, I would have chosen the Ashanti, Zulu or Yoruba traditions. At least the Yoruba just mark your face and you keep pushing forward. But near death?! We laugh out loud and realize that greater things shall come from this.

On July 15th I walked out of the Daniel Freeman Hospital, one month after I checked myself into the emergency room. One of my doctors and a few therapists expressed concern over my leaving. (They wanted to keep me a few more days, put me in a mock apartment, etc.) But for anyone who has been in a hospital for a prolonged period of time, you know how debilitating it can be. I told the doctor he could speak with my brothers when they arrived. He then seemed happy and willingly agreed to do so. My doctor didn't know that I wasn't playin'. Rev. Leon Campbell showed up with about ten of my Agape brothers. Isaiah was also there to show his support along with some close friends. The doctor took one look and knew, just like everyone else in attendance, that my strength was their strength and vice versa. I left the Daniel

Freeman Hospital that day with a smile on my face and determination in my heart.

My life has been altered forever and I'm sure everyone who experienced this with me has been transformed as well. My body is improving little by little every day. Please continue to keep me in your prayers and know that you are in mine. By October I should be back to throwing children in the air—one of my greatest pleasures. In the future, look for me directing films, continuing to heal the planet through my humanitarian efforts, and early next year I'm traveling back to Sierra Leone to build a high school with several colleagues.

For those of you who have called, please forgive me for my tardiness in getting back to you. Thanks so much for your kindness and know that you are in my thoughts. Recovery takes time, so please be patient with me.

And to those who do not believe that God is still in the miracle business, I am here to tell you that God has once again spoken and it feels so good to hear his voice.

Thanks again for your love, support, prayers and well wishes.
Your brother,
Adisa Khepra
PS: Please forward to any friends and colleagues I might have forgotten. Thanks!!

My spirit began to smile after reading Adisa's words of encouragement. I was humbled by his support. I later learned that during his battle with the deadly hantavirus, Adisa died and was revived three times. Adisa kept his word about finding "his purpose on the planet." He has since cofounded Finaza Foundation, an organization that, per its Web site, "is committed to the enrichment of impoverished children's lives throughout the world and to help galvanize communities that are in need of resources as a means of empowerment."[10]

The organization provides scholarships, produces an annual soccer tournament, and works with local NGOs. Adisa has traveled to Sierra Leone several times providing services for the Sierra Leone children and completed a documentary about his Finaza Football Tournament. He is truly a miracle.

CHAPTER 16

Blood Diamonds

I poked my head into Sonya's office. "Did you call the duchess back?" she asked.

"What? I thought that was a prank call from you," I replied.

"No, hon," she said, "it's the Duchess of York, all right; just spoke with her assistant last week. You haven't been checking your e-mails again?"

"Wow, should I call her back? What does she want?"

"She says her daughters are huge fans and they want an autographed photo of you," she explained.

"Wow, okay. Um, I'll call her when I get back to the set."

On November 2, 2006, the Duchess of York, Sarah Margaret Ferguson, would come to visit me on the set of my TV show. She wanted me to give her a personal tour.

One day, while I was getting clearance from my boss, Shonda Rhimes, for the duchess to tour the set, she asked, "What are you doing? Running for president?" She was becoming increasingly intrigued by my relationships with Sierra Leone, Capitol Hill, and now the Duchess of York.

"No." I answered, "that's not in my DNA." I walked out of her office and headed back to my trailer to wait for the duchess to arrive. My cell phone rang. It was E.H., a lobbyist from DC. He asked if I knew Leonardo DiCaprio, Djimon Hounsou, or Ed Zwick. "No," I said, "not personally, why?"

"Well, this movie *Blood Diamond* could kill the diamond industry," he explained. "And that would kill a lot of jobs in Sierra Leone, Liberia, and all of the diamond-mining countries."

Yes," I said, "I received a letter from the president of Botswana expressing his concern, but what does that have to do with me?"

"Isaiah," he said, "you are in a very powerful position right now. Your name is on the lips of every person, newspaper, and tabloid around the world. Use it to your advantage. Can you call Ed Zwick and try to convince him to put out a disclaimer stating that his movie isn't historically accurate?"

"Why would I do that?" I asked. "Ed Zwick isn't going to listen to me."

"Isaiah, nonconflict diamond mining is the only way Sierra Leone is going to get out of its present condition."

"I don't agree with that, sir. I'll make a call, but don't expect anything."

"Thanks, buddy," he said. "I'll make sure your foundation is earmarked for this."

"Yeah, sure," I said, and hung up.

I scrolled through my contacts and dialed my agent at the Innovative Artists agency, Ben Press.

"Izayyyyyyaahhhh, how ya doing, buddy? Ya hanging in there?" he asked.

"Yeah, I'm all right," I told him. "Look, I need a number for Ed Zwick's office."

"Surrrrre," he said, "wanna tell me what the call is about?"

"I'm just going to call him. I promised someone that I would *call* him," I said.

"Okaaaaaayyyyyyyy, hold on, here it is, a ready?" I grabbed a pen and wrote down the number.

I dialed the number Ben gave me.

"Hello, this is Isaiah Washington calling," I said when the receptionist answered. I could hear the air leave her body.

"Can I ask what this call is regarding?"

"Yes, I promised someone that I would *call* Mr. Zwick's office. I've done that."

"I'm sorry, I don't understand what the message is," she said, confused.

"There isn't one," I answered. "I just need you to document that I *called*."

"Well...okay...sure."

I hung up and began reading an article on jcrs.com about the Duchess of York on my laptop:

Sarah Ferguson, the Duchess of York, recently launched a collection of moissanite jewelry. On top of the trend, *Good Housekeeping* has called moissanite the new "it" jewel. Moissanite is a naturally occurring mineral. In 1893, Henri Moissan discovered minute silicone carbide crystals in a 50,000-year-old meteor in Arizona. Later, the crystalline substance was named after him. In fact, moissanite can be considered a huge success story for lab-grown gems. Moissanite producers say it has more luster and brilliance than diamond, perhaps twice the fire of diamond, and it is almost as durable. (On the Mohs hardness scale, moissanite ranks 9.5—right between diamond, the hardest known mineral, which ranks 10, and sapphire, which ranks 9.)[11]

I met the Duchess of York with my publicist, Cynthia Snyder. We took a few pictures and I introduced her to a few of my cast mates. The whole thing seemed a little bizarre to me, but not as bizarre as it was going to get.

The duchess seemed to enjoy her tour by "Dr. Preston Burke." We exchanged hugs and mobile phone numbers, and then her bodyguards escorted her back to her car.

I could have cut the tension on the set with a high-powered chainsaw and it would not have made a scratch. There was a full-scale war brewing outside the studio walls and it was focused on me. And then there was the other war to escalate, the one between Hollywood and the diamond industry. I found myself standing right in the middle of both conflicts. My relationship with Sierra Leone and the dustup I'd had with Patrick Dempsey made me a perfect target for the media. I had become a pawn on an extremely broad and lethal media chessboard. I knew that I would soon have to pick a side.

On November 20, 2006, the Google alert I'd set up on De Beers popped up on my computer revealing an article in *Time* magazine. The article covered how Leonardo DiCaprio prepared for his role in *Blood Diamond* by spending a month in Africa and described the movie, noting:

> The movie follows the fortunes of a soldier turned diamond smuggler who works with both warlords and an international diamond corporation.... Along the way, many unromantic acts are perpetrated in the pursuit of the gemstones....The film is historical, but the history is recent. And since a diamond's worth is intimately connected with its significance for romance, the gem industry knows it can't be too careful about the film.

The article went on to describe how the World Diamond Council (WDC) was countering with a $15 million crisis PR campaign.

> "I'm not worried at all by the film as long as people get to know the facts," says Eli Izhakoff, head of the W.D.C. "We see this as an opportunity to make sure that people are aware of all the good stuff the industry has done." Rosalind Kainyah, until recently De Beers' London-based director of public and corporate affairs, is a little more direct. "I'm sure that Warner Bros. wouldn't want to harm Africa," she says. "So I believe they'll want to put the movie in a historic context."[12]

"Warner Bros. wouldn't want to harm Africa?" I said out loud. "Wow, Rosalind, how much are they paying you?" Right then and there, I made my choice. I picked a side. I wanted no part of the diamond industry or its money. I just wanted to build a school for the village of Njala Kendema in Sierra Leone. I changed the phone number on my mobile phone and turned my attention to my job, my family, and getting the school built.

The clock was ticking. Five months had passed since I pledged to build my school according to my 365-Day Plan. I needed to focus. My military training began to kick in; I had to prepare for battle because in my mind I was now at war. I sat down at my computer and pulled up my investment portfolio. The Bausch & Lomb shares I decided to buy the day I sat waiting for Jeffrey Sachs at Jean Georges had yielded some very nice dividends. I also owned shares of Disney and those were making money too. I Googled the Walt Disney Company, ABC's parent company, and read that Disney had reported a fourth-quarter net profit of $782 million, or 36 cents per share, compared to $379 million, or 19 cents per share a year before.[13]

And then a headline in the stock news section caught my eye: "Wenner Media Acquires Disney's 50% Stake In *Us Weekly*."[14] Disney had sold its stake in *Us Weekly* to Wenner Media. *Us Weekly* was one of the tabloids printing much of the negative press about me!

I picked up my office phone and called Steve McPherson and Mark Pedowitz, two top executives on my TV show, to discuss the increasingly negative and inaccurate stories that the magazine was publishing about me.

Us Weekly had recently paid Disney $300 million to regain its full ownership again.

"Yeah, Michael Eisner would have sold his grandmother when he was in office," said Steve. "We don't do business like that anymore."

"I see that Disney and our show are doing very well," I said.

"Yes, we are making money."

"Hey, this thing is growing legs in the wrong direction; the tabloids got it all wrong. I never attacked T.R. What's going on? I think I need to talk. Tell my side of what happened. This thing is hurting everything connected to me," I explained.

"Shit happens," Steve said nonchalantly. "You still have that bottle of Gaja I sent you?" he asked.

"Yes, I do," I answered.

"Now would be a good time to open it. Buy a big hat and keep quiet. We are handling this."

I hung up and called Mark Pedowitz. "Hey, Mark, this thing with the tabloids is killing me, my family can't go out of the house. Cameras are everywhere. My wife had to turn the radio off this morning so the kids wouldn't hear my name."

"I know, Isaiah," Mark said. "Just stop talking to the press. Change your number yet?"

I said I had. "Good man," he said.

"Mark, *Us Weekly* is *killing* me, and Disney was in business with these guys just three months ago. Do you think I should buy some Wenner Media shares?"

"Why not, couldn't hurt, I guess," Mark said. "Once you become a major shareholder maybe you can ask them not to bother you anymore."

We both laughed and I hung up. "This is crazy," I thought to myself. What the hell was I laughing at? Disney stock value was going up and at the same time my personal stock value was plummeting. I stood up, opened up the cabinet in my office, and opened that bottle of wine Steve had given me.

My agent called to remind me that I had been invited to attend the *Blood Diamond* premiere and after party at the Roosevelt Hotel later that evening. I knew everyone attending would be dressed in traditional suits and evening gowns as usual. But I didn't have time to go home and change into a shirt and tie. So I went dressed in my dark blue coveralls, Wellie boots, and a baseball cap. With each sip of wine, I resigned myself to the idea of appearing underdressed. In fact, I began to think that my present attire would actually be fitting for what was happening in my life. Because of the derogatory way the media was portraying me and the way the baggy dark blue coveralls looked, I felt like an abused field hand, street sweeper, or mechanic, maybe even a garbage man or prisoner of some sort. So why shouldn't my attire match my feelings?

I arrived to the theater late, to give the press time to exhaust themselves on the red carpet, and then I slipped into the theater. Maybe it was just my imagination, but I felt some people were looking at me as if I had lost my mind. I didn't care. I had consumed half a bottle of a 2005 Gaja Barbaresco and had a bit of alcohol courage going. I sat in the darkness of the theater and felt as if people around me were whispering. Were they talking about me? When I returned a few of the stares, eyes were quickly diverted.

The movie truly hit home with me. I felt something on my face and thought someone had sprayed me with spittle. I wiped at my face only to realize that it was my own tears running down my cheeks. No matter how many times I saw or read an illustration of the pain and suffering the African people were subjected to, I never hardened to it. Each time, it hurt me to my core. I ducked out of the theater before the credits started rolling.

I headed over to the after party at the Roosevelt Hotel and was immediately stopped by security. The guard asked to see my ID. He looked at it with his flashlight and then back up at me. "My apologies, Mr. Washington," he said. "I didn't recognize you, please come right in, sir."

The first person I ran into was the composer for the film, James Newton Howard. He was polite. I waited for several minutes to introduce myself to Ed Zwick, but he was preoccupied with well-wishers. Someone pointed out Sorius Samura, the director of *Cry Freetown*. A young lady named Nzinga Blake introduced herself; she was a Sierra Leonean American actress from Sierra Leone.

"Hello, did you enjoy the movie?" she asked.

"Very much so," I replied.

"I'm a little upset," she said.

When I asked her why, she replied, "They didn't shoot anything in Sierra Leone."

"Wow," I said, "that's too bad. Sierra Leone could have used the money."

"I'm a host for Al Gore's *Current TV*," she continued. "Are you familiar with the show?"

I told her that I wasn't.

"Maybe I can interview you one day. I know what you have been doing for Sierra Leone."

"Actually," I explained, "all I've done is travel there and ask a lot of questions. I do plan on building a school there soon. Maybe we can talk about that."

She agreed and gave me her number. Nzinga introduced me to her cousin and then I excused myself and began to mingle. I ran into Djimon Hounsou, who was as poised and immaculately dressed as usual. He slowly looked me up and down and then asked, "You all right?" I guess he wasn't feeling my outfit.

"Don't believe what you read, man. It's all being handled," I said. "I want to talk, but they want me to keep my mouth shut."

Djimon placed his right index finger up to his lips and mimed a silent but irrefutable sssssshhhhhhh. I congratulated him on a great performance and made room for some of his well-wishers. He winked at me. I winked back and walked away.

On December 8, 2006, the film *Blood Diamond* opened in theaters around the nation, grossing $57 million in the United States. The film had cost $100 million to make.

The diamond industry spent millions upon millions of dollars bracing for the negative backlash it thought the film would create. The thinking was that if the world saw the atrocities and abuses committed by machete-wielding rebels during the war in Sierra Leone, the average diamond purchaser would be completely turned off.

I don't know if diamond dealers' cash registers slowed or even stopped ringing, but I do know that my phone continued ringing off the hook. I was getting messages from managers, publicists, and attorneys. I even received a message from Susan Whitson, Chief of Staff for the Office of First Lady of the United States Laura Bush.

The next day, during a break on the set, I returned Susan Whitson's call. "Isaiah!" she said, cheerfully answering the phone, "how are youuuuu?"

"I could be better, but God is good," I replied.

"He sure is," she agreed. "I'm calling you on the behalf of the First Lady to let you know that she was interested in having you as our master of ceremonies for the first White House Summit on Malaria that she is hosting."

I paused to think. Malaria was a serious issue in Sierra Leone, as it was in many countries in Africa. This could be a wonderful opportunity to get some exposure and support for the work I wanted to do there.

"Hello. Isaiah, are you still there?" she said.

"Yes," I finally answered. "I would love to support the First Lady on one condition."

"Oh," she said. "Well, I hope we can accommodate you."

"I will agree to emcee if I can talk about Sierra Leone and my organization, the Gondobay Manga Foundation."

"Isaiah, I don't think that will be a problem at all," she said. "We think you would be perfect to emcee this historical event. Do you have any information on the foundation that you can send?"

"Yes, I will have my office forward the TGMF mission statement and my Web site address to you today."

"Thank you so much for doing this, Isaiah. The First Lady will be very pleased, as I am as well. We are all just such big fans of your show. I will be in touch with your publicist to make all of the arrangements. See you soon, bye-bye!"

On December 14, 2006, at the Grosvenor Building in Washington, DC, I once again served as a voice for the people of Sierra Leone, making the following speech:

Greetings and good morning, and in my newfound language, *Bu Waa!* out of Sierra Leone. What a wonderful, wonderful, wonderful song. I've been to Africa and I met many, many joyful children like these who are bound by our common hope to see the African children grow up.

Defeating malaria is an urgent calling and an achievable goal. Malaria, a completely preventable and treatable disease, kills a child in Africa every 30 seconds. At least one million infants and children under five in sub-Saharan Africa die each year. We have eliminated malaria before, and with the help of people across the United States and around the world, we can do it again. It's hard to believe now but just a few generations ago, malaria plagued the Southeastern United States, but after a sustained public effort the United States was declared malaria-free.

In Panama these same techniques were used last century during construction of the Panama Canal and infection rates for workers dropped 80 percent in two years. Malaria has an enormous economic impact. Malaria makes workers weak and fills hospitals. When individuals cannot work, economies suffer and impoverished nations are subject to conflict.

The President and Mrs. Bush's Summit will examine the challenge of malaria facing Africa today. Our public-private partnerships and multi-lateral efforts are addressing this challenge and how we can mobilize grassroots efforts so that individuals can be a part of saving the life of another in Africa. We know we can save millions of lives. We have already begun. I would now like to introduce a woman who has said herself that our first challenge is to inspire the people of all free nations so that we may unite in a common cause to solve common problems. With honor, I introduce to you Secretary of State Condoleezza Rice.

Secretary of State Condoleeza Rice then spoke:

Good morning and thank you to Isaiah Washington both for that kind introduction and for the dedication and commitment that you have shown to this and so many causes. I'm honored to join all of you here today at the White House Summit on Malaria. I'm also pleased by the tremendous support that this Summit has received from America's business community, religious leaders, and other concerned citizens.

The idea of public-private partnerships is at the heart of so much of President Bush's vision for America, and I want to welcome all of you and to thank you for joining us today. What brings us together today is our basic belief that all human beings are free by nature and equal in dignity. That every life is precious, and as President Bush has said that, "No insignificant person was ever born." We are led, therefore, to this fundamental conviction, that the child suffering from malaria in Africa possesses the same matchless value as the most powerful and prosperous among us.

This is a profound and revolutionary idea—a vision of dignity that has transformed our nation, and is transforming our world. It is the idea that is also at the heart of America's public diplomacy, the work that we are doing to help save and transform lives across the world. President Bush has put compassion at the top of our agenda, the American people's concern for equality and dignity at the center of our nation's foreign policy. It is these principles that lead us into the world to support the liberty and human rights of all people, to confront heinous crimes like trafficking in persons, and to fight dreadful diseases that steal human life indiscriminately and tragically; HIV/AIDS, tuberculosis and of course, malaria.

Last year the President resolved that America can and must play a greater role in the global fight against this curable disease, so he launched the President's Malaria Initiative, a historic commitment to work with developing nations in Africa and around the world to fight to end malaria, just as we did in this country two generations ago. The President also made it clear that our effort could only succeed if we reached beyond government and mobilized the good faith and the hard work of private partners. Judging by this great audience and this great response, I would say that we are already succeeding together.

One person who has taken tremendous leadership in our fight against malaria is the woman I have the honor of introducing to you today, the First Lady of the United States, Laura Bush. In my four years at the White House, and now in my past two years as Secretary of State, I've had the honor of working closely on some of the most important issues facing the international community, from the promotion of education and literacy in every country in the world to the empowerment of women in places like Iraq and Afghanistan, to the fight against extreme poverty in Africa.

In the past year, it has been my privilege to work with the First Lady shoulder-to-shoulder to help advance her vision and the President's vision of a world in which no human life is lost to a disease that we can prevent with something as simple as a well-covered place to sleep. I've seen the passion and the conviction with which the First Lady has tackled this fight against malaria. She has worked tirelessly to mobilize the resources and the goodwill of the American people, and she has done a great deal to make this Summit today a reality. Along with countless others, I have experienced the First Lady's decency, her generosity and her commitment to human dignity. And in that time I have gained an even greater joy, the honor of calling her my friend. So today it is my privilege to introduce to you, a great woman, a compassionate woman—First Lady Laura Bush.

First Lady Laura Bush then made her speech, beginning by thanking Dr. Rice and several key people in attendance. She continued, saying:

Educators, business leaders, philanthropists, researchers, activists, and distinguished guests, welcome to the White House Summit on Malaria. Today's gathering presents us with a historic opportunity to end the suffering of millions. Governments, the private sector, and concerned citizens have all united in one place, ready with unprecedented commitments that can turn the tide against malaria. We're here because eradicating malaria is an urgent calling. The disease claims 1.2 million lives every year. It devastates people living with HIV/AIDS, pregnant women, and especially young children and babies.

Malaria kills 3,000 children in Africa every day. Parents grieve for their sons and daughters, communities mourn, and developing countries lose generations of productive citizens. Adding to the urgency is the fact that malaria is treatable and preventable. The disease once sickened men, women, and children in many parts of the United States, but through advances in science and technology, we learned that the cause of such enormous suffering is a microscopic parasite carried by an insect. We learned how to stop the spread of malaria, and the disease was eliminated in the United States nearly 60 years ago. The challenge now is to use this scientific progress so that it benefits people still at risk.

In June 2005, President Bush launched the President's Malaria Initiative, a five-year, $1.2 billion program to combat malaria in 15 of the hardest hit African nations. This initiative calls on developed countries, private foundations and volunteer organizations to join to reduce the suffering and death caused by malaria. Private foundations and corporations have responded with millions of dollars for prevention and treatment. Civic groups and religious organizations have mobilized thousands of volunteers. Through early PMI partnerships with the first three focus countries, aid from the American people has reached about six million Africans. Next year, 30 million more will receive lifesaving medicines, sprays and nets as the program expands. These partnerships save lives and spread hope. Last year in the Tanzanian villages of Kambini and Kiwani, during the peak infection month of June, local health workers documented more than 450 cases of malaria. This June, one year into PMI, the number of cases plummeted to eight. In some PMI areas, malaria researchers have actually complained that they no longer have enough cases to sustain their studies. They're the only ones complaining.[15]

Sierra Leone wasn't one of the fifteen countries to receive some of the $1.2 billion in aid to fight its malaria problem, but at least I was there to represent the Sierra Leonean people in front of some of the most powerful individuals in the world. Sierra Leone and TGMF were still moving forward and my school was getting closer to being built. I met some amazing people that day including Special Agent Christman, who was assigned to protect President Bush. He was a fan of my work as an actor and as a humanitarian. We would cross paths again on yet another important trip to DC.

But before that was to happen, disaster struck again....

CHAPTER 17

Denial

January 15, 2007, was supposed to be a birthday celebration for two people who were very important to me. It was the birthday of the great civil rights leader and one of my personal idols, Martin Luther King Jr. It was my amazing wife, Jenisa Marie Washington's birthday as well. It also happened to be the day of the Golden Globes. My TV show was up for several awards. The evening would prove to be simultaneously one of the greatest and worst of my entire life.

Just twenty-four hours before, I had visited the Century City Hospital. My mother-in-law had just undergone brain surgery after suffering from several life-threatening aneurysms. She is okay now, but, ironically, when she collapsed, she was attending the wake of Swami Turiyasangitananda (Alice Coltrane), my wife's and my spiritual leader.

The day marked the fifth consecutive week of tabloid and media attacks against me. Headlines such as "Grey's Anatomy Star Uses Anti-Gay Slur, Is Rebuked" seemed to be everywhere.

In the car on the way to the event, I did something I had never done in my career. I drank some limousine liquor. I was thinking, "It's time for a celebration of health and life." For the next four hours I drank and I drank. I had arranged for a birthday cake to be brought out for my wife while at the *In Style* viewing party. I had also arranged for the on-duty security professionals to "clear a path" for me if my TV show won a Golden Globe. They agreed to do it.

At the Golden Globes, I listened quietly as the names of the nominees were read. And then, something miraculous happened. The presenter said, "And the Golden Globe for Best TV Drama goes to *Grey's Anatomy*."

I ran full speed like a running back on red turf. All of the security professionals had their positions locked off for me to make a smooth entrance into the dinner room, where I saw my boss and the show's creator step up to the microphone to give her acceptance speech. Everything seemed to be happening in slow motion as I walked as fast as I could toward the stage. I locked eyes with actor Hugh Grant, who was seated right next to the stage. He knew exactly what to do. Hugh parted his legs on his chair so I could step up between them and use his seat to unceremoniously hoist myself onto the stage and join my cast mates in the winner's circle.

One of the show's producers looked at me and said, "Where the hell did you come from?" The whole cast proceeded backstage. I saw Eddie Murphy and shook his hand. Then I shook hands and got a hug from Jamie Foxx. My phone rang. It was Susan Whitson and her entire staff calling from the Office of the

First Lady of the United States screaming their congratulations. I saw Disney President Bob Iger and shook his hand too. Disney executive Ann Sweeney was there, I shook her hand as well. It was an exciting moment. It was such a rush, such a high after the negativity that had stalked me for the previous few weeks. I walked up on the stage set up for post-award press interviews, sweating from the run and all of the excitement and adrenaline. Shonda stood at the mike, carefully cradling her Golden Globe statue as if it were a brand-new doll.

She looked so happy standing there smiling, shoeless, before the entire world. Then came the questions. First question: "What designers are all of the ladies wearing?" Second question: "Can you talk about the fight that happened on the set where Isaiah called T. R. Knight a homophobic slur?"

"NO, NO, NO! This can't be happening. Not here, not now," I thought to myself. I felt my breath leave my body. I heard grumbling in the room. I saw T.R. step up to the microphone. Trying to defuse the situation, he said, "Fight? What fight? There was no fight."

Then came a statement from Ted Casablanca, a gossip columnist: "No, Shonda, we are not going any further until you tell me why Isaiah"—he pointed at me—"called T. R. Knight a homophobic slur!"

Shonda just stood there, looking totally vulnerable and horrified. I blinked and when I looked again, standing right there under the hot bright lights, I saw Muh' Dear. She was refusing to let me back in the house if I did not return and fight the Frazier sisters who called me names, stole my money, and beat me up. Blink. I saw my mother jammed up against the wall, her feet dangling in midair, being hit and abused by my father and my stepfather. Blink.

For months I heard this *nasty word* being burned into my soul against my will, *threatening* to become synonymous with my name. Blink. I saw my biological father lying in a casket. Blink. I saw the faces of limbless children in Sierra Leone. Blink. I saw the children I promised a school and new hospital. Blink. Blink. I saw my boss being humiliated because of *me*....

"GET! OFF! MY! MAMA!" is what I heard myself say into the mike as I broke ranks from the rest of the cast, stepped in front of my heroine, the woman who believed in me and my talent, and who supported me—a strong, dark-skinned man. I tried to defend a precious moment in time for her. I was wrong. The world heard differently...and I would soon discover that no one needed *me* to be a hero that day.

The next day all hells of hell broke loose. The wrath I would receive from around the world came back at me even more strongly, burning out of control like a raging wildfire in the Southern California hills aggravated by the Santa Ana winds. I was sleeping less than four hours a night, filled with an indescribable level of anxiety. All I could do was operate as a human being, one minute at a time. I prayed constantly, in between GLAAD (the Gay & Lesbian Alliance Against Defamation) meetings, writing and rewriting letters of apology, filming PSAs, and dealing with what had become media insanity. I was forced to pay thousands of dollars for "crisis management."

I was in big trouble. I was now considered a monster. Everywhere I went, my car was trailed by photographers. I was hunted down with calls from Diane Sawyer and every other major talk show. They all wanted me on their sofa. They all wanted me to cry on air. I believe that most people's sanity would not have survived under similar circumstances. I was eviscerated daily and, at the same time, could feel the hatred inside of my own organs. In a strange way the evisceration started to feel humane. It's hard to explain, but the attacks began to mollify me. I fell upon a quote from Gandhi.

The weak can never forgive. Forgiveness is the attribute of the strong.

—Muhatma Gandhi

After discovering it, I began praying less for forgiveness and instead started praying to forgive.

Even though the outrage had boosted the ratings to twenty-four million viewers, up 31 percent from the season before, it was clear that my days on my TV show were numbered.

One day I drove home and, rather than going inside, remained sitting in the car in the garage for about an hour. As time went on, I did that more often. It took great amounts of energy and courage just to be able to walk through my own door and face my wife and children. I started to feel that I could no longer protect my own family. I wouldn't wish that feeling on my worst enemy, not even on the very people that seemed hell-bent on destroying me, my name, and everything connected to me.

I called my friend Denial and he set me straight. Denial can work as a powerful ally when your faith in yourself is shattered to the core. Denial is at least kind enough to keep your head up when the world has dropped on it. "This thing will blow over," Denial told me. "Soon life will return to normal."

Once Denial and I finished our conversation, I dialed Congresswoman Barbara Lee, whom I now considered a friend. I asked her what she thought of what was going on. She said, "Isaiah, I think you should resign as soon as possible. This thing is not going to end the way you think it is."

"ABC knows what they are doing, they told me that it all will blow over soon," I assured her.

"Isaiah, I don't know about that," she said.

I thanked her for her advice and hung up. I just continued sitting there in my garage. I didn't tell her that I was under a "gag order."

In late January 2007, I asked Shonda to release me from my contract. I apologized to her for bringing so much pain and chaos to her doorstep. It was never my intention. I thanked her for giving me and my family the greatest opportunity of my career. I asked her to allow me to clear my name.

"They want me to fire you, but how do I fire a man who is trying to change the world?" she said. I walked out of her office, away from "the Flagpole" (the nickname for the writers' offices) straight to my trailer. I closed the door, locked it, sat down. I cried harder than I ever had in my life.

At least TGMF was still moving forward. Sonya was able to plan a trip back to Sierra Leone with Breton F. Washington, the architect of the future Foday Golia Memorial School in Njala Kendema. The news of the school moving forward was inspiring, but every day the cast and crew tried to move forward meant another day they were subjected to screams and petitions calling for me to not only be dispatched from the TV show, but from the Earth.

I called my attorney, Peter Nelson. "I want to check myself in for counseling," I told him.

Peter asked, "Why would you want to do that, Isaiah?"

I said, "I will write my own letter of apology since they won't let me go on camera and defend myself. This is about my name. I want my name back. I will do the executive counseling that they offered. The world needs me to be crazy, so let me be crazy. But I have to write my *own* letter of apology. The people want to hear from me, not the network anymore. Can you make that happen?"

"I don't know, Isaiah. They seem to have their minds made up. They are dealing with a firestorm of bad press over this."

"Can you set up a deal with the network about my letter?"

I spoke to Shonda and she agreed to let me have time off for counseling, but the network PR people couldn't resist. They released a statement about me "needing help with my issues." Those who knew me recognized that the network-released statement didn't sound like me at all. But it was too late. I had been branded around the world as an angry black man, damaged goods, a fuckup, a bigot, a coward, a liar, a bully, a monster; someone not worthy of forgiveness, let alone a five-million-dollar-a-year salary.

I knew my tenure at ABC was over, but my life was not over. I had been severely bludgeoned and battered by the words "reportedly" and "allegedly" in the press, but I was still breathing. I had my friend Norrell Walker drive me to the private counseling location in Newport Beach.

I was watching the Screen Actors Guild Awards when my cast mate Chandra Wilson thanked me in her acceptance speech. "First of all, it's about those ten cast members sitting over there and the other one in rehab, I mean y'all just hold me together! I thank y'all so much!" The next day the press went crazy over the word "rehab." It was another nail in my proverbial coffin. I said aloud, "No, Chandra, it's 'executive counseling.'" I reached for my mobile phone, grabbed a cigar, walked outside the private residence, sat down on the patio, and cried some more. I had spoken with Chandra earlier that day just after she finished the red carpet. I texted her a note of congratulations for her win. There was a time delay so she got the text well after.

I checked out of the counseling facility after six days. While there I participated in:

- three psychiatric sessions
- four psychotherapy sessions with a clinical psychologist
- one spirituality session
- two life-coaching sessions
- three energy psychology (emotional release) sessions

- three amino acid therapy biochemical evaluations
- one tai chi session
- three massages
- three personal-training sessions
- three stress-management sessions
- two yoga sessions
- one nutritional consultation

I was diagnosed with an Axis I: 309.9 Adjustment Disorder. The recommended treatment was a six-month program of weekly follow-up meetings; weekly psychotherapy; weekly stress management, yoga, or meditation; weekly sessions with a personal trainer; and life-coaching sessions every other week.

On February 8, 2007, Sonya called me from Sierra Leone excited that she and Breton had broken ground for the new Foday Golia Memorial School, in Njala Kendema. The sun was shining brightly as I sat in my SUV in the parking lot on the set. Suddenly, it seemed out of nowhere, it started to rain. I looked at the beads of water on my windshield shimmering in the California sunlight like tiny diamonds, and said, "The devil is beating his wife!" I had witnessed this scene so many times in my life, in Houston as a boy, and thousands of miles away in Africa as a man. Now, here it was again in LA. But now it was happening in more ways than one. It was sunny outside and construction on the school was finally under way, and that was a good thing; but at the same time it was raining on my career and on my soul.

I climbed out of my SUV and walked into my trailer. I had some calls to make. I called my manager, Eric Nelson, and told him that I didn't want him to have to screen calls and duck the media anymore. I told him that he was great to work with, but I thought rather than fending off the press and defending me all day his time could be put to better use. I released him as my manager against his wishes. Next I called my publicist, Cynthia Snyder, one of the sweetest and most honorable people I know. I knew this situation was taking a toll on her. I also knew that she was in way over her head, but that she would try and weather the storm with me. Cynthia didn't need this in her life, no one did. I released her against her wishes as well. Of course the media reported otherwise. They wrote that I blamed her for my bad press!

I lit up a cigar, sat down, and opened up my laptop. My inbox was flooded with my crisis. I noticed one from a friendly source, my old friend Antonio K. Hubbard. He had sent me the following poem:

The Bridge Builder

An old man, going a lone highway
Came, at the evening, cold and gray,
To a chasm, vast, and deep and wide,
Through which was flowing a sullen tide.
The old man crossed in the twilight dim—
The sullen stream had no fears for him;

But he turned, when safe on the other side,
And built a bridge to span the tide.
"Old man," said a fellow pilgrim, near,
"You are wasting strength with building here;
Your journey will end with the ending day;
You never again will pass this way;
You've crossed the chasm, deep and wide—
Why build you this bridge at the eveningtide?"

The builder lifted his old gray head.
"Good friend, in the path I have come," he said,

"There followeth after me today,
A youth, whose feet must pass this way.
This chasm, that has been naught to me,
To that fair-haired youth may a pitfall be.
He, too, must cross in the twilight dim;
Good friend, I am building this bridge for him."

—W. A. Dromgoole[16]

My new publicist, Howard Bragman, and his team at Fifteen Minutes advised me on the dos and don'ts for my arrival at the 38th Annual NAACP Image Awards. He said that I would have to skip the red carpet and take my seat much later than everyone else. I was seriously considering not going at all, but Howard said that there was a very strong chance I would win an award. He predicted the media would pounce on me even more if I didn't attend.

Damn. No way out.

On March 2, 2007, I attended the awards and my friend Clarence B. Jones, former speechwriter and counsel to Martin Luther King Jr., personally wrote my acceptance speech in case I should win. He said, "Son, you shot yourself in the foot with this, but I'm going to walk with you."

It turned out I was able to use that speech. I was honored to be named Outstanding Actor in a Drama Series for *Grey's Anatomy*. That night eonline.com posted an article noting:

> The wrap-up music cut Washington off before he was finished. So, we'll never know whether he was about to acknowledge the recent conflict that prompted him to seek treatment for his "issues."[17]

The next day I received a call from Vic Bulluck from the NAACP. He said his phone had been ringing off the hook.

The cancer had spread. People were angry and outraged that the NAACP would give me an Image Award, and they were even more outraged that the entire audience gave me a standing ovation.

I guess it's true. People do believe everything they see on TV and read in the tabloids. I had apologized numerous times. I taped a PSA about the power of words for GLSEN (the Gay, Lesbian, and Straight Education Network), I played a gay character in a Spike Lee film ten years before, went through counseling, but it still wasn't enough.

I had been back at work for over six weeks. I didn't understand what it was about me that the world felt it needed to hate no matter what I did. I started to understand that this was deeper than the color of my skin or even my behavior. I knew now that DNA had memory. Could it be that it also had "enemy memory"? I thought back to the Canada Lee Award I had won in 2005, and his meteoric rise to fame and subsequent fall from grace. I started to wonder if the award that I thought was the key to discovering who I was instead was in fact some kind of horrific omen.

I continued to focus on my work with TGMF. It was the one place I felt that I could accomplish something, where I still had some measure of control. My work in Sierra Leone and the Foday Golia Memorial School were like heavenly blinders for my psychic peace. Not only did the people of Sierra Leone need me, I needed them.

CHAPTER 18

Cease and Desist

There was an announcement over the PA system that we would land in Liberia. "Why are we flying over Freetown into Monrovia, Liberia?" I asked.

The Astraeus Airlines flight attendant explained, "President Ellen Johnson Sirleaf's son Dr. David Sirleaf and other family members have had a death in the family and need to arrive in Liberia as soon as possible."

I walked over and introduced myself. Dr. David Sirleaf was very nice and offered me some champagne. After we had a few glasses together, he tried to convince me to get off the plane with him in Monrovia. He had heard about the work I was doing in Sierra Leone and wanted me to meet his mother. I was extremely honored, but I told him that I was on a tight schedule and had to get to Sierra Leone and return to the United States within a certain time frame.

"Maybe you can visit Liberia when you complete your stay in Sierra Leone," he said. I told him that would not be possible. I was scheduled to shoot my new film, *The Least of These,* in June. But I was excited. The good word about what I was doing was getting around!

May 24, 2007, marked my second trip to Sierra Leone. I was very happy to see Dr. Sheku T. Kamara and the staff at Hotel Barmoi again. I was given the same VIP room as before. Dr. Kamara arranged to have a live band playing music that night on the patio just for me. He even had some Bundu dancers.

Since my last trip, I had made some new additions to my team. Antonio K. Hubbard could not make this trip to run security, so he recommended another former marine, Malcolm "Mike" Bradford. Malcolm was a top criminal investigator in the United States Marine Corps. He held the rank of Master Sergeant while stationed at Camp Pendleton in California. He was amazing to travel with because he was very quiet and watchful. He could be in a room and yet have an amazing ability to be so unassuming he was virtually invisible at times. I also had a great new cameraman, Martin Proctor, and a soundman, Mark T. Laurent. Martin was an all-around great guy and proved to be a very good photographer in spite of being tormented by the Sierra Leonean children who constantly called him, *"white man."* In reality, Martin was a "light-skinned" brother. In spirit and rage, Martin was "blacker" than me! The renowned Academy Award–winning documentarian Chuck Workman, who reminded me so much of Harry Poe, was also on board as my filming director.

The legendary blogger/activist for lesbian, gay, bisexual, and transgender (LGBT) rights Jasmyne Cannick was also traveling with us. Jasmyne started a petition to keep me on my TV show. She was the only voice from the LGBT community who came to my defense and publically charged GLAAD and the media with racism. This would be Jasmyne's first time in Africa. Dr. Andre Panossian could not make the journey either, so I had Dr.

Zoanne Clack, also a writer/producer on my TV show, travel as my team physician.

Our first day of filming took place in downtown Freetown with Joe Opala. I was very anxious to get to BO and see the progress of the school in Njala Kendema. When we arrived at the school, Sonya and I waited for my tribal brother Raymond Scott-Manga. Raymond was running unusually late, even for "Africa time." Sonya was going over the ledger for the school with Raymond's younger brother, Josie Manga, and detected a discrepancy in the budget. There was $1,500 unaccounted for.

I sensed this was going to be a problem that could become a bigger issue if I didn't address it head-on. Sparks began to fly when Sonya confronted Raymond. As an American, you are often expected to accept "things as they are in Africa." I knew there were going to be some severe decisions to make that day. As if I didn't have enough to deal with already, going through hell back in America. The "media liability" speech Eric Nonacs had given to me before my first trip to Sierra Leone now applied to me, and I wasn't in the mood to give it to myself.

I was thinking, "If my money can 'disappear' then my potential investors' money could disappear too." I wasn't interested in hearing anyone tell me "I told you so" about trying to do business in Africa with Africans. So I decided to get creative while on the school site.

I was directing now; Chuck had had to get back to the States after we finished filming in Freetown. I knew empirically that I had to confront Raymond, his brothers Alieu and Josie, and Chief Lamin publically. They were very powerful in this village, but I needed to make a stand. I did.

There were protests in English and in Mende against my "implication" that one of them, if not all, had taken the $1,500. At one point I thought, "Isaiah, it's only $1,500, give them a break." I shot that thought down. That kind of rationale had stifled this country for centuries. The tension grew with every passing second.

The interpreter I had hired in Freetown was not a part of the Njala Kendema village. This fact proved to work to my advantage. I had quietly asked my interpreter to secretly ask the villagers working on the school if they had been paid and given their agreed upon stipends and food items. The answer came back a resounding no.

Someone was lying. I pressed them hard to find answers. I must admit that I truly appreciated how the brothers stuck together, but they knew I too bore the proud name of Manga.

Alieu eventually spoke up. "There were extenuating circumstances," he said. There was that phrase again. It was the same reason he had given when I had asked how they could have sold their brothers and sisters into slavery. I forgave then but never accepted it as right. And I didn't accept it now. Alieu put his head down and walked away from the conference circle. Aware that my cameras were capturing every moment, I decided to push Raymond harder for more drama. I had to sacrifice him. Yes, he was the man responsible for bringing me to Sierra Leone, but I could not allow this transgression to go unaddressed.

I watched Raymond step away from the conference circle in an attempt to escape my cameraman. On pure instinct, Martin pointed the camera in his direction without me saying a word. It hurt me, but I had to make my point. I said, "You see? This is what I was saying before my induction. This is why I forgave you for selling my ancestors."

Their muted grumbling shot around the village like a rabid bat and made my body twitch slightly. I could feel my adrenaline and heart rate begin to spike a bit. I eventually found my bearings and pushed on. I said, "Alieu, you see? DNA does have memory. You said the exact same thing to me the night before my induction and now you take money from me?"

There were extenuating circumstances. . . .

That did it for me. After that, the moments passed at lightning speed as Chief Lamin, the site manager, stepped in, stoically outraged. He was looking at me with hurt or concern in his eyes, holding both arms up waving them in a "now hold on" or "that is enough" fashion. At this point, I didn't care which.

I knew I had just broken a major rule in Africa. I just embarrassed my family in front of Sonya, my "white woman." Those words "white woman" are an important element of this story. Later in my dealings with the Manga brothers, they would become quite ironic. I would also discover that exposing them in front of Sonya was more of an insult than my accusing them of any fiscal impropriety.

I thought that because they had made me a chief that I was one of them. I thought that I could live and die by their rules. I didn't think that anyone would cut my throat on the spot, but they might possibly attack me when I left the country. And of course, history showed my people clearly knew how to hold a grudge. They had fought each other for eleven years.

I ascertained by their body language that if I were somebody other than Chief Gondobay Manga, I would have been instantly run out of this village, escorted by men wielding machetes and rocks. I knew without a shadow of a doubt that they understood that I was here out of love; I was here because I cared and desired to change this country one village at a time.

Armed with this new information about financial impropriety, I stood on the red dirt addressing the brothers. Slowly, the villagers were gathering around. The workers and my chief builder, Pa Musa, slowly assembled under a shade tree a few feet away. I knew that they had no idea what I was saying, but they could certainly feel that it wasn't good. The chief wasn't happy and I had a good damned reason not to be.

I pushed on, "How dare you. How dare you. I've come all the way across the ocean for this?"

Once, when charging through a particularly dense thicket, I stalled and lurched off my bike, landing hard on the dirt.

"My name, my reputation, my career is being destroyed in America as I speak."

My body itched and ached from the angry burrs that held fast to my clothes, skin, and hair. It was as if they were chastising me for disrupting their order. But, I remained undaunted, ignoring the pain of the razor-sharp weeds tearing at my hands. . . .

This cannot happen, you understand?"

. . . I yanked my bike's chain, pedals, and wheel spokes away from their snaking grasp and ripped them away from my legs.

"Raymond? Didn't I promise you that I would build a school? Isn't that what you wanted?"

Raymond mumbled, "No, I never told you to build a school."

I was unwilling to give up and lose face—I learned that from my grandmother Muh' Dear.

"What? Didn't you tell me that the only way I could show the people that I wanted to help them was to build something that they needed?"

Raymond said, "Isaiah, I don't remember telling you that."

"You don't remember? You don't remember, because it was bullshit! Once you saw that I was putting all my money into this school and not your agricultural center, you got mad. You mad at me? Then be mad, because I'm keeping *my word.*"

I remembered:

"Hmmm. You are a man of your word I see," he said.

"Yes, I am," I said.

"Be careful," he warned. "Men have died here trying to keep their word."

"If I die here keeping my word, that can only mean I will be in better company than I am now."

I turned and looked right at Raymond. "This school will be built with or without you."

I reached down and grabbed a piece of glass from a broken bottle I found lying on the ground near my leg and used it to chop away the weeds that still entangled my bicycle and me. Once free, I began to run using the bicycle as a makeshift plow, pushing and ripping my way forward as if my life depended on it. I had no idea where the hell I was or the path I took to get there.

If I knew anything about African men and their pride, and I did, I knew that this wasn't going to be the end of this. Either way, they now knew what kind of African American man I was.

Dr. Clack and I began to set up shop in one of the mud huts that currently served as the children's school. I always tried to offer some medical attention and examinations when I came to Sierra Leone. It might have been on a small scale, but something was better than nothing at all. Dr. Clack and I noticed that many of the children were suffering from some sort of skin disorder, lesions. It looked frightening and very painful.

Dr. Clack could not identify the virus. Still, word of our work had spread to the neighboring villages, and people started bringing their children for help. We were completely overwhelmed and unprepared. When I saw that we were about to run out of Tylenol and antibiotics I tried to slow down the process. There was a line of about a hundred women and children waiting outside for medical assistance, but I needed to save some of the supplies for my village, Ngalu.

The heat was unrelenting. I needed a distraction. I asked my driver, Mohamed, to start slipping some of our goods out of the examining area. The villagers were playing music. I walked out into the middle of the village and began to dance to the beat. The locals began to form a close circle around me. We all fell in line, circling and singing, circling and singing.

Meanwhile, Mohamed was slipping the goods into his Land Rover. I was still singing and dancing, the heat no longer affecting me as much as the rising dust, stirred up from our movement, making it harder for me to breathe. But I kept on dancing anyway. I began slashing at the air with my *Tikpoi* (staff) as if it were a spear. The villagers went crazy, singing louder and playing harder.

I could feel my lungs tightening, but I kept going. I could feel the people around me filling me up with all that they could afford to give me...their love, their respect, their gratitude. I could feel the spirit of each and every one of them latching on to mine, strengthening me. I looked over at Jasmyne, who was also dancing; she had a beautiful blissful look on her face, like she was in heaven. A *Ngoboi* dancer showed up covered in raffia and replete with the ancient spirit to "clear my path." I danced along with the *Ngoboi,* and the villagers went even crazier, dancing and singing and cheering at a frenzied pace. My interpreter pulled me aside later and told me that the villagers wanted me to know that the dance moves I was using, unbeknownst to me, were ancient *Ngoboi* moves.

When I finally stopped and caught my breath, I could see that Mohamed had succeeded at his mission. I started to help pack up the other Land Rovers with supplies. As I hoisted a carton into the back of one of the trucks, I felt something bumping into my leg. I turned around to find little Ambrose Wudie, the little boy who had had the granuloma on his face, the one that Dr. Panossian and I removed last year. He just stood there, looking at me, smiling the biggest, most beautiful smile.

Ambrose tagged alongside me as I made one last walkthrough of the school and thanked the construction workers before I left. Ambrose's father walked up to me and gave me a live chicken and a pineapple as gifts to take with me.

I gave Ambrose a gentle handshake and told him I would see

him soon. The team mounted up and headed for Ngalu. Raymond, chastised but still cordial, led us all to the village, past Pandoh Mountain and through the tall grassy lands of my ancestral country.

When we arrived, Nyande Manga, Raymond's mother, and my tribal mother, was there to greet us. I gave her a hug and a kiss. Unloading some bed nets we had brought along with us, we began to distribute them. I took the live chicken and the pineapple Ambrose's father had given me and gave them to Mama Nyande. She smiled, said thank you, and then disappeared into the house. I could hear her barking orders to the women cooking in the backyard.

Raymond wanted to show me the rice fields that were being plowed, and pointed out the massive acreage filled with palm nut trees. It was a beautiful sight. He also took me on a ride on a tractor that I had helped purchase. When I hopped up on it, dressed in my dark blue coveralls and boots, the very same ones I had worn to the *Blood Diamond* premiere, I felt like a cross between a field general and a construction worker. Raymond had good reason to be proud. I could see the years of his hard work and passion for this farm. There were rows and rows of rice growing for as far as the eye could see.

When it was time to eat, I, following custom, had to eat first because I was chief. After I had my fill of rice and goat's meat, everyone else joined in. And eat they did. The meat we ate came from the goat given to me during my induction ceremony when I became chief. It is customary for the newly made chief to eat the goat upon his return. "Sorry, goat," I thought as I ate, "but I had to come back."

After lunch, Dr. Clack and I set up shop in the same house where Dr. Panossian had done his examinations during our first visit to Sierra Leone. After we handed out the last of the Tylenol and antibiotics, I gave my last hugs, thumbs-ups, and winks; it was time to head back to Freetown.

We traveled back along a northern route, driving through Makeni, Sierra Leone's fifth-largest city. Makeni is mostly inhabited by the Temne people. Something told me to ride in the very last Land Rover in our convoy. I would later learn why I had this inkling. After driving for nearly two hours, we pulled over for a pee break. I walked through some abandoned buildings that I remembered being filled with villagers the last time I had passed through. Suddenly, about twelve children appeared, seemingly out of nowhere, and immediately began to beg. I smiled but ignored their requests and returned to my SUV. We all piled back into the trucks and started to drive off.

The children started running alongside our convoy. I watched in awe at how fast they moved. They were actually keeping up with the pace of the Land Rovers, so much so that they had outpaced mine and were now running in front of it. I saw something fly out of the window of the truck ahead. Then I saw the group of children descend on whatever it was, struggling over it on the ground. As we got closer, one of the little boys fell right in front of my Land Rover's huge black tires. The driver yanked on the steering wheel and swerved so hard to the left that our vehicle nearly tipped over from the centrifugal force of the maneuver, missing running over the fallen boy's head by only inches.

The object of the struggle was now apparent—it was an empty plastic water bottle. In Sierra Leone, tossing a plastic bottle on the ground is equivalent to throwing money out the window. The bottles were very valuable. They could be sold for a great deal of money or used to store clean water or palm wine.

I told my driver to flash his headlights and signal to the driver ahead of us to pull over and stop. I got out and calmly walked up to the vehicle in front of us. "Who threw the bottle outside?" I asked. No one answered immediately. Then, finally, Martin, my cameraman, admitted that he did it. I was shocked. I knew he had traveled to Africa just as much, if not more, than me.

"Did you see what happened?" I asked, trying to stay calm.

Martin looked confused. "See what?"

"The children started fighting over the bottle you tossed out the fucking window, Martin! My driver almost ran over a boy! Do you have any idea how fucking bad that would have been?"

"I was just—" he started to say.

"No! You fucked up! The next time you want to *help,* try getting out of the fucking truck and place the bottle in the child's hand! Treat them like they are human beings!"

He tried to speak again, "I thought—"

I cut him off. "I know what you thought and you were wrong! Don't let it happen again! Do you understand?"

He nodded. "Yes."

I was so shaken by the image of what could have happened to that child, not to mention the thought of even more media scrutiny back in the States, that I just turned and started walking. I walked past and ahead of the lead SUV. I kept on walking until I was about one hundred yards away from my team. Then I veered off the road and into the bushes, bent over, and threw up. When I finished, I took a deep breath and I thanked God for sparing us and that little boy's life. I stepped back up onto the street and stood for several minutes looking at the convoy of SUVs lined up behind me. "Why the hell am I doing this?" I thought. "God, tell me why am I here doing this?" I stood there for a few minutes more, trying to pull myself back together.

Dr. Clack got out and started walking toward me, but I motioned for her to go back. I silently made my way toward the convoy, walking past everyone without saying a word. Back at my SUV, I opened the back door and grabbed my satchel. I looked inside, reached in, and pulled out my Tibetan prayer beads. I had purchased them back in LA and used them as spiritual protection. I sometimes even wore them on my body.

I climbed into the cramped backseat of the Land Rover and

told my driver to take the lead. As we picked up speed I looked back at the winding convoy following behind us and clasped my beads in my hands. I started to pray a Hindu chant called "*O bhagavan.*" It means God Supreme Being.

We arrived back in Freetown safely and without further incident.

I asked Mohamed to take me to Paddy's, the famous restaurant and music hall. Malcolm, Dr. Clack, and Jasmyne joined us. I ordered the fish and rice dinner from the waitress, who recognized me from my trip the previous year and began to spread the word that I was there.

A few tables over was a group of about twelve Chinese men engaged in a very intense debate over the price for some prostitutes. The air in the restaurant was becoming very tense. The men were loud, cursing in their own language. I was concerned for the women's safety. I left the table and headed to the restroom to wash my hands. As I stood at the sink, a man—tall and sinister looking, his energy very dark—appeared behind me. He said the manager wished to speak with me. Without telling Malcolm, I agreed to the invitation and allowed the man to escort me into a back room of the restaurant.

As I stepped through the door he locked it behind us. He asked me to stand near the now locked door as he proceeded to unlock yet another one and gestured for me to walk through. As I stepped into the second room, a cramped little pantry-like space, he closed that door behind me and I heard him click another lock shut. Lying on the floor next to my right foot was a huge chainsaw caked with what looked like blood on its caustic blade.

"Now that's really a good deterrent. I gotta remember that one," I thought to myself.

I heard the jangling sound of keys and the click clack of opening locks on the other side of the door in front of me. As it opened, a heavyset man stood there with a wide smile and invited me in. "Mr. Washington," he said, "I see you made it back to our great country. How have you been?"

I thought maybe he was the manager of Paddy's.

"I'm back, just as I promised," I said, "but life has been a little rough on me these days."

"Yes, yes, so I've heard," he replied. "What the hell, you are home now. If you need anything, and I mean anything, you just call on me, okay?"

"I will keep that in mind. So, I see that you keep a chainsaw in your...ah...waiting room."

He laughed. "This is Sierra Leone; you can never be too careful, no?"

"Yeah, I guess you're right. So...is there anything you need from me?"

"No, I just want to make sure that you are having a good time."

"Yes, I am! So far, so good. Thank you. Now that I think about it, I guess you can help me out with something."

"Anything," he said.

"The Chinese guys out there, who do they work for?"

He rolled his eyes. "Oh yes, the Chinese! They are slowly taking over. They are fishermen, pumping fish out of our waters twenty-four-seven. There is tension growing between the workers and the people here."

"Yes, I noticed."

"They work on the fishing boats for months and when they come to the mainland, they have lots of money to spend," he explained.

"I see."

"Well, I will let you get back to your guests, eh? Please enjoy your meal, the drinks are on me."

When I told him that wasn't necessary, he said, "Please, please I insist!"

I shrugged my shoulders and agreed. "Okay. As you wish. Thank you."

With that he unlocked the door and walked me out of his office. The man who walked me in was waiting for me on the other side. We went through the entire locking and unlocking process again in reverse. Finally, I washed my hands and returned to my table. My food was there waiting, and I was very hungry now. I sat down and devoured it.

My team returned to Bunce Island, this time on official business. The power of the engines rumbled and growled. I watched the American and Sierra Leone flags flap loudly in the wind as it beat against my face. Bunce Island grew larger and larger as we approached the shore, riding in the boat generously donated by Ambassador Thomas Hull. He had heard about the little boating incident from our last visit to the island, when we had to return to shore navigating by the stars, and offered up use of his private vessel.

Chuck staged some really nice shots for me, and Joe Opala gave us the exact same tour as last time. Jasmyne became very agitated and hurt by what she heard and saw, affected much in the same way I was when I first heard the history of Bunce Island.

As the tour ended, I was told that the little boy from whose back Dr. Panossian and I removed the tuberculosis cysts had arrived. I was overjoyed to see him. Dr. Panossian had been sure he was too sick to survive, but there he was, standing right in front of me! I hugged him gently and shook his father's hand. I couldn't stop staring at him. "He survived. He survived," I thought to myself. I gave them some money, careful to make sure no one else saw me. Then we loaded back into the boat and headed back to Freetown.

★   ★   ★

This second trip was successful. There were no major incidents, we had no media liability, and the school was 75 percent complete. But traveling back to the United States this time wasn't as simple. While in Gatwick Airport, Mark, my soundman, had been stopped and was being held at security. Sonya sent the flight attendant to discreetly give me the message. She whispered for me to get off the plane and follow her. I arrived at the boarding gate back in the terminal and was greeted by a woman dressed head to toe in black. She went by the name "the Dragon Lady." She escorted Sonya and me back to the security area. I could see Mark standing there surrounded by the London police.

"What's going on?" I asked one of the officers. One of them produced the steel expandable police baton that a special agent had given me for our first trip to Sierra Leone. I had been carrying it in my backpack and had given it to Mark to walk through the security line because I had two other bags to carry. Mark apparently told them it was camera equipment. And they didn't buy it. I had completely forgotten about it.

The police then turned their focus on me and asked if it was mine. "Damn," I said, "I thought I lost it!" For the next hour and a half, I was held for questioning right there in the open. I was asked to sign all kinds of police reports. Even though I was surrounded by London's antiterrorist unit, passing fans wanted to take photographs and have me sign autographs.

Obviously they couldn't hold the plane and my team had to return home without Mark, Sonya, and me. Eventually the commanding officer came over, looked me up and down, and then gave me a stern verbal warning. They confiscated the baton and let us go. Sonya arranged for a hotel and we spent the night in London.

Sonya and I weren't back in Los Angeles for a week when we received a call from Mohamed with news that Chief Lamin and Josie Manga tried to "rehire" themselves and return to the site of the school. When I hired Mohamed at the school, it was because I knew I could trust him. He told us that the chief of Njala Kendema had run them off. When Raymond Scott-Manga found out about what had happened to Chief Lamin and Josie he was not happy about it to say the least.

I knew when I confronted them about the missing $1,500 that the Manga brothers couldn't cut my throat in front of the villagers, but I also knew Raymond Scott-Manga was pretty upset, and as the older brother of us all, he would have to retaliate to save face. Raymond emphatically explained to me that by firing Chief Lamin and Josie without bringing the matter to a village council for a vote or a fair trial I had broken a traditional African custom. "Raymond, I don't have time for all of that," I responded. "Sonya and I gave you all ample time to come up with the missing money, prove that the ledger was wrong, or at least offer an apology for the error. But all we got was anger and denial. The bottom line is that fifteen hundred dollars is not accounted for and if I do not show 'zero tolerance' for this now, how can we expect anyone to believe that business practices have changed in Sierra Leone? It is clear to me that if I cannot maintain proper oversight in building a school in my own village, with my own money, how, in good faith, could I solicit future donors and future investors to invest in Sierra Leone? I told you that I am here to help the people of Sierra Leone, not help hurt them. Like it or not, Mohamed Kamara is the new project manager, end of story!"

After receiving a series of very nasty e-mails and threats from Raymond, including banning Sonya from the village, demanding that I fire her, and labeling her a "white she devil" (which I thought was ironic since my good brother Raymond had been married to a white woman for over twenty years), I had had enough. I figured that it was time for me to show my power—my American power. I needed to remind Raymond, quickly and decisively, that I did not *live* in Sierra Leone and was one of the few African Americans willing to engage this war-torn nation in a respectful and serious way. I needed to let him and *others* know that I fully intended on asphyxiating any form of corruption from the ground up, one village at a time. Once he saw that I was not going to fire Sonya and side with him, my dear brother Raymond declared war!

That was exactly what I didn't need, more media liability.

As the president of TGMF, Sonya sought Bradford's advice to find a way, without actually filing a lawsuit, to stop Raymond from launching his verbal assaults. The press would have a field day with anything even closely resembling legal action against Isaiah Washington's foundation.

Sonya characterized Raymond's e-mail attacks as similar to "a child throwing a tantrum in the grocery store," embarrassing, yes, but she could handle them. Her concern, our concern, for TGMF was making sure our professional contacts didn't get caught up in the drama. We wanted them to continue to have faith that the foundation was legitimate and well run with regard to all business matters.

Bradford advised that as she was the president of TGMF, any attacks against Sonya almost bound her to protect her image, thereby protecting that of our organization. He recommended employing some kind of legal remedy to protect both TGMF and her. He also pointed out that any terroristic threats from Raymond should be taken very seriously. In our current day and age, they were, in fact, illegal.

Bradford advised Sonya to have all letters and e-mail traffic reviewed by our lawyers. I had noticed Sonya's attitude toward the "natives" and had mentioned it to her more than once. It came out sometimes in her tone when she spoke to the Sierra Leonean people. A bit of a control freak, Sonya would get frustrated with the language barrier and doing things in "Africa time." I took full responsibility for the cultural fallout. I was certain that Sonya's heart was in the right place. Unfortunately for me, I was stuck between two allegiances and I had no time to make everything right for Raymond. If I had to sacrifice my relationship with him in the short term, then so be it. I knew that in the long run, as long as I continued my work in Sierra Leone, Raymond Scott-Manga was going to be my brother for life. In my heart of hearts I knew that his tactics were just over-the-top posturing. But I also knew that I could not allow him to hurt himself, or what he and I had planned to do for Sierra Leone. I don't know who took the money. I only know it was missing. This illustrates how difficult it can be sometimes to give aid in Sierra Leone. It was a difficult time. Thank God Raymond and I would later make amends. However, in that moment, Sonya was the president of TGMF and TGMF was me. I had to protect her and myself immediately.

So, we proceeded with legal action as advised and a cease and desist order was issued to my brother Raymond Scott-Manga. I quickly found out that being a true leader and a Mende chief was not for the faint of heart.

My life *evolved* on June 7, 2007, four days after I returned from Sierra Leone to Los Angeles. I got a call from Shonda telling me to call my publicist, agent, and attorney.

"Isaiah," she said, "I have been fighting for you for the last three hours and I can't stop it. It's been released to the Associated Press. You're not coming back to the show."

"Shonda, you've got to be kidding me! After all we've been through? After all that I've done to make it right? Okay, FINE.

You know I have to clear my name now. You know I'm going to fight to clear my name!"

I heard Shonda sigh as if I had just kicked her in the stomach. She knew that this wasn't going to go away anytime soon for her either. I hung up and called Howard Bragman, my new publicist. I said, "I'm mad as hell and I'm not going to take it anymore!" Unfortunately, Howard used my comment to *him* as my response statement to the Associated Press. It backfired tremendously. No one got that it was a reference to the movie *Network*. I was now viewed as the angriest black man on the planet!

It seemed that there were issues coming at me from all four corners of the earth—someone or something constantly wanted or needed my full attention. I knew that for every action there is a reaction; and everything that was happening to me was happening because of *my* actions, but it is important to note that I was not "fired on the spot," as it has been reported. My contract was not renewed after I returned to the show *eight months* after the incident with Patrick Dempsey, where he admits to provoking me vehemently in front of thirty-five fellow employees. You should also know that on June 7, 2007, when I received the news that I would not be returning to my TV show, I was working on the independent film *The Least of These* and shooting a scene where my character overhears a private conversation among his superiors on how he was going to be allowed to take the fall for something he did not do and be thrown to the wolves within the press. Some people might say ironic, or another story hard to believe. It was yet another of the many defining moments that have guided and prepared me for the huge transitions and changes that have characterized my life. Personal growth and change are never easy. To *evolve* is the key to life. I no longer subscribe to the revolutionary concept of living life. Historically, I realized that all "revolutionaries" died violently or were co-opted by subversive tactics.

★   ★   ★

In all of the turmoil that resulted from leaving my TV show, I found an invaluable gift. I had already cleared out my trailer and successfully completed all the episodes and contractual obligations by the end of the season in May 2007. I realized that my resistance in life was never against authority, my stepfather, father figures like Harry Poe, coaches, COs in the air force, as I had once thought. *My resistance was always against ignorance and fear.* I now knew that I was born to confront any construct that prevents change. To *evolve* is necessary for all progression and for the survival of all living things. If I survived, I lived, and if I lived I had to evolve. To evolve made me a part of an *evolutionary process.* To participate in the *evolutionary process,* to proactively and positively participate in life as a global citizen, to discover and know where my origins are on that great African continent have made me an *evolutionary.* People often ask me how I feel about what happened, to tell them what my thinking is about it all today. To be honest, it is still evolving just as I am. Perhaps as I grow and change I will be able to describe it in my next book. For now, I have written all I want to say about it. I am still learning more every day about the responsibilities of my newfound identity and hope that all the parties involved during the debacle surrounding my former TV show have evolved and found peace with the past as I have.

CHAPTER 19

It's Raining, It's Sunny, the Devil Is Beating His Wife...Again

It was eight weeks later when I received a delightful call from Sonya. I was in Vancouver working on my new TV show, NBC's *Bionic Woman*. Sonya told me that the IRS and Department of the Treasury had sent the Gondobay Manga Foundation its tax exemption identification number.

The letter was dated August 6, 2007, just three days after my forty-fourth birthday. It was official. TGMF was now a bona fide nonprofit organization. I congratulated Sonya for her hard work. I hung up and called my pro bono accountant Steve Churchwell of DLA Piper, Rudnick, Gray, Cary, LLP, and thanked him for all of his efforts to push the TGMF application through.

I hung up the phone, walked to my hotel window, and exclaimed, "The devil is beating his wife!" I gazed out, and, once again, with all the rain pouring down in my life, the sun was figuratively still shining through. This was a victory.

Another symbol of the sun shining through entered my life in the form of Maria Elena Lamas. Maria was a huge supporter of my work and me on my former TV show and a member of an online fan site called bangsanatomy.com. Maria had learned about my work in Sierra Leone and decided that she wanted to become involved with TGMF. She had a bright and shining smile, complemented by her equally bright and shining spirit. She spoke very fast and had an enthusiasm and a sense of urgency about helping people and getting things done that matched my own. I knew that she was a godsend, a Cuban angel, when I first met her, I just didn't know to what extent. Maria Elena Lamas would soon become *the* driving force behind TGMF.

On September 17, 2007, Dr. Ernest Bai Koroma was successfully democratically elected as the new president of the Republic of Sierra Leone. Howard Bragman, my new publicist, called me from his LA office to say that CNN and the BBC wanted a comment from me regarding the election. I declined. I was concerned that the media would somehow use me to turn this wonderful event in Sierra Leone into a negative.

The attacks from the media had amped up with my presence on *Bionic Woman*. In fact, there was a full-scale war of words in the media between my new boss, Ben Silverman at NBC, and my old boss, Steve McPherson at ABC.

I thought back to the conversation I had had with Moza Cooper when she called to tell me I was the perfect person to receive the Canada Lee Award. When Canada Lee was blacklisted in Hollywood and became the subject of the era's yellow journalism, it destroyed his reputation forever. Lee died penniless at forty-five years old. I thought to myself, "Oh my God, I'm forty-four!"

While I was pumping gas into my SUV one day, someone screamed out of their passing car, "Hey, Isaiah, you're in the news more than President Bush!" I placed the nozzle back in its resting place, climbed back into my vehicle, and noticed that I had a missed call on my cell. It was from Pamela G. Alexander from Ford Motor Company. She left a message that she was calling to invite me to be her special guest at the 37th Annual Congressional Black Caucus Dinner in Washington, DC. I immediately called her back and accepted the invitation.

I had attended the CBC dinner as the master of ceremonies, along with actress Sheryl Lee Ralph, the previous year. The event was particularly special because Senator Barack Obama, Senator Hillary Rodham Clinton, and Representative Nancy Pelosi were all there under one roof.

My celebrity was well received there. I was even a little embarrassed at all of the attention I got from fans. But what I needed was the attention of the African American corporate executives who had either sponsored the CBC Foundation or were members.

I collected more than twenty-five business cards that night, but, unlike at other previous events, not one of the card owners wanted to take a photo with me. I knew I was "radioactive" when it came to corporate sponsorship but I still had to try.

As the evening came to a close, I thanked Pamela for her many introductions that evening and returned to Los Angeles knowing that I was a *marked man*. I personally made follow-up calls to every single one of the corporate executives I'd met at the dinner that night. Not one of my calls was ever returned.

On October 19, 2007, my new friend Zainab Bangura, whom I had first met in the airport waiting for our flight back to the United States after my first trip to Sierra Leone in 2006, was sworn in as the Minister of Foreign Affairs. In an article published by ipsnews.net, she was quoted saying, "I am the architect of Sierra Leone's multilateral and bilateral relations with the international community and this is a challenge I am prepared to shoulder."[18]

*   *   *

In November, I traveled to DC again to put all of my positive energy and focus on the preservation of the Slave Castle
ruins on Bunce Island, part of my 365-Day Plan. No matter
what was happening in the rest of my life, I had to stay focused
on my work in Sierra Leone. Joe Opala had set up the day of
meetings, bringing about twenty-five people together from the
United States, United Kingdom, and Sierra Leone. The sum-
mary of the day published on the Web site bunce-island.org.uk
noted:

> By the end of the meeting, it was clear that the urgent
> priority is to carry out an engineering survey to estab-
> lish the possibility and cost of stabilization work, while
> working with the relevant authorities in Sierra Leone to
> establish a longer-term plan for conservation and devel-
> opment of the site. The meeting also led to the develop-
> ment of a strategy for the US and UK to work together
> in support of Bunce Island.[19]

That same month the Writers Guild strike started. More than
twelve thousand writers hit the picket lines. My deal at NBC
was fulfilled, *Bionic Woman* was canceled, and I was officially
unemployed again with no prospects in sight. All of my efforts
in Sierra Leone were being severely threatened as was my ability to support myself and my family. My business manager was
in full crisis mode and was insisting that I shut down TGMF.
He begged and pleaded for me to stop funding the organization
with my own money. My wife, Jenisa, stepped up her concerns
and began to apply pressure to shut down TGMF as well.

I ignored their pleas and pushed on. I had to finish what I
started. I had given my *word*.

"If I die here keeping my word, that can only mean I will be in better company than I am now."

On November 15, 2007, the Foday Golia Memorial School was completed and opened for the children of the village of Njala Kendema. The TGMF project manager, Mohamed Kamara, sent me some very inspiring photos of the students standing in front of the school smiling and waving. I was very happy, but my smile would soon be wiped away by the media attacks that continued from around the world.

There was a petition circulating on the Internet in January 2008, one year after my Golden Globes moment. It was signed by over five thousand fans essentially voicing their concerns over what they believed was the deterioration of the plot line of my former TV show. Unfortunately for me, the result was that my name was brought up all over again on various blogs as the *reason* my former TV show began to decline in the ratings.

I wanted to pull my hair out as I watched my name and my brand slowly and methodically become two of the most negative words in the world. The continued demonization was impacting everything. I was running out of political clout on the Hill as quickly as I was running out of money. I had a huge overhead I was trying to maintain. Without my five-million-dollar-a-year salary, I had to make some sacrifices.

In an attempt to quell the voices of discontent from my wife and business manager, I released Sonya of her duties as TGMF president and closed the TGMF doors. I was devastated.

After one hundred days on the picket lines, the Writers Guild strike ended on February 12, 2008. But the damage was done. Not only was there a work shortage in Hollywood, but for me personally, my name was no longer on the short list as a potential choice to be an actor for *any* project.

I was now my own worst nightmare, a *media liability.*

In spite of all this, there was one person from the Hill who reached out to me, Ms. Jackie B. Parker, deputy legislative director for Senator Carl Levin. Ms. Parker called and invited me to speak about my work in Sierra Leone and my "DNA Has Memory" theory before members of the Senate Black Legislative Caucus (SBLC). I wholeheartedly accepted her invitation.

I started thinking about whom else I could meet while I was in DC. While I had to close down TGMF for financial reasons, there was no reason I couldn't continue with my vision to help the people of Sierra Leone, my people. Besides, my acting career was in ruins, it's not as if the phone were ringing off the hook with offers for movie or TV roles.

I remembered that I had once received an invitation to play golf with HUD Secretary Alphonso Jackson. I had met him through Ann Walker Marchant of the Walker Marchant Group. Ann spent six years in the White House, where she served as Special Assistant to the President and Director of Research and Special Projects for Communications for President Clinton. She was responsible for developing and implementing communications strategy in support of key presidential initiatives and she was, and remains, very supportive of my mission for Sierra Leone.

As soon as I hung up with Ms. Parker, I called Secretary Jackson's office to see if I could set up a meeting with him regarding my work. Secretary Jackson not only agreed to a meeting with me, but reminded me that he was committed to the pledge he made when we met the previous November to help preserve Bunce Island.

Secretary Jackson reached out to Secretary of the Interior Dirk Kempthorne and asked him to join us. The next call I made was to the office of Congressman John Conyers Jr., House Committee on the Judiciary of the U.S. House of Representatives. I spoke with his chief of staff Cynthia Martin Esq. and arranged a meeting between Congressman Conyers and Sierra Leone's newly democratically elected president, Ernest Bai Koroma, for later in the year.

On February 27, 2008, I spoke before members of the Senate Black Legislative Caucus in the Senate Building. Ms. Parker thought that it was a great success. Immediately after the meeting, I left the Senate Building and had my driver, Lorenzo Miller, drive me to the U.S. Department of Housing and Urban Development.

Lorenzo said, "Wow, Mr. Washington. I just want to say that I am very proud of you and what you are doing for Africa. I wish that there were more brothers like you."

"Well, if I can help rebuild Sierra Leone before the world," I said, "then hopefully it will inspire more brothers like me to do the same elsewhere. I'll call you when I am ready to go. Wish me luck!" I said as I jumped out of the car.

"Good luck and God bless you, brother!" Lorenzo called after me.

I walked into the building and was instantly struck by the beautiful photographs and artwork that lined the walls. Secretary Jackson's assistant came down to greet me and escorted me up to his office.

It was an old building and I could feel the long history of development deals from over the years emanating from the hallways as we walked toward the secretary's office. Just outside the waiting room an armed guard stood watch. "Why does the HUD secretary need armed security?" I wondered.

Just then, I heard Secretary Jackson's booming and confident voice inviting me in as his office door flew wide open. "Isaiah, I'm so glad that you could make it. How have you been?" he said.

FLASH! The house photographer snapped my photo as I stepped in the room and embraced Secretary Jackson. He asked if the Secretary of the Interior had arrived yet. "He's not running late, is he?" he said to one of his staff members, who replied that he was on the way.

"Come over here to the window," Secretary Jackson said. "Have you ever seen such a beautiful view of Washington?"

"No, sir, this is quite spectacular," I agreed.

"I absolutely love this view," he explained. "It reminds me every day how important my job is. I just love it."

At that moment Secretary of the Interior Dirk Kempthorne walked in and said, "I see you are showing off your view again, Alphonso."

I turned to face him and shook his hand. *FLASH!* I was nailed again by the house photographer. The three of us posed for a photo and then proceeded into the secretary's private chamber to have lunch. The dining room was magnificent; its windows opened to the same beautiful view of the Potomac as the one from his office.

Secretary Jackson jumped right in and immediately explained to Secretary Kempthorne about my efforts and accomplishments in Sierra Leone, and expounded on the Bunce Island preservation committee. Secretary Kempthorne listened attentively. As Secretary Jackson began to wind down his pitch, he looked at me, and I took the baton and gave Secretary Kempthorne my theory on DNA having memory.

I asked Secretary Jackson what country he felt most comfortable in, insisting that he answer as honestly as possible. I noticed that he looked very Asian. "Well," he said, "I feel very connected to Africa—"

I interrupted, "Sir, please, if I may reiterate. I want to know what country *you* feel the most comfortable in, where you would have no problem living and dying."

Secretary Jackson thought for a moment, "Well, Isaiah, that country would be China." Secretary Kempthorne looked on with great curiosity. "That's very interesting," he said. "You know I have been thinking about this connection we feel with other peoples and I feel a strong connection with the Nez Percé" (Native Americans living in the Pacific Northwest). "I think you are on to something here."

"Dirk," Secretary Jackson asked, "is there any money available to help Isaiah preserve Bunce Island?"

"No, there is no funding left, it's all going to the Iraq War," he replied. "But I do know of an organization that may be able to help. Isaiah, have you heard of the African American Experience Fund program?"

I said that I hadn't.

Secretary Kempthorne offered to give me some contacts there and suggested they might be able to assist me.

"Thank you, sir, that would be very helpful," I said.

We all began eating our lunch and mused about DNA having memory. After we finished, I thanked Secretary Kempthorne and Secretary Jackson for their time and gracious advice. They both wished me well.

I called Lorenzo, who asked if I planned to go back to the Hotel George. "No," I told him, "drive me to the Hart Building. I can't come to this town and have a friend and fan find out I was here and didn't stop by and say hello."

That friend was Ms. Ashley Tate-Gilmore, who had helped facilitate my meeting with Senator Barack Obama when I was lobbying on the Hill in June 2006. A huge supporter of my efforts in Sierra Leone and a fan of my former TV show, Ashley also happened to work for Senator Obama. Lorenzo dropped me off at the Hart Building and the security guards waved me in saying, "We know who you are, Mr. Washington, you don't have to go through the metal detectors. You're in town lobbying for Sierra Leone, aren't you?"

I laughed and said, "Aren't I always?"

One of the guards said, "You're going to Senator Obama's office, right?"

"Yes, sir!" I replied.

I walked into Senator Obama's office and sat with Ashley at her desk. The rest of the staff members looked on in awe that Ashley knew "Dr. Preston Burke." As we caught up on the latest CBC gossip, I noticed stacks and stacks of Barack Obama's book *The Audacity of Hope* surrounding her work area.

"Oh my God," I joked, "are all these signed for me?" We both laughed. We talked about how cold it was outside, and I began to share my opinions on the campaign. Ashley and a senior Obama staff member, who was sitting nearby, quickly hushed me. "Isaiah, this office has ears," Ashley said. "If you want to talk politics we will have to do it in the senator's office." She escorted me away from the area of cubicles and walked me into the senator's empty office.

I realized that I had been running all day and had not checked my e-mails. I asked if it would be okay to use the computer. She said, "As long as you are *just checking your e-mails* it shouldn't be a problem." She put in her security code and left me alone. I was in Senator Barack Obama's office; I couldn't believe it. I just sat there in awe of all the family portraits of his wife, Michelle, and their daughters placed prominently on the huge wall. I noticed a Holy Bible grounded at the upper right-hand corner of his desk. There was a huge photograph of Muhammad Ali knocking out Sonny Liston, and another of Senator Obama and Nelson Mandela. I sat at the computer and began to feel as if I were privy to something very sacred.

I felt as if my body wanted to get up and leave, as if I were invading his sanctuary, his sacred place. But I stayed, sitting there, waiting for my Yahoo mail icon to pop up. I got up to use the bathroom, but once I walked in I thought, "No way, I can't pee in this man's toilet without his permission, now that would be crossing the line." I turned off the light and willed my bladder to hold it. Back at the computer, Jackie B. Parker had sent me a couple of e-mails reminding me that she had an invitation for me to attend an event at the Smithsonian's National Museum of African Art later that night.

My next stop was Congressman John Conyers Jr.'s office. Connecting President Koroma to this most influential congressman could help to raise awareness about the plight of the people in Sierra Leone and raise money for economic development. His staff members Melanie Roussell, Veronica L. Eligan, and Lou DeBaca were also there.

Congressman Conyers listened intently as, in twenty minutes flat, I went through the history of Sierra Leone, its connection with the development of early America, and African Americans' connection to Bunce Island. I also told him that Sierra Leone was the poorest country in the world, about my connection to the Mende and Temne peoples, my mission and vision for Sierra Leone's future, and my theory on DNA having memory.

"Well, young man," the congressman said, "you seem to be pretty informed and versed in the history of Sierra Leone." The staff members all laughed, because they all had heard it from me before, in the longer version.

"Thank you, sir," I replied. "I know your time is valuable and I'm trying to be respectful of that. I am also wondering if you would be interested in meeting with the newly democratically elected president, Ernest Bai Koroma, when he arrives here in the United States for the first time this coming September?"

"Sure," said the congressman. "I would love to meet President Koroma and introduce him to some people who may be able to help him. I mean, we live in one of the greatest countries in the world with access to trillions of dollars. I don't understand how we could not provide some guidance to Sierra Leone and its people."

I saw Congressman Conyers's staff look at each other as if they wanted to run for the hills. Whether it was a hard commitment or not I was grateful to put Sierra Leone on Congressman Conyers's personal radar. After the meeting, I asked Melanie Roussell if I could count on Congressman Conyers keeping his word about wanting to meet with President Koroma.

"The chairman always keeps his word, Isaiah," she said. "Sometimes I think he tries to do too much, but if he says he's going to do something, he does it."

As Lorenzo slowly pulled up to the Smithsonian National Museum of African Art, I sat in the car, thinking about how blessed I was to be able to see and experience Washington, DC, in such an unbelievable way. I recalled my time at Howard University and wondered what Harry Poe would say if he could see how far I had come in his city.

Tears began to well up in my eyes as I stepped out of my Lincoln Town Car. The sharp cold night air hit my face and reddened my nose as my tears tightened in diamond shapes under my eyelids, making me look like a harlequin. I wiped at my face with the inner part of my glove and told Lorenzo I would call him when I was ready to leave.

FLASH! The moment I stepped inside the museum the pictures started. *FLASH!* The house photographer said, "Do you mind? I need to get a photo of you and our director."

FLASH! I looked around the room but saw no familiar faces. The place was in full party mode—excited chatter, many people greeting each other and shaking hands; the room was electric. Ms. Parker walked over singing, "Izaaayyyyyyaahhhh! You made it! Let me introduce you to Sharon."

A beautiful, calm, and elegant storm of a woman walked up to me and smiled. It turned out she was the director of this very new and special place, Sharon F. Patton PhD. "Hello, Mr. Washington. It's a pleasure to meet you."

"The pleasure is all mine. So, you are the creator of all this wonderfulness?"

She laughed and said, "I have a great staff."

"This would be the perfect place for me to do my first fundraiser in Washington and raise awareness for Sierra Leone," I said.

She agreed it would be. We discussed February 2009, Black History Month, as a good date, and she agreed to check the schedule and get back to me. "You should walk around and see our exhibit," she said as she left.

As an African singer kept the crowd enthralled with her beautiful voice, I slipped downstairs to admire the collection. It contained some of the most amazing African art that I had ever seen, from all over Africa.

I looked down at one huge mask from Sierra Leone and noticed that it was owned by Walt Disney. I looked at another piece, it was owned by Disney as well. Then another piece and then another. I stopped and looked around to see if Ashton Kutcher from the TV show *Punk'd* was going to jump out and let me off the hook. I walked farther and saw a security guard standing there. "Hey, man," I said. "I see Walt Disney on all of these art pieces."

"Yeah, Walt Disney owns all six thousand," he answered, pointing to a sign above one of the entrances. I looked past his finger; "Walt Disney–Tishman Collection" was inscribed above the door. "Deep, ain't it? Mickey Mouse owns all of our shit," he said.

"Not me," I said.

"What you say?" he asked.

"Disney doesn't own me, he's helping me."
"Helping you? Helping you do what?"
"Reach my destiny."

On March 5, 2008, I sent out an e-mail blast to all of Minister Zainab Bangura's key supporters and to my TGMF board members saying:

> Dearest TGMF Board Members and Friends,
>
> I am happy to report that my time on Capitol Hill last week was not a waste of valuable time. It turned out to be more informative and productive than I could have hoped. I have to give a special note of thanks to Secretary Alphonso Jackson for introducing me to the Secretary of the Interior Dirk Kempthorne and Ms. Jackie Parker from Senator Levin's office. She was very supportive in helping me spread the word with the United States Senate Black Legislative Staff Caucus and with my introduction to Sharon F. Patton, PhD, the Director of the Smithsonian Institution National Museum of African Art.
>
> I was also able to get a full commitment from Congressman John Conyers Jr. and some of his key staff members regarding the Bunce Island Exhibit being shown on Capitol Hill this year and support of Sierra Leone and its newly elected President Ernest Bai Koroma. In addition, I have just received a very complimentary letter from the Secretary of the Interior Dirk Kempthorne. He has asked the National Park Service for further background on Sierra Leone and what their current involvement has been. Kempthorne has also recommended that we look into the African American Experience Fund Web site: http://www.nationalparks.org/who-we-help/aaef/

Thank you all for your continued support of the Gondo-
bay Manga Foundation.
  Let's keep pushing!
  Chairman
  Isaiah Washington

Things were starting to look up. But, a few weeks later, on March 23, 2008, I received a frightening e-mail from Maria Elena Lamas, my Cuban angel and the biggest donor to TGMF, that she was in a severe car accident. She sent out an e-mail via her iPhone from an ICU. She fortunately had no internal injuries but was in great physical pain. Despite that, she vowed her fund-raising event for TGMF would still go on as planned.

I was not alone. It was clear that this thing was getting much bigger now, much bigger than my solitary vision; now others were embracing the vision as well. I *had* to continue with TGMF.

I called Jasmyne and asked her if she could answer the phones at TGMF while I looked for a nonprofit specialist. Sonya needed more money to return to TGMF and I just couldn't afford it. Everything was coming directly out of my pocket. That was a tough decision to make. Sonya *was* TGMF. She did all of the heavy lifting.

On April 1, 2008, Ms. Lorne S. Wellington was hired as executive director of TGMF. Lorne had recently returned from working with an organization in South Africa and had extensive knowledge of the nonprofit world. Jasmyne stayed on as marketing director. I called my broker at Morgan Stanley and sold all of the Bausch & Lomb shares I had purchased the day I had met Jeffrey Sachs for lunch back in New York, but Lorne let me know that the major threats to TGMF's success were a lack of *money* and *focused leadership*. I knew that the proceeds from selling the stock wouldn't last for long, but I needed to get TGMF ready to be taken seriously in the world.

I finally found work. Filmmaker Tim Story cast me in the film *Hurricane Season,* starring Academy Award–winner Forest Whitaker. It was Forest who had put me in his directorial debut film that had caught the attention of Spike Lee. And now it was Forest Whitaker giving me a chance to *continue* my film career in spite of the forces that seemed to be conspiring to keep me from ever working again. The income I earned from the film was a third of what I usually made, but I didn't complain. It was good work. Things were getting tough in Hollywood and around the world, and I was very grateful for the opportunity to work.

In April, I was invited to sit on a panel at Harvard University. David Sengeh, a native Sierra Leonean, had created the Harvard College Sierra Leone Initiative (HCSLI). The other panelists included the legendary, ninety-three-year-old Dr. John Karefa Smart, Eleanor Thompson, and author Ishmael Beah.

By May, Maria Elena had made a miraculous recovery and held the fund-raiser for TGMF in her home in Miami, Florida, as scheduled. Lorne attended on my behalf because my film schedule would not allow me to be there in person. I also had to cancel my third scheduled trip to Sierra Leone. I wasn't happy about either circumstance, but I was doing what I had to do to keep my family afloat, as well as continue moving forward with TGMF. Feelings were hurt, and I felt terrible that there was nothing I could do to avoid it.

While working on the film in New Orleans, I received daily calls from Lance, my business manager, about my dire financial situation. The prognosis wasn't good. All of the projects I tried to produce outside the Hollywood system fell through. I went through my entire portfolio, including my retirement monies, and it still wasn't enough. I received a frantic call from Lance saying, "Isaiah, don't you care about your family? You are going to lose everything!"

"I'm doing this in Sierra Leone for my family," I said.

"This is madness," he said. "It will take years before you see a return on anything in Sierra Leone."

I hung up and recited a quote from Albert Einstein to myself. "Great Spirits have always found violent opposition from mediocrities. The latter cannot understand it when a man does not thoughtlessly submit to hereditary prejudices, but honestly and courageously uses his intelligence."

I watched helplessly as project after project fell apart. I had come to the end of the line. TGMF was over. I had to resign myself to the fact that I had kept my *word*. I had built the school. My larger plans for Sierra Leone would have to wait or maybe, I finally had to accept, might never happen.

I composed an e-mail and sent it out to all of my TGMF board members and supporters.

Sent: Wednesday, July 2, 2008 10:39:43 PM
Subject: Re: the next steps
     The hard reality is that I can no longer "afford" this effort alone past August 1, 2008. If a substantial amount of cash (and I mean substantial) doesn't come in this month, I will have to throw in the towel…again. Maybe I am supposed to fail. W.E.B. Du Bois did and died broke and exiled in Africa trying to accomplish what I am trying to do. So be it. I know when I have been beaten. I have my family to think about.

Within twenty-four hours e-mails were coming in from around the world urging me not to give up. One of my supporters alerted me to what was written on my Wikipedia page.

I typed in the Web address and took a look. I couldn't believe my eyes! Someone had leaked my e-mail. Who? I wondered who hated me so much and why? I sat there in complete shock as I read how my effort in Sierra Leone, TGMF, and my career failure were considered a media "victory." My weariness, my resignation to give up, fell away and was replaced by inspiration and determination to continue to fight, and to push forward with TGMF, my vision, and my mission for the people of Sierra Leone.

Among the rest of my e-mails I found this one from a fan, Kristle Jenkins:

To: iwashington@africanancestry.com
Date: Thursday, July 3, 2008, 6:46 AM

This does not sound like the man I know. You are not one to accept defeat at all. From what I DO know about what's going on, this is just a stumbling block in the wonderful mission that you are trying to accomplish. My mother always used to tell me that life and death lies in the power of the tongue. It may sound far-fetched but with God and enough faith, we have the ability to speak into existence what we want to happen and it can happen. The only way something will not come to pass is if we give up and let go of the ulti-mate calling that God himself has placed on our life.

So yes, you may not be able to accomplish THIS particu-lar task RIGHT NOW but keep working at it. For everything there is a time and a season. If a farmer plants a crop out of season it will not grow and he will not reap a plentiful har-vest. So maybe it is not the time for this particular project/ harvest to be sown. Maybe it's supposed to happen at a later date and God will do something greater than what even you expected. I know I probably sound preachy right now, but I just truly believe that sometimes our own desires and expectations get in the way of us listening to what the Lord is trying to tell us.

Yes, maybe W.E.B. Du Bois failed and died broke and exiled in Africa, but you are Isaiah Washington. Take what happened to him and learn from his mission, his mistakes. Make sure you don't make the same mistakes that caused him to die in that condition. YOU CAN BE BETTER THAN HE WAS, AND BE SUCCESSFUL AT WHAT HE WAS TRYING SO HARD TO ACCOMPLISH. At the same time, I understand that you DO have a family to think about. Just because you may not accomplish what YOU want does not mean you have not made a difference or an impact on people. So don't call it throwing in the towel, that makes it seem like you have FAILED a task. You cannot fail.

Think of these types of situations as a retirement, not as throwing in the towel . . . you have put in your time and effort, and given it your all so now it's time to step back and enjoy what you HAVE accomplished. This goes for everything you do, not just this particular endeavor. I know it's in you, just don't let a little disappointment make you forget your potential, who you are, and who God is! Check this out:

"Stand still that I may REASON with you." (I Sam. 12:7)

"Stand still that I may SHOW thee the Word of God." (I Sam. 9:27)

"Stand still and HEAR." (Numbers 9:8)

"Stand still and CONSIDER." (Job 37:14)

"Be still and KNOW that I am GOD." (Psalm 46:10)

Basically, shut up, clear your mind, and listen to the next move that GOD is telling you to make! Luv ya!

On August 5, 2008, Lorne and Jasmyne proudly presented me with the new TGMF brochures, the new TGMF budget plan, and the creation of the new reachonemillion.org Web site that they had worked tirelessly to create. Finally, it started to feel as if we were winning.

Jasmyne sent out a press release.

August 5, 2008 Reach One Million Campaign

Actor and philanthropist Isaiah Washington is using the occasion of his 45th birthday to kick off a national campaign entitled Reach One Million. Spearheaded through the nonprofit organization he founded, The Gondobay Manga Foundation, the campaign is the brainchild of Washington, who has set a goal of raising $250,000 to help improve the lives of one million children in Sierra Leone—one village, one region, at a time.

Launched online via ReachOneMillion.org, the Reach One Million campaign will engage and educate everyday Americans on the plight of the children of Sierra Leone, where 47% of the country's children under the age of 5 are afflicted with malaria and 28% of the population is unable to meet basic food requirements.

The campaign calls for Americans to help "reach one million" children in Sierra Leone by making a donation in the amount of $5 to $5,000, to aid in providing food, education, protection from malaria, and clean drinking water.

The Reach One Million campaign comes on the heels of Washington discovering his genetic link to the Mende tribe of Sierra Leone. After his initial visit to Sierra Leone in 2006 where he saw firsthand the extreme poverty and the needs of the children of Sierra Leone, he made a pledge to do more to help the country. One year later in 2007, Washington opened the Chief Foday Golia Memorial School near the village of Njala Kendema in the Bagbwe Chiefdom. Currently, there are 300 students out of a total population of 2,150 from six villages in the Chiefdom attending class every day.

Later this year, Washington will travel back to Sierra Leone where he will receive dual citizenship from the Sierra Leonean government.

"This is a historical moment in time for me, the people of Sierra Leone, and Africa," commented Washington. "DNA has memory and we all can do our part to make life a little better for those less fortunate. While I am very much focused on helping the underserved here at home, it's also important to me now that I know where I come from, to help my people in Sierra Leone as well."

Two days later, I received a call from my business manager telling me that I was completely bankrupt. I asked him to send me all of my account records and bank statements.

On August 20, 2008, I released Lorne and Jasmyne as employees of TGMF. "Lorne," I said as we sat down to talk, "I can't afford to pay you any further. I'm shutting the office down."

"What? You telling me you are not solvent?" she said.

"Yes. I know you're upset, but I've pulled money from everywhere and I'm tapped out. It's over."

When I told Jasmyne, she was equally shocked. "You're kidding, right? We just launched the Reach One Million Campaign on your birthday. Give it some time," she said.

"It won't be enough to cover your salaries. I'm sorry."

Eventually, they both left.

I walked to my office, closed the door, and sat there alone for a very long time. I began having some very selfish, very dark, and very serious thoughts of blowing my brains out to quell the pain and rage I felt. But I knew that would be exactly what my enemies and the media could capitalize on. If I did that, then they would win. "Hell no!" I thought to myself. "I'm a good person." I had made mistakes. I had apologized. I had been cornered. I had been abused. I had been disappointed and down before. So, I sat there quietly and thought, "If you are down and not underground, sooner or later there is only one way you can go...and that's up!"

"Be still and KNOW that I am GOD." I recited the scripture out loud.

Things continued to get worse. In September, not only was I without money, I also found myself with no publicist, no agency, and no business manager—the kiss of death for an actor.

It's amazing how quickly your so-called *friends* disappear when the money is gone. When I called people I thought I could rely on, they simply didn't answer, or never called back. Despite feeling the bone-shattering hurt and anger, I had little time to dwell on it. I had to keep my head held high. I had to keep trying to find ways to keep moving in a forward motion for my family, for TGMF, for Sierra Leone, for my fans, and for myself.

When the calls from creditors began to overwhelm me, I had our home phone and mobile phones disconnected. It was a move that proved only to make things even more difficult. Trying to find a working pay phone in Los Angeles was no easy task. The only working phone I had access to was the one in my office at TGMF. Anytime I had to make an important call meant a trip to my Burbank, California, office. I was stuck in a $3.5 million house that I could afford to neither stay in nor move out of. I had $500,000 worth of personal debt.

There was some good news: TGMF was doing better, thanks to the money raised by my Cuban angel, Maria Elena Lamas.

And President Koroma was coming to New York to attend the 63rd Session of the United Nations General Assembly at the UN headquarters, to make his debut as the new democratically elected president of Sierra Leone. I had worked hard for six months to get President Koroma and Congressman John Conyers Jr. in one room.

I received an e-mail from Minister Zainab Bangura asking me when I was arriving in New York. I didn't have the heart to tell her that I could not afford a plane ticket. I felt numb and crestfallen with the thought that I was going to miss this historic moment, a moment I had worked so hard to be a part of. But it was not about me, it was about bringing awareness to the people and problems in Sierra Leone. I kept my focus on that.

I received a call from Noelle LuSane from Congressman Donald Payne's office asking me if the congressman should meet with President Koroma and Sierra Leone's ambassador to the United States, Bockarie Stevens.

I told Noelle that President Koroma was the real deal and a true change agent for Sierra Leone. I hung up. I left the TGMF office in Burbank and drove the twenty-six miles to Venice to the UPS Store where I had my new P.O. box. I walked in, stuck the key in the lock, pulled open the door, and lifted out three envelopes with the Screen Actors Guild Residual Department return address on them. I ripped open the envelopes and found three checks from Disney totaling $17,000!

I felt a wave of relief wash over me, much like breathing air after a near-drowning experience. My body felt buoyant and alive again. I just kept repeating, "God is good all the time. God is good all the time." Not my time, but His time. Then I walked calmly and quickly out of the UPS Store and jumped into my SUV and drove straight to the bank!

★　　★　　★

I made sure my family had plenty of food in the house, paid the back rent, the overdue car notes, and the overdue utility bills, and, finally, I had my cell phone turned on again. With my family secured, I purchased an economy ticket and arrived on the red-eye into LaGuardia Airport in New York on Friday, September 25, 2008. As soon as I landed I placed a call to my wife, Jenisa, telling her I had made it safely, and then I called Minister Zainab Bangura. When she answered I said, "Hello, madam, I am here in New York and Congressman John Conyers Jr. and Congressman Donald Payne are set to meet with President Koroma."

"Well done, Isaiah!" she said. "I am sending Souley Manah-Kpukumu over to your hotel in an hour. He will take you to get your credentials as a Sierra Leone adviser to the president for entry into the UN. You will be a part of his delegation now. I will see you there."

I reached for my "black bible" and read over my notes on Sierra Leone. I knew that I had just forty-eight hours to impress President Koroma and convince him that I should be given dual citizenship as soon as possible. I was ready. It had all of my notes on the history of Sierra Leone and its connection to the building of what would eventually become the United States of America. I was versed on Pan-African leaders, their histories, and their philosophies. I had my research and clippings on De Beers and the Sierra Leone diamond history. I had everything! I felt emboldened and secure as I presented my case as to why I should be the one, the first one, to receive a dual citizenship from him.

I meditated for forty-five minutes to center myself. I had just stepped out of a hot shower when the phone rang. It was a woman from the front desk calling to ask me for another credit card. I told her I would pay cash upon checking out and to turn off the phone and other services in the room. She seemed satisfied and hung up.

Shortly after, my cell phone rang. It was Souley, whom Minister Zainab Bangura had assigned to help me get my credentials, telling me that he was downstairs waiting for me. I got dressed and met him in the lobby.

He asked me to follow him and together we walked three blocks to a building where I had to hand over my U.S. passport, was photographed, and handed a badge with my name on it. Souley smiled at me. I followed him along a series of shortcuts through Manhattan's East Side streets and walkways.

I looked up and saw the massive United Nations Building looming in the distance, getting closer and closer as we walked.

As we went down a flight of stairs in one particular walkway, I found my eyes being guided to some lettering on a wall. It was a verse from Isaiah 2:4. "They will beat their swords into plowshares and their spears into pruning hooks. Nation will not take up sword against nation, nor will they train for war anymore."

I nearly fell to the ground seeing my name etched so gallantly into the aged and heavy stone. I picked up my pace and hurried down the rest of the stairs. Souley had already spilled out onto the congested sidewalk leaving me a few paces behind.

There were so many people on the street, all of us being shuttled like cattle between the royal blue NYPD barricades. Police vehicles, with lights flashing, were parked on every corner and at every intersection. Sirens blared from convoys of speeding black SUVs with tinted windows and suited men with wires connected to their ears inside.

Souley and I finally made our way through security and into the building. We boarded a crowded elevator that took us up several floors. I tried to keep pace and follow behind Souley, walking along a huge concave wall, but was separated from him when I was almost run over by several bodyguards surrounding Microsoft founder Bill Gates. When I turned around, I found myself face to top of head with the president of Iran, Mahmoud Ahmadinejad.

"Oh pardon me, Mr. President," I said as his Secret Servicemen swarmed around him. President Ahmadinejad smiled and kept going. I watched him disappear into a sea of brawny men all dressed in dark gray suits. I finally caught up with Souley and there was President Ernest Bai Koroma standing tall in an immaculate dark blue suit and a bright red tie.

"Hello, Mr. President," I said, "I'm Isaiah Washington."

"Yes, yes, I have heard a great deal about you," he said.

"I hope it's been good things, sir."

"Oh yes, very good things. Welcome."

With that, President Koroma was escorted to his seat on the floor of the United Nations. *FLASH!* A woman who worked at the UN took a photo of me and started screaming for her coworker to come take a photo of her standing with me. "I hope you don't mind!" she said.

"No." I smiled. "I don't mind." *FLASH!*

Suddenly a burst of loud applause emanated from the huge UN Assembly floor. Every head of state from the free world was clapping as Bill Gates walked to the podium. I was stunned at how casual everything and everyone was. I looked around the room and saw Sweden, Sudan, and Sierra Leone signs, with men and women adorned in headphones sitting proudly behind each sign. There were two massive Jumbotron screens separated by the map of the world on polar azimuthal equidistant projection and surrounded by two olive branches, both symbolically significant. The olive branch can be traced back to ancient Greece and serves as a symbol of peace. The world map is a symbol of the area with which this organization is concerned in achieving its main purpose: peace. Which was exactly what I felt my entire time inside the UN. Peace.

I watched as heads of state from São Tomé and Principe, Comoros, and China spoke about global warming and their concerns. Then President Koroma took the podium. I sat next to his sister, who was beaming with pride, as he serenely and spectacularly delivered his speech. He spoke about a new Sierra Leone, agricultural opportunities, tourism, and education of the country's youth.

After the reception where President Koroma greeted his constituents and supporters, I returned to my hotel, got some money from the ATM, and checked out paying with cash. Souley picked up my bags.

There seemed to be some confusion as to who from the delegation was allowed to take the van to the train station in order to head down to DC. I jumped in a cab and had the driver take me to Penn Station. I arrived at the same time as the president. We were all escorted by New York's finest into a VIP room. One police officer winked at me and asked me if I wanted a stick of chewing gum. I accepted.

As we waited for the train to Washington, Minister Zainab Bangura introduced me to the president's personal assistant, Brian Gilpin, and other members of his delegation. The special agents signaled that it was time to board our train and we walked single file to the gate.

I strategically positioned myself directly in front of President Koroma as we walked. Once we arrived on the platform I turned to him and asked, "Mr. President, how is everything going, sir?"

"It's a lot of work," he answered, "but someone has got to do it."

CHAPTER 20

Making History

Our train rolled slowly into the station and came to a complete stop. I could feel the level of tension among the policemen and special agents rise suddenly as the disembarking passengers started to crowd around us, trying to get a look at the tall and regal-looking man the large team of officers was protecting.

One of them looked at me and said, "What did you do now?" I laughed and chewed my gum harder. I was getting used to that. It seemed no matter where I went or what I was doing, someone had something to say about me or my departure from my TV show.

We finally boarded the train and Minister Bangura made sure that I sat directly in front of President Koroma. I was nervous, but I was determined not to show it or, at the same time, appear too confident. As the train pulled out of the station I could see that Minister Bangura and President Koroma were tired. I knew I had to make my case, and quick.

Before I could finish my spiel on the importance and historical significance of obtaining my dual citizenship, President Koroma smiled at me and said, "I understand what it is that you are trying to do and I support it. I am aware of W. E. B. DuBois's teachings and I am of the same school of thought. I have had many ask me, 'Why are you giving this man citizenship?' and I say to them, 'What are you all so afraid of?'"

I sat there silent for several seconds and then said, "My sentiments exactly, sir. Thank you for your time. I will shut up and let you rest."

I got up and walked toward the back of the secured car. I saw one of the special agents and asked him, "Hey, what are you carrying?"

"Oh just this lil ol' thing," he said as he slightly opened his coat revealing his Sig Sauer P226.

"Yeah, that's little all right," I said, laughing. "Hey, do you know Special Agent John R. Christman?" We had talked at the White House Summit on Malaria.

"Of course," he said. "He's our special agent in charge. You want me to call him?"

"Yeah, tell him Isaiah Washington says hello."

The special agent dialed his phone. "Hey...yes. We are on our way now. You have Isaiah Washington asking for you."

"He says to ask you, 'What the hell are you doing with the President of Sierra Leone?'"

"Tell him I am advising him," I said.

The special agent handed me the phone and I chatted briefly with Special Agent Christman and promised that I would call him while I was in DC.

Once I finished my conversation, Special Agent Mark T. Lewis and Special Agent Raymond J. Sturm Jr. handed me their cards and introduced themselves. "What do you guys think of my new president?" I asked them.

They both agreed that President Koroma and his delegates were good guys. Special Agent Sturm said, "We have been with these guys for a while now and, you know, people tend to relax and talk a lot in front us. They are *good guys*, Isaiah."

"That's good to know," I answered. "Thank you for watching out for him."

We pulled into Union Station in DC and I watched as President Koroma and Minister Bangura were escorted to their vehicles driven by the United States Secret Service. I grabbed my bags and walked the short distance to the Hotel George. I checked into my usual room, dropped my bags, collapsed on the bed, and passed out from exhaustion.

The next morning did not go as smoothly as I'd hoped. Unfortunately, President Koroma arrived in Washington at the same time the Senate and the House of Representatives were scrambling to pass the Emergency Economic Stabilization Act of 2008. Despite what his staff had told me about Congressman Conyers always keeping his word, he kept President Koroma waiting for two hours and then finally had to cancel the meeting. Minister Bangura was very disappointed. I was able to arrange for Congressman Conyers and President Koroma to talk on the phone before he left for Sierra Leone so all was not completely lost.

A few days later, on September 29, 2008, the Dow Jones lost 778 points, the biggest single-day point loss in history, after the House of Representatives rejected the government's $700 billion bank bailout plan. I lost what was left of my portfolio. The sweetness of my victory with President Ernest Bai Koroma began to fade; it wasn't just me facing a financial crisis anymore, now the whole world was having a financial meltdown.

A few days later, on October 5, I received a refreshing e-mail from Professor Joe Opala that let me know my efforts were not going unnoticed. Sierra Leone was moving forward as planned.

The devil is beating his wife, again.

Over the next few weeks I spent countless hours at the TGMF office trying to figure out what my next move would be. The only thing that kept me distracted from thinking about my own situation was watching presidential candidate Barack Obama on the campaign trail making some of the most incredible speeches I have ever heard.

The day before the U.S. presidential election, I was in my office working on invitation letters for the TGMF Inaugural Dinner planned for April 23, 2009, in Washington, DC. We had yet to discover that Barack Obama would be the forty-fourth president of the United States. Ironically, I received a copy of an e-mail from Iris Max-Macarthy from the office of the Permanent Mission of the Republic of Sierra Leone to the United Nations in New York. Iris told me that she sent it out to all Sierra Leoneans on her contact list who may have had doubts or reservations about voting for presidential nominee Barack Obama. After I read it, I knew that my work in Sierra Leone was indeed my *destiny*. Meeting Senator Obama and having access to his office was no *coincidence*. The senator wanted positive *change* in Sierra Leone and in the world. That was directly in line with the *change* I had worked for my entire adulthood. Then it hit me, I remembered something he had said to me when we met briefly outside of the Senate chamber: "I'll see you at the crossroads."

I had arrived in Sierra Leone for the first time on May 22, 2006. Just eighteen days before, without my knowledge, Senator Barack Obama had written to Gaddi Vasquez, director of the Peace Corps, to request that he reinstate the Peace Corps program in Sierra Leone. Could Sierra Leone be at its "crossroads" for the betterment of itself its people? Will President Barack H. Obama, President George W. Bush, President William J. Clinton, and I all see each other again...in Sierra Leone?

★　　★　　★

It was about 8:30 in the morning on December 15, 2008, ten days before Christmas. I was driving on the 405 North on my way to the TGMF office when my mobile phone rang. I pressed the speaker phone and heard Minister Zainab Bangura's voice. She told me that President Koroma had agreed to initiate my immigration and naturalization paperwork to make me a citizen of Sierra Leone.

I almost careened off of the freeway, nearly blinded by the burst of my own tears of joy. "I'm sorry, Minister Bangura," I said, "but can you please repeat that?"

She did. "Oh my God." I said, "Do you know what this means historically? Oh my God! This is the best news ever! Thank you! Thank you! Thank you! And please tell the president I said thank you!"

I arrived at the TGMF office in Burbank, jumped out of my SUV, and ran inside the building. I was so excited I could barely get my keys into the lock. I closed the door behind me and locked it. I fell to my knees. The tears ran down my face as I prayed. I thanked God for an early and amazing Christmas gift. It was done and there was *no turning back!* I managed to regain a modicum of composure, went to my computer, and composed an e-mail that I blasted out to my entire contact list.

Hello ALL,

Well…as I sit here in the TGMF office completely numb yet elated, I am at a loss for words. Minister Zainab Bangura has phoned me from New York to "officially" tell me that I am now a citizen of Sierra Leone and that I need to send her 2 photos for the Sierra Leone Passport that awaits me in Freetown. I could go on and on about how much that phone call means to me, but I will simply refer you all to my "Recent Work" section on

Wikipedia. (lol) President Koroma now goes down in history
as the "first" African President to issue an African American
full citizenship based on DNA. Congrats to all who have been
on this historical journey with me. Mission Accomplished. That
said, I'm so moved right now that I am literally wiped out with
the gravity of this new reality. Going home to celebrate my "dual
citizenship" with my family...One Love

    IW

On April 23, 2009, I held my long-planned Gondobay Manga Foundation Inaugural Dinner in Washington, DC. We honored Forest Whitaker; Rick Kittles PhD and Gina Paige of African Ancestry; Congresswoman Barbara Lee; and Professor Henry Louis Gates Jr. The Duchess of York, Sarah Margaret Ferguson, was the keynote speaker. Ken Harvey, Etan Thomas, and Jeffrey Wright were the presenters and Esther Vassar gave the opening remarks. Seventy-five percent of the event was sponsored by Maria Elena Lamas using her personal money. TGMF raised $100,000 that night during the height of the recession.

In his acceptance speech, Professor Henry Louis Gates Jr., recipient of the 2009 TGMF Sankofa Award, expressed his gratitude for the award and thanked me and TGMF. He spoke eloquently of the importance of memory and remembering one's personal history, one's family history, and one's people's history, and how vital it is to keep those histories alive.

He talked of Carter G. Woodson, known as "the Father of Black History," who wrote that "a people cannot determine their future unless they know their past." He talked of Alex Haley and his quest, through television, to connect the "African past with the African American future." And he talked about his own passion for DNA ancestry tracing and his acclaimed PBS series.

I stood there listening, and thinking that this is what it was all for. All of the times I wondered, all of the times I cried, all of the times the people who loved me suffered for what I was trying to do, all of the times I wanted to give up, this was the reason why I didn't. Here I stood, the first African American man in history to achieve dual citizenship from the United States and an African country. I had realized a dream that phenomenal African American men like W. E. B. DuBois, Edward Wilmot Blyden, Marcus Garvey, Martin Luther King Jr., Malcolm X, and Reverend Leon H. Sullivan had long before I was born.

The debt collectors, the money worries, and my acting career—none of that mattered to me in that moment. I just looked around the room and took it all in. This was the culmination of a journey that started with a seemingly meaningless award named after a mostly forgotten man. It was then that I realized that Canada Lee was not forgotten—his spirit, his DNA, was alive in me. It was alive in every other black man who ever stood up and risked his life, reputation, and income, dreaming that his life could be about something bigger than himself.

Professor Gates was finishing his speech:

Isaiah Washington has taken this journey. And this foundation is the splendid result of what he has found. Isaiah Washington not only talks the talk, he walks the walk. No one embodies the spirit of Sankofa more fully and completely in our generation today than does Isaiah. And I ask you to give it up for our host this evening, a man of enormous vision and dedication to restoring and reconnecting our African American sisters and brothers with their African heritage.

Applause roared, filling the room, and I knew that some say, may your dreams come true. Well I say, stay true to your dreams.

NOTES

1. http://www.paff.org
2. http://www.archives.gov/education/lessons/amistad
3. http://www.sierra-leone.org/villagenames.html
4. Information taken from www.stanford.edu: "Blood Diamonds: The Conflict in Sierra Leone" by Eric Johnson, *Edge,* December 6, 2002, and "Amputation Is Forever: Blood Diamonds and the Civil War in Sierra Leone," by Cordel Robbin-Coker, *Edge,* June 2, 2005.
5. http://www.imdb.com/character/ch0032902/quotes
6. http://www.pbs.org/kcet/tavissmiley/archive/200506/20050627_washington.html[0]
7. http://www.kimberleyprocess.com
8. http://www.ddiglobal.org
9. Excerpt from the speech taken from "Transcript of Bush's Address to N.A.A.C.P.," July 20, 2006, www.nytimes.com.
10. http://finazafoundation.org/Finaza_Foundation/About.html
11. http://jcrs.com/newsletters/2007/2007_01.htm
12. Simon Robinson and Jeffrey Ressner, "Hollywood Plays Rough With Diamonds," *Time,* November 27, 2006, page 64.
13. "Disney Profit Jumps on Strong Results from Networks, Studios, Parks," www.usatoday.com, November 9, 2006.
14. http://www.usatoday.com/money/companies/earnings/2006-11-09-disney_x.htm
15. http://www.kaisernetwork.org/health_cast/uploaded_files/121406_whitehouse_malaria_transcript.pdf[0]
16. http://www.putonthearmoroflight.com/2010/01/bridge-builder-by-w-dromgoole.html
17. http://www.eonline.com/uberblog/b54551_greys_ugly_are_hot_image_awards.html
18. http://ipsnews.net/news.asp?idnews=44113
19. http://www.bunce-island.org.uk/page3/page3.html

ABOUT THE AUTHOR

Actor, producer, and human rights activist Isaiah Washington is an NAACP Image Award– and Screen Actors Guild Award–winning American actor. A veteran of four acclaimed Spike Lee films, *Crooklyn, Clockers, Girl 6,* and *Get on the Bus*, Washington is best known for his role as Dr. Preston Burke on the ABC medical drama *Grey's Anatomy.*

Washington's other feature film credits include *Hurricane Season, True Crime, Romeo Must Die, Out of Sight, Ghost Ship, Welcome to Collinwood, Bulworth, Love Jones, Dead Presidents, Stonewall, Strictly Business,* and the acclaimed *Dancing in September,* in which his performance earned him an NAACP Image Award nomination for outstanding actor.

On television, he has guest starred in several series, including *NYPD Blue, Law & Order, Homicide: Life on the Street, Ally McBeal, New York Undercover, Living Single, Soul Food,* and *Touched by an Angel.*

Washington acted as master of ceremonies for the first White House Summit on Malaria to fight the war against malaria in fifteen African countries. In September 2008, he attended the 63rd United Nations General Assembly in New York City as an adviser to President Ernest Bai Koroma of the Republic of Sierra Leone.

Isaiah is the recipient of several international awards: Planet Africa's 2009 Marcus Garvey Memorial Award, The Daily Voice 2009 Hope Award, Oliver Hill Foundation 2009 Speakers Award, Reverend C. T. Vivian 2009 Passing the Torch Award, the African Achievement 2009 Philanthropy Award, National Organization of Sierra Leoneans in America 2009 Diamond Award, the African Focus 2009 Goodwill Award, Who's Who in Los Angeles 2009, Satellite Award, the Black Oscar Family Tree Award, the Noble Johnson Legendary Award, the Harvard College Sierra Leone Initiative Award, and the first person given a full African citizenship based on DNA.

Isaiah Washington will also become the first African American to lead the Africa Alternative Investment Fund designed to rebuild the infrastructure of Sierra Leone with his new company HIRA International Investment Group, LLC, overseeing a multibillion-dollar investment fund.